Effective Teacher Leadership

Effective Teacher Leadership

USING RESEARCH
TO INFORM AND REFORM

Edited by Melinda M. Mangin and Sara Ray Stoelinga

Foreword by Mark A. Smylie

Teachers College, Columbia University
New York and London

Published by Teachers College Press, 1234 Amsterdam Avenue, New York, NY 10027

Library of Congress Cataloging-in-Publication Data

Effective teacher leadership : using research to inform and reform / edited by Melinda M. Mangin and Sara Ray Stoelinga ; foreword by Mark A. Smylie.
    p.   cm.
  Includes bibliographical references and index.
  ISBN 978-0-8077-4840-4 (cloth : alk. paper)
  1. Teacher effectiveness.   2. Educational leadership.   I. Mangin, Melinda M.
II. Stoelinga, Sara Ray.

  LB1025.3.E355 2008
  371. l—dc22   2007025922

ISBN 978-0-8077-4840-4 (cloth)

Printed on acid-free paper
Manufactured in the United States of America

15   14   13   12   11   10   09   08   8   7   6   5   4   3   2   1

To our husbands:
Timothy M. Snyder and Timothy M. Stoelinga

Thank you for your enduring patience and loving support.

Contents

Foreword

TEACHER LEADERSHIP is big news again. After a lull in the mid-1990s when our attention was focused squarely on standards-based reforms and accountability, we have returned to teacher leadership with full force. Schools and school districts are looking again to teacher leadership as a vehicle for teacher professional development and improvement in school organization and classroom instruction. They are investing substantial amounts of human and financial resources in efforts to develop it. Moreover, opportunities for teacher leadership have grown in new and exciting directions. They have expanded from roles focused primarily on administrative tasks and participative decision making to roles focused more specifically on school organizational and instructional improvement; from appointing a few individual teachers to leadership positions to encouraging groups of teachers to engage in leadership work; and from considering teacher leadership as something that is separate from and added to teachers' classroom work to redesigning the basic nature of teachers' work to incorporate school-level leadership.

With this renewed attention to the development of teacher leadership has come renewed attention to teacher leadership in the academic and professional literature. A brief search of the Educational Resources Information Center (ERIC), the largest education database, reveals that the total number of articles, papers, and technical reports written about teacher leadership has increased by nearly 50% during the past 10 years. The number of research articles, papers, and technical reports has increased at a similar rate. According to *Books in Print*, 20 new books devoted specifically to the topic of teacher leadership have appeared since 2000.

This book stands out as a very different and significant contribution to the literature on teacher leadership, inasmuch as the existing literature can be characterized as conceptually murky and atheoretical, broad but insufficiently deep, more descriptive than explanatory, and lacking in methodological range and rigor. Melinda Mangin and Sara Ray Stoelinga have assembled an unusually coherent set of papers prepared by a diverse and talented group of scholars, and as a result they have accomplished something rather unique. Instead of having relatively little to say about a number of different forms of teacher leadership, these papers have a lot to say about one particular form of leadership that is gaining substantial currency in schools and school districts across the country: nonsupervisory, school-based, instructional teacher leadership roles. Instead of focusing on teacher leadership through one particular lens, these papers bring multiple theoretical perspectives to bear on a common subject. Instead of one particular research design and methodology, this collection of papers presents evidence from multiple designs and methodologies, both qualitative and quantitative. And instead of focusing on only one dimension of these teacher leadership roles, this set of papers explores multiple dimensions and in the process advances our knowledge and understanding of teacher leadership with a depth and comprehensiveness rarely found in the literature.

In addition, this is an important how-to book on teacher leadership but not in the conventional sense. Most how-to books on teacher leadership are designed to promote and guide action. They suggest concrete steps that schools and school districts might take to develop and support the practice of teacher leadership. While there is a lot of practice advice to be gleaned from these pages to inform the doing of teacher leadership, what distinguishes this volume from other how-to books is that this is a "how-to-think" book. Mangin and Stoelinga provide us with different ways to think more clearly, more systemically, more strategically, and more effectively about teacher leadership in general and about instructional leadership roles in particular. We are shown new ways to think about the design of teacher leader roles and how the content and procedural knowledge of teacher leaders relate to the development and exercise of those roles. We are shown new ways to think about the organizational contexts of teacher leadership. In particular, our attention is drawn in new and informative ways to think about formal and informal networks, communication structures, and social influence relationships as elements of those contexts. We are also presented with new ways to think about external support of teacher leaders and their work, including social support and data and information support. By helping us become better thinkers about teacher leadership, we will likely become better at the doing of teacher leadership. And that is all for the good if the promises of teacher leadership for educational improvement are to be fulfilled.

Mark A. Smylie
University of Illinois at Chicago

Acknowledgments

THIS BOOK would not have been possible without the encouragement and support of many people. First and foremost, we would like to thank our mentors: Bill Firestone, Mark Smylie, and Charles Bidwell. When Mark introduced us to each other in 2002, we had no way of predicting the synergy of our scholarship or the evolution of our friendship. We are grateful for his foresight. Once we were connected, Bill encouraged us to move forward with this edited volume, helping us gain greater clarity about our aims and intentions as we crafted our initial proposal. We deeply appreciate his wisdom and insights. Bill, Mark, and Charles have all spent countless hours reading drafts of our work, chairing various related symposia, and offering their encouragement. Thank you.

The success of this project is inextricably linked to the contributing authors' dedication to high-quality research. We would like to thank all the contributors for their hard work and exemplary scholarship, not to mention their tolerance for seemingly endless e-mail messages. Their cooperation and receptivity made organizing this project a rewarding endeavor.

We have also benefited from the support of our colleagues. M. Cecilia Martinez was an early enthusiast, whose confidence in our efforts helped propel this project forward. Jennifer York-Barr, Eric Camburn, and Mike Copland provided us with valuable feedback on initial drafts of several chapters. Similarly, comments from James E. Taylor and Jennifer Goldstein sharpened our thinking about instructional teacher leadership. Gary Sykes offered timely advice about the publication process. We hope to reciprocate the generosity of each of these colleagues.

Moreover, we would like to thank our respective institutions for their continued assistance. Michigan State University has provided Melinda with many opportunities for professional growth, offering the resources to make this and other scholarship possible. Over the past 12 years, The Consortium on Chicago School Research at the University of Chicago has repeatedly served as Sara's home institution, providing a stable base for conducting educational research. Both of us appreciate the support we have received from our colleagues at these institutions.

Without a doubt, this volume has benefited immeasurably from the collective efforts of the Teachers College Press editorial team. Thoughtful comments from three anonymous reviewers, careful editing by Wendy Schwartz, and Brian Ellerbeck's astute guidance have all contributed to the end result.

Finally, and most important, we wish to express our deepest gratitude to our families. Their patience has allowed us to attend to this important educational issue, and their impatience has motivated us to bring this project to fruition. We are forever grateful.

Teacher Leadership:
What It Is and Why It Matters

Melinda M. Mangin and Sara Ray Stoelinga

CLASSROOM TEACHERS in schools across the nation are working hard to foster student learning and academic achievement. Pressure to perform comes
from all directions: parents, principals, local communities, policy makers,
and the media. To succeed, teachers must be able to address students'
unique instructional needs and learn and utilize current best practices.
Teachers need to assess what their students know and what they have yet
to learn. They must have the capacity to use this information to reflect
upon and alter their teaching practice accordingly. Without adequate resources, it seems unlikely that teachers will be able to consistently meet
the ever-increasing expectations for improved instructional performance.
What professional supports are available to help teachers meet the demands
of the current educational context?

　　This book explores instructional capacity building through the examination of nonsupervisory, school-based, instructional leadership roles.
These positions—frequently referred to as teacher leaders, specialists, or
coaches—offer two unique benefits. First, they bring some level of special knowledge about teaching to the school setting. And second, they
do so outside the line of school authority, with the goal of promoting
the development of trust between teachers and the instructional leader.
The goal of these positions is to provide teachers with the skills and
knowledge necessary for continued instructional improvement and,
ultimately, enhanced student learning. This book investigates how instructional teacher leadership roles might contribute to instructional

improvement efforts and the conditions that promote or hinder their success.

In this chapter we articulate the motivations and intentions that underlie the book and provide a framework for the interpretation of instructional teacher leadership roles. The framework includes an explication of the types of teacher leadership positions considered as well as a discussion of the contextual and historical conditions that laid the groundwork for the development of teacher leadership roles, the assumptions behind their development, and their intended outcomes. Building on that framework, we present an overview of the ensuing chapters, drawing linkages across the chapters and highlighting their contribution to the field of teacher leadership.

WHY TEACHER LEADERSHIP?

Much has been made of the contributions that teachers can make to school leadership in general and instructional leadership in particular (Crowther, Kaagan, Ferguson, & Hann, 2002; Harris & Muijs, 2005; Hart, 1995; Katzenmeyer & Moller, 1996; Lieberman & Miller, 2004). Teachers' connections to the classroom—creating learning opportunities for students, assessing student performance, and adapting their teaching practice accordingly—provide them with a situated perspective on the core technologies of teaching. This knowledge, combined with teachers' ability to influence instruction, implies that teachers may be the logical leaders of promoting and supporting change in teaching practice. Distributed theories of leadership further emphasize teachers' leadership potential by defining leadership as the process of people's interaction with one another and with their situation (Gronn, 2000; Spillane, 2006; Spillane, Halverson, & Diamond, 2004). As such, teachers, in interaction with one another, have the potential to lead instructional improvement efforts despite a lack of positional leadership authority.

While much of the literature on teacher leadership trumpets the ability of all teachers, regardless of position, to contribute to school improvement, there has been a resurgent interest in the formalization of instructional teacher leadership roles. Leadership roles for teachers were a common reform strategy in the 1980s and early 1990s. Positions such as master, lead, and mentor teacher were seen as a way to decentralize authority, include teachers in shared decision making, improve morale, enhance teachers' work, and tap into previously underutilized resources (Conley, 1991; Firestone & Bader, 1991; Hart, 1995; Heller & Firestone, 1995; Lichtenstein, McLaughlin, & Knudsen, 1992). Despite the possible benefits, these positions were criticized for focusing on individual job enhancement rather than collective engagement and for directing teachers' energy toward managerial tasks rather than instructional domains (Hart, 1990; Smylie, 1997). Thus new roles—aimed at instructional improvement and collective work enhancement—began to emerge, putting teacher teaming, teacher as researcher, and coaching initiatives at the forefront of school reform efforts (Smylie, Conley, & Marks, 2002). These new teacher leadership roles constitute the focal point of this book.

With increasing frequency, districts and schools are creating new leadership positions—such as coach or coordinator roles—that formally expand responsibility for instructional leadership to teachers (Murphy, 2005). These positions have received support from federal initiatives including Reading First and the Math Science Partnership; private foundations such as the Small Schools Coaches Collaborative funded by the Bill and Melinda Gates Foundation; large-scale comprehensive school reform models such as America's Choice and Success for All; and professional organizations like the National Staff Development Council. As a result, formal teacher leadership roles have been evident in large-scale school reform efforts as seen in New York, San Diego, Boston, and Chicago (see Datnow & Castellano, 2001; Elmore & Burney, 1997; Hightower, Knapp, Marsh, & McLaughlin, 2002; Stein, 1998; Stoelinga, 2006) as well as in more localized contexts (see Mangin, 2005, 2006, 2007).

The proliferation of instructionally focused teacher leadership roles has been fueled by education policies that pressure school administrators and district leaders to seek effective ways to increase student achievement. This pressure has become especially pronounced in the high-stakes testing environment associated with the No Child Left Behind Act of 2001 (Public Law 107-110). One way to enhance learning outcomes is to improve instruction. The notion of instruction as the pathway to reform has gained increased acceptance as scholars and educators alike recognize that previous reform efforts—focused on school restructuring and district-level accountability—did not necessarily improve student achievement (Elmore & Burney, 1997; Stoelinga, Fendt, & Wenzel, 2005). Hence districts increasingly focus their reform efforts on improving instruction. Instructional teacher leadership roles can facilitate instructional improvement by providing teachers with effective professional development—sustained, supported, and school-embedded opportunities to learn about the core technologies of teaching (Cohen & Hill, 2001; Hallman, Wenzel, & Fendt, 2004; Hawley & Valli, 1999). Thus conceived, instructional teacher leadership roles can potentially improve teaching practice and enhance student achievement outcomes.

THE NEED FOR RESEARCH

Despite the emergence of instructional teacher leadership roles, evidence of their enactment, successes, and constraints remains thin. In a recent review of the literature on teacher leadership, York-Barr and Duke (2004) found that the existing research is largely asynchronous, atheoretical, and incomplete. Nevertheless, districts continue to invest both human and financial resources into the creation of these positions. For example, in 2001 the Chicago Public Schools launched the Chicago Reading Initiative (CRI), which included the implementation of 114 school-based reading specialists, a number that expanded to 160 by 2003 (Alliance for Excellent Education, 2003; Kelleher, 2002). The cost of hiring and training the school-based coaches was estimated at nearly $20 million dollars. In addition to the steep financial cost of human resources, instructional leadership positions also prompt a shift, and potential loss, of scarce human resources as teachers move out of classrooms and into specialized roles. Given these human and financial considerations, there is a clear need for increased understanding of how these roles interact with and influence existing systems of leadership and instruction.

The task of building a coherent body of research that can inform the development and implementation of teacher leadership roles is complicated by the confusing array of terms used to describe these positions. Titles such as coordinator, facilitator, specialist, helper, trainer, lead teacher, master teacher, mentor, and coach are all used to identify nonsupervisory, school-based, instructional leadership roles. Moreover, use of the same title does not ensure comparable roles and responsibilities. The absence of a common vocabulary and common understandings undermines the potential of these positions and the development of a coherent body of research that links roles, actions, and outcomes. Thus we delineate a set of parameters that characterize the kind of instructional leadership roles we aim to investigate. These positions are (a) nonsupervisory, (b) focused on instructional improvement, (c) aimed at teachers' capacity building, and (d) working at the school level.

OVERVIEW OF THE BOOK

This book presents new research on instructional teacher leadership roles. In the chapters that follow, the contributors provide evidence of the enactment, design, conditions, constraints, and successes of nonsupervisory, instructional teacher leadership roles. Each chapter draws from a different data set while holding constant the characteristics described above;

hence contributing to a unified body of research. This comprehensive set of data provides a complex understanding of how these roles contribute to improved teaching.

To begin, in Chapter 2 James Taylor reviews the history of instructional coaching and examines its current status in the field of education. The chapter includes a comprehensive investigation of the various types of coaching, the conditions under which they operate, and their potential for improving instruction. Taylor's thorough treatment of the literature sets the foundation for the subsequent chapters, which provide empirical evidence of instructional teacher leadership.

Christopher Manno and William Firestone present the first set of research findings in Chapter 3. The authors examine teacher leaders' content knowledge and how teacher leaders leveraged that knowledge in their work. They draw on data from a 2-year study of eight mathematics teacher leaders—four content experts and four nonexperts—and the teachers with whom they worked. The findings indicate that teacher leaders' content knowledge can influence teachers' receptivity to the role and the overall effectiveness of teacher leadership initiatives. Specifically, content experts recognized deficiencies in their colleagues' content knowledge, they viewed their work as advocating for teaching all children, and their specialized knowledge helped them develop trust and rapport with colleagues.

In Chapter 4 Brian Lord, Kate Cress, and Barbara Miller present findings from their 3-year investigation of mathematics and science teacher leadership models to consider teacher leaders' procedural knowledge. Their analyses indicate that teacher leaders draw heavily on their own experience as classroom teachers in their efforts to help colleagues change instructional practice. Teacher leaders essentially "show and tell" teachers how to change—they "show" through direct modeling and they "tell" through planning and advising. The authors demonstrate that showing and telling can provide images of complex instructional practice; yet they are seldom sufficient for establishing the kind of collegial critique or reflection that promote continuous improvement on a large scale. Finally, the authors examine the conditions that contribute to teacher leaders' show-and-tell strategies.

Turning to contextual aspects of teacher leadership, Melinda Mangin examines how the design of teacher leadership initiatives can influence enactment in Chapter 5. Mangin studied variations in mathematics teacher leader role design in five districts. The investigation focused on three primary design components: (1) employee selection and professional development, (2) resource distribution, and (3) communications management. Mangin's analysis of districts' design decisions draws on concepts of rational decision making and bounded rationality. The findings highlight factors that constrained districts' ability to optimize teacher leadership design, the trade-offs inherent in different designs, and designs that offered greater potential for advancing effective instructional teacher leadership.

In Chapter 6 Sara Ray Stoelinga uses social network analysis and qualitative data analysis to investigate the institutionalization of a literacy coordinator position. Stoelinga found that the alignment between formal and informal leadership roles and the positionality of the literacy coordinator within informal communication structures influenced the character and depth of institutionalization. Stoelinga demonstrates that informal teacher leadership can be extremely powerful, either in support of or in opposition to the goals surrounding formal teacher leader roles.

In Chapter 7 Eric Camburn, Steven Kimball, and Rebecca Lowenhaupt present a case study of a literacy coach initiative that was implemented in a large, decentralized urban district. They first assess the initiative's potential by viewing it through three lenses: literature on instructional coaching, social and situative learning theories, and arguments about instructional improvement in decentralized contexts. Next, the authors employ mixed-method evaluation, including survey and regression analyses, to describe variation in coaching across the district and examine factors that supported coaching. Their findings show that a series of developments at the district level, as well as competing demands at school sites, diluted the effectiveness of the initiative.

The final two evidence-based chapters present new ways of thinking about teacher leadership roles. In Chapter 8 Jonathan Supovitz applies social network analysis to a national sample of 14 high schools, examining the allocation of instructional leadership across positions, the characteristics of those positions, and the extent to which teachers relied upon them. To elucidate his findings, Supovitz uses the lens of French and Raven's typology of social influence. The findings suggest that instructional leadership comes more informally from colleagues and peers than from the top down or even through formal leader-follower channels and that different leaders emerge depending on the nature of the expertise needed. These findings suggest the need to rethink leadership concepts, including what it means to be a leader, the range of leadership activity in schools, and the complexity of instructional assistance networks.

In Chapter 9 Richard Halverson and Christopher Thomas examine a different kind of instructional leadership in their investigation of how school leaders created data-driven systems to improve instruction. Relying on data from a 5-year National Science Foundation Study, the authors found that school leaders turned to the practices and expertise of student services personnel—school counselors and psychologists—who possess data analysis and utilization expertise as a result of training associated with Individualized Education Programs (IEPs). As such, student services personnel played a role in developing and maintaining support programs to help all students and teachers meet the demands of high-stakes accountability.

Taken together, the chapters in this book serve three main goals. First, they prioritize teaching and learning as a pathway to school improvement. Second, they establish a common understanding of nonsupervisory, school-based, instructional leadership roles. Third, they provide empirical evidence of the conditions and contexts that influence the effectiveness of these roles. As a result, this body of research can inform the development and implementation of future instructional leadership roles and establish a solid foundation for further investigation of their influence on improved instructional outcomes.

REFERENCES

Alliance for Excellent Education. (2003). *Chicago Reading Initiative—Chicago, IL.* Washington, DC: Author.

Cohen, D. K., & Hill, H. C. (2001). *Learning policy: When state education reform works.* New Haven, CT: Yale University Press.

Conley, S. (1991). Review of research on teacher participation in school decision making. In G. Grant (Ed.), *Review of Research in Education* (Vol. 17, pp. 225–266). Washington, DC: American Educational Research Association.

Crowther, F., Kaagan, S. S., Ferguson, M., & Hann, L. (2002). *Developing teacher leaders: How teacher leadership enhances school success.* Thousand Oaks, CA: Corwin Press.

Datnow, A., & Castellano, M. E. (2001). Managing and guiding school reform: Leadership in Success for All schools. *Educational Administration Quarterly, 37*(2), 219–249.

Elmore, R. F., & Burney, D. (1997). *Investing in teacher learning: Staff development and instructional improvement in Community District #2, New York City.* Paper prepared for the National Commission on Teaching and America's Future. Philadelphia, PA: Consortium for Policy Research in Education.

Firestone, W. A., & Bader, B. (1991). Professionalism or bureaucracy? Redesigning teaching. *Educational Evaluation and Policy Analysis, 13*(1), 67–86.

Gronn, P. (2000). Distributed properties: A new architecture for leadership. *Educational Management and Administration, 28*(3), 317–338.

Hallman, S. R., Wenzel, S. A., & Fendt, C. R. (2004). *CMSI/CUSP elementary school development, 2003–04: The Specialist Report—Report B.* Chicago: University of Illinois–Chicago, CMSI Evaluation Project.

Harris, A., & Muijs, D. (2005). *Improving schools through teacher leadership.* New York, NY: Open University Press.

Hart, A. W. (1990). Work redesign: A review of literature for education reform. In S. B. Bacharach (Ed.), *Advances in research and theories of school management and educational policy* (Vol. 1, pp. 31–69). Greenwich, CT: JAI Press.

Hart, A. W. (1995). Reconceiving school leadership: Emergent views. *Elementary School Journal, 96*(1), 9–28.

Hawley, W. D., & Valli, L. (1999). The essentials of effective professional development. In L. Darling-Hammond & G. Sykes (Eds.), *Teaching as the learning profession: Handbook of policy and practice* (pp. 127–150). San Francisco: Jossey-Bass.

Heller, M. F., & Firestone, W. A. (1995). Who's in charge here? Sources of leadership for change in eight schools. *Elementary School Journal, 96*(1), 65–86.

Hightower, A. M., Knapp, M. S., Marsh, J., & McLaughlin, M. (2002). *School districts and instructional renewal.* New York: Teachers College Press.

Katzenmeyer, M., & Moller, G. (1996). *Awakening the sleeping giant: Leadership development for teachers.* Thousand Oaks, CA: Corwin Press.

Kelleher, M. (2002, April). Chicago Reading Initiative: Building a program under the gun. *Catalyst Chicago, 8*(7), 4–5, 7.

Lichtenstein, G., McLaughlin, M., & Knudsen, J. (1992). Teacher empowerment and professional knowledge. In A. Lieberman (Ed.), *The changing contexts of teaching: 91st yearbook of the National Society for the Study of Education*, Part 1 (pp. 37–58). Chicago: University of Chicago Press.

Lieberman, A., & Miller, L. (2004). *Teacher leadership.* San Francisco: Jossey-Bass.

Mangin, M. M. (2005). Distributed leadership and the culture of schools: Teacher leaders' strategies for gaining access to classrooms. *Journal of School Leadership, 15*(4), 456–484.

Mangin, M. M. (2006). Teacher leadership and instructional improvement: Teachers' perspectives. In W. K. Hoy & C. Miskel (Eds.), *Contemporary issues in educational policy and school outcomes* (pp. 159–192). Greenwich, CT: Information Age Publishing.

Mangin, M. M. (2007). Facilitating elementary principals' support for instructional teacher leadership. *Educational Administration Quarterly, 43*(3), 319–357.

Murphy, J. (2005). *Connecting teacher leadership and school improvement.* Thousand Oaks, CA: Corwin Press.

Smylie, M. A. (1997). Research on teacher leadership: Assessing the state of the art. In B. J. Biddle (Ed.), *International handbook of teachers and teaching* (pp. 521–592). Dordrecht, The Netherlands: Kluwer.

Smylie, M. A., Conley, S., & Marks, H. M. (2002). Exploring new approaches to teacher leadership for school improvement. In J. Murphy (Ed.), *The educational leadership challenge: Redefining leadership for the 21st century; 101st yearbook of the National Society for the Study of Education*, Part 1 (pp. 162–188). Chicago: University of Chicago Press.

Spillane, J. (2006). *Distributed Leadership.* San Francisco: Jossey-Bass.

Spillane, J., Halverson, R., & Diamond, J. B. (2004). Towards a theory of leadership practice: A distributed perspective. *Journal of Curriculum Studies, 36*(1), 3–34.

Stein, M. K. (1998). *High performance learning communities in District 2: Report on year one implementation of school learning communities.* Pittsburgh, PA: Learning Research and Development Center, University of Pittsburgh.

Stoelinga, S. R. (2006). *Seeking the "S" in CMSI: History and implementation of the science initiative*. Chicago: The PRAIRIE Group.

Stoelinga, S. R., Fendt, C. R., & Wenzel, S. A. (2005). *Analysis of schools on probation implementing CMSI curricula*. Chicago: University of Illinois–Chicago, CMSI Evaluation Project.

York-Barr, J., & Duke, K. (2004). What do we know about teacher leadership? Findings from two decades of scholarship. *Review of Educational Research, 74*(3), 255–316.

Instructional Coaching:
The State of the Art

James E. Taylor

INSTRUCTIONAL COACHING, or teacher leadership of instruction, is one of the most prominent and promising practices in education today, and yet it is not well understood. The purpose of this chapter is to define the phenomenon of instructional coaching, consider its origins, examine why it might work, and explore how it fits into contemporary American schooling.

Improved student learning outcomes is the ultimate goal of most school reform efforts; in this respect coaching reforms are no different. One of the strongest determinants of improved student learning outcomes is improved instruction (e.g., Gamoran, Porter, Smithson, & White, 1997; Sanders & Horn, 1998; Westbury, 1993). However, instructional practices are resistant to change and the instructional improvement process is complex (Berman & McLaughlin, 1978; Fullan, 1991). A widely accepted conclusion of research on school reform and instructional improvement is that local school leadership is critical to the implementation and sustainability of reform (Bodilly, 1998; Bryk, Camburn, & Louis, 1999; Kirby, Berends, & Naftel, 2001). Yet much of the existing research exclusively focuses on the instructional leadership provided by the principal (e.g., Edmonds, 1979; Hallinger & Murphy, 1985; Lipham, 1981) and concludes that such leadership is in short supply because a large portion of the principal's day is consumed by managerial tasks (e.g., Kmetz & Willower, 1982). These constraints point to a pessimistic prognosis for school reform. Instructional improvement appears possible only in schools with an extraordinary or "heroic" principal.

Increasingly, both practitioners and researchers are looking to teacher leadership and other distributed forms of leadership as a promising strategy for instructional improvement because of the increased leadership capacity beyond the principal (Elmore, 2000). Distributed leadership takes many forms, ranging from the creation of assistant principal positions to nonsupervisory instructional leadership roles, to teacher collaboration initiatives.

The current dominant strategy of distributed leadership is to activate additional formal and informal teacher leadership roles to expand responsibility for leadership over instructional issues beyond the principal. Researchers, reformers, and practitioners use a wide variety of terms to refer to these roles. I will use the term *instructional coaching* because of its widespread use by practitioners.

The creation of instructional coaching roles is a growing trend (Coggins, Stoddard, & Cutler, 2003; Guiney, 2001; Neufeld & Roper, 2003). Although highly visible examples of literacy coaches in New York City, San Diego, and Boston indicate that these positions hold promise for promoting change (Elmore & Burney, 1997; Hightower, Knapp, March, & McLaughlin, 2002; Stein, 1998), little empirical evidence for the effectiveness of coaching and distributing leadership exists. This strategy of adding nonsupervisory, instructional leadership positions to increase the total amount of instructional leadership capacity in schools is especially prominent in schools implementing Reading First projects (Toll, 2006), National Science Foundation Math/Science Partnerships (Osthoff & Cantrell, 2005), and comprehensive school reform programs (Camburn, Rowan, & Taylor, 2003; Poglinco et al., 2003). Furthermore, as the No Child Left Behind Act of 2001 (Public Law 107-110) prompts states to identify more schools as in need of improvement, districts are likely to intensify their interest in instructional coaching as a means to improving low-performing schools by examining data, developing teachers' skills and improving classroom instruction.

Despite the great interest in this strategy, instructional coaching roles remain ambiguous and complex. It is difficult for coaches to enact roles they don't fully understand and it is difficult for researchers to develop a body of evidence around a phenomenon that they have yet to fully articulate.

WHAT IS INSTRUCTIONAL COACHING?

It is no easy feat to define instructional coaching. There is a broad array of coaching models and an even wider variety of ways in which coaches and others in similar positions have enacted those models (Poglinco et al., 2003). One of the largest obstacles to understanding instructional coaching is the lack of a clear definition of the phenomenon or agreement on what counts as coaching. Although I cannot resolve all disagreements here, I will articulate a definition.

Instructional leadership is the performance of a set of functions that establish goals for instruction and engage others in the processes of classroom instruction and instructional improvement. *Instructional coaching*—one form of instructional leadership—is characterized by nonsupervisory/nonevaluative individualized guidance and support that takes place directly within the instructional setting. This support is intended to promote teachers' learning and application of instructional expertise. Four key components make up the definition of instructional leadership and coaching: (1) the meaning of leadership, (2) the objective of leadership, (3) the functions of leadership, and (4) the sources of leadership.

The Meaning of Leadership

Leadership fundamentally means setting a direction and getting others to head in that direction. There are many ways to set a path and get others to follow it; coaching relies on developing the motivation and capacity of individuals to choose to follow that path.

The Objective of Leadership

There are a wide variety of types and subtypes of school leadership but the terms I've defined prioritize instructional leadership. This priority exists because setting instructional goals, developing instructional expertise, and promoting the application of expertise in the service of those goals are a primary means of improving student learning outcomes. Other types of leadership are valid and may complement or supplement instructional leadership.

The Functions of Leadership

There are certain leadership functions or activities that significantly influence instruction and the environment for instructional improvement (e.g., Bossert, Dwyer, Rowan, & Lee, 1982). Although researchers have suggested numerous instructional leadership functions (e.g., Hallinger & Murphy, 1985; Heller & Firestone, 1995), consensus on some basic leadership functions helps sustain the integrity of the instructional leadership construct. Sheppard (1996) found that most researchers identify lists of instructional leadership functions that largely overlap with those in Hallinger and Murphy's (1985) pioneering work on the Principal Instructional Management Rating Scale (PIMRS). In this work, the main functions of instructional leadership included framing and communicating school goals, supervising and evaluating instruction, knowing and coordinating curriculum, monitoring student progress, setting standards, modeling expectations, protecting instructional time, and directing professional development.

The core functions of coaching draw heavily from the notion of instructional leadership. However, the literature on coaching stresses that coaches operate outside the formal line of authority and do not hold supervisory or formal evaluative roles (e.g., Coggins et al., 2003), thus distinguishing them from the instructional leadership positions of superintendents, principals, and department chairs. The supervisory and evaluative functions outlined in the instructional leadership literature are reconceived in coaching as collegial interactions focused on providing constructive feedback and prompting self-reflection.

Another hallmark of coaching is the emphasis on working within the classroom setting. Coaches typically situate their work within the physical classroom or within artifacts (e.g., simulations, videotape, lesson plans, student work) of classroom instruction, often enacting the role of the classroom teacher through planning lessons, modeling lessons, coteaching, and observing instruction.

For coaches, the instructional leadership function of directing professional development is a central component of the role. Whereas the typical instructional leader (e.g., principal) might ensure that teachers receive staff development, coaches work directly to develop teachers' instructional expertise, frequently working one-on-one with teachers to deliver individualized professional development. Although personalized attention may be provided by principals, it serves as a hallmark of coaching in a way that isn't true of instructional leadership more generally.

Coaching also involves other instructional leadership functions: framing and communicating goals, knowing and coordinating curriculum, using data to monitor student progress, setting standards, and protecting instructional time. Collectively, these functions can be referred to as developing instructional capacity—the heart of coaching.

The Sources of Leadership

The true sources of leadership have been obscured by the tendency to confuse function with position. The functions of instructional leadership are performed collectively by multiple sources and by both formal and informal roles (e.g., Heller & Firestone, 1995; Spillane, Halverson, & Diamond, 2001). Until recently, researchers had rarely looked beyond the principal as a source of instructional leadership. Distributed leadership theory has called on researchers to identify the potential sources of social influence on instruction, such as administrators, district staff, instructional coaches, teachers, and even the teaching materials and artifacts that teach-ers use (Spillane et al., 2001). Thus researchers have begun to investigate how individuals in positions other than the principalship provide school leadership.

WHAT ARE THE MAIN TYPES OF COACHING?

Given this multitude of potential sources of instructional leadership, which positions fit the definition of instructional coaching? Table 2.1 shows a classification of common educational leadership positions organized by the typical focus of their leadership activities. Positions in the lower right cell of the table tend to be nonsupervisory and focused directly on instruction; therefore, they most closely fit this definition. Of course, formal positions and titles do not strictly determine roles and actions. Similarly named posi-

Table 2.1. Focus of various leadership positions.

	Indirect or Noninstructional	Direct Instructional
Supervisory/ evaluative	Superintendent	Department chair
	Assistant superintendent	Assistant superintendent for instruction
	Principal	
	Assistant principal	Principal (instructionally focused)
	Chief financial officer	Assistant principal for instruction
	School board	
	Teacher on special assignment	Peer evaluator
		Teacher on special assignment
Nonsupervisory/ nonevaluative	Professional developer	Coach
	Peer teacher	Facilitator
	Other nonteaching staff (e.g., school secretary)	Coordinator
		Specialist
	Union representative	Consultant
	Teacher on special assignment	Professional developer coach
		Higher ed instructor (internship)
		Mentor
		Master teacher
		Peer teacher
		Teacher on special assignment

tions may perform dissimilar functions in different places or even within the same jurisdiction by different individuals (accordingly, *teacher on special assignment* appears as an all-encompassing term in all four cells of the table). Ultimately, observation is the only way to determine if a particular position functions as an instructional coach role. Even among formally labeled coaching positions, there is still great variety in the functions being performed. Table 2.2 lists the key dimensions on which instructional coaching positions vary.

WHAT ARE THE ORIGINS OF INSTRUCTIONAL COACHING?

Instructional coaching originates from an attempt to remedy the problematic organizational realities of schooling. As a form of instructional leadership, coaching is intended to tighten the traditionally loose coupling between leaders and the core technical work of the school organization. Furthermore, coaching aims to distribute responsibility for school leadership across a broader set of individuals, thereby augmenting the overall capacity for instructional improvement.

Loose Coupling

A seminal finding of organizational design research is the "loose coupling" of the school organization first suggested by Bidwell (1965) and extended by Weick (1976) and Meyer and Rowan (1978). Loose coupling describes schools as having a variety of instructional tasks which the actors in a school are uncertain about how to complete. Therefore, leaders in a school have only weak connections to the tasks of instruction and teachers have weak control over instructional tasks and outcomes. In Rowan's (1990) words, "in loose coupling theory, the uncertain and poorly understood technology of instruction is seen to result in a lack of either bureaucratic or professional controls over classroom instruction" (p. 355). Complementary work done on the sociological nature of American schools revealed norms of teacher isolation and privacy, a lack of bureaucratic or professional controls on teachers (Lortie, 1975), and a fragmented, compartmentalized structure (Jackson, 1986) that is essentially stable and unchanging (Goodlad, 1984). Essentially, schools were described as ineffective organizations where leaders lacked influence over the core work of the school: instruction.

These challenges prompted the development of the "effective schools" literature (for a review see Purkey & Smith, 1983) in an effort to identify the characteristics that distinguish effective from ineffective schools. One of the most critical characteristics of effective schools was strong principal

Table 2.2. Dimensions of Instructional Coaching

Dimension	Classification
Basic dimensions	
Type of coach	Specialist ↔ Generalist
	Coaches typically either specialize in a particular subject, grade level, or component of a program or generally lead the school's reform effort (Neufeld & Roper, 2003). Specialists often are known as content coaches or subject specialists, while generalists are often called change coaches, reform facilitators, change agents, program coordinators, or, somewhat confusingly, turnaround specialists.
Purpose	Organizational ↔ Collegial ↔ Personal growth
	Organizational (technical assistance for transfer to practice) vs. collegial (collaboration for building professional culture) vs. personal (challenge coaching for individualized problem-solving and growth) (Garmston, 1987, pp. 18–21)
Knowledge and skills	Content knowledge ↔ Pedagogical knowledge ↔ Curricular knowledge
	Most coaching is focused on developing teachers' pedagogy or instructional skills, strategies, and techniques. Coaching may also focus on building teachers' knowledge of subject matter.
Type of coachee	Novice ↔ Learner ↔ Expert
	Many coaches adapt their actions and their form, orientation and style to the particular type of coachee and beyond that to the nature of individual coachee's needs as well as their receptiveness to advice.
Procedural dimensions	
Form	Technical ↔ Collaborative ↔ Problem-solving ↔ Simple support
	Technical coaching is characterized by the coach as expert or mentor. Collaborative coaching puts the coach and teacher both in the role of reciprocal learner. Coaching as problem solving involves mirroring in a facilitative style and requires expertise in coaching but less expertise in the subject matter as the coach mainly prompts the teacher to reflect and solve the problems themselves based on this introspection (e.g., cognitive coaching). Support is provided in all forms of coaching, but coaching as simple support is defined by providing support and encouragement as an end in itself (e.g., provide materials so that teachers can conduct lessons) rather than as a means to building rapport or changing technical practice.

(continued)

Table 2.2. (*continued*)

Dimension	Classification
Orientation	Active ↔ Passive
	Individuals can perform coaching functions either by actively seeking out people to develop and problems to solve or by passively responding to requests for assistance or questions when asked.
Style	Directive ↔ Facilitative
	Individuals can perform coaching functions either by telling teachers what to do or by asking and eliciting self-reflection. It may be that coaches continuously adapt their orientation to their coachee or their purpose.
Structural dimensions	
Authority	Formal ↔ Informal
	A formal coach performs the functions of coaching within a structure of dedicated time and a position designed to provide instructional leadership. An informal coach performs the functions of coaching but is a peer or mentor with no dedicated time and serving in the position of teacher.
Location	On-site ↔ Off-site
	Most attention has been paid to coaches located at the school site. Many Comprehensive School Reform models, Reading First projects, and some districts have created a position located at and dedicated to a single school in order to enhance coaching at that school. However, there are examples of push-in or pull-out coaching where coaches periodically visit the school site (e.g., AIR, 2005) or teachers travel to another school site to be coached. In other situations videotape or distance-learning technology can enable teachers to retain the inside-the-classroom setting but leave the school site to receive coaching.
Ratio/span of control	One teacher to: One grade ↔ One school ↔ Multiple schools
	Most attention has been paid to coaches working with one entire school (although they may begin with only a few teachers and gradually phase in other teachers and grades). However, there are examples of smaller teacher to coach ratios (e.g., AIR, 2005) as well as many examples of coaches with much larger ratios, given that they work with multiple schools.
Duration	Full-time ↔ Part-time
Frequency	Continuous ↔ Regular or periodic ↔ Rare
Span	Multiyear ↔ One year ↔ Less than a year
Grade level	Elementary ↔ Middle ↔ High
Subject	Literacy ↔ Math ↔ Science ↔ Other

leadership, which spawned a literature on instructional leadership. However, as noted above, this instructional leadership literature focused on the principal and typically found strong principal instructional leadership to be in short supply. In addition to the literature on effective schools, the problem of loose coupling also resulted in a move toward site-based management in an effort to move decision making closer to the technical core; however, such decision making rarely focused on instructional matters (Robertson, Wohlsetter, & Mohrman, 1995). Similarly, loose-coupling prompted the creation of various professional teacher leadership roles, which also lacked direct connections to instruction (Smylie, Conley, & Marks, 2002).

Like these other developments, coaching is intended to tighten the traditionally loose coupling between leaders and the core technical work of the school organization. To do this, instructional coaching configures additional formal and informal roles to formally expand responsibility for instructional leadership beyond the principal.

Distributed Leadership

The distributed leadership perspective recognizes the reality of multiple sources of instructional leadership. Smylie, Conley, and Marks (2002) and Weise and Murphy (1995) note that ideas of distributed leadership date back to the early 1900s. The distributed leadership literature can be divided into four distributions of leadership: source-based, total, dispersed, and configurational (Taylor, 2004). Coaching has its roots in the source-based literature on teacher leadership (e.g., reform facilitators and change agents) but has important connections to the other distributions of leadership as well. Below, I review these four leadership distributions and the relationship of coaching to each.

Source-based distributions. The original source-based conception of leadership drew upon the instructional leadership literature and the portrayal of principals as the sole source of leadership. More recently, researchers have argued that a solitary principal cannot perform all the tasks that effective school leadership demands and that other sources of leadership must be activated (Kaplan & Owings, 1999; Rallis & Highsmith, 1986; Shachar, 1996). These researchers typically reject the "heroic" view of the principal in favor of administrators acting in pairs or teams. Rallis and Highsmith (1986) stress that administrative management and instructional leadership are two fundamentally different tasks that require distinct skills rarely present in a single individual. For this reason, they conclude that more than one leader is needed for effective school leadership. Kaplan and

Owings (1999) suggest using assistant principals as a source of instructional leadership. Focusing on the district level, Floden et al. (1988; see also Wimpelberg, 1988) suggest that instructional leadership can be performed by superintendents and other district staff. At the secondary level, Hallinger (1989) examines the decentralization of instructional leadership into teams in secondary schools. Bird and Little (1986) show that secondary school principals delegate instructional leadership responsibilities to teams of administrators and teachers.

In research on educational program implementation, researchers suggest that school-level staff are an important source of leadership. Gersten, Carnine, and Green (1982) conclude that instructional leadership is a set of functions rather than an aspect of the principalship, stating "that it is less important who performed the functions than it is to what extent they are performed" (p. 20). Joyce and Showers (1983) stress the potential influence of school-site coaches on organizational norms and teachers' instructional change. However, in contrast to the idea that it does not matter who performs the functions, Joyce and Showers stress the special set of functions associated with coaching, noting that the coach is uniquely situated to provide instructional leadership. Cox (1983) highlights the role of external change agents (e.g., facilitators, consultants) and central office staff (e.g., curriculum coordinators, program directors, and specialists) in providing expertise, resources, external linkages, and school- and classroom-level assistance. In their research on reform implementation, Hord and Huling-Austin (1986) report that "the principal was not the sole change facilitator" (p. 112). Hord and Hall (1987) suggest that, whereas the principal was the primary intervener on teachers as a faculty, the "second change facilitator" was the primary intervener on individual teachers and did the most to develop supportive organizational arrangements, provide consultation and reinforcement, and monitor and evaluate in most of the schools studied.

Others have suggested that the source for expertise needed to lead instruction lies in teachers (Carnegie Forum on Education and the Economy, 1986). Hart (1995) outlines several purposes for promoting teacher leadership: an ideological commitment to democratic or communitarian philosophies of organizational participation (Sergiovanni, 1994); an attempt to tap the underutilized resource of teacher expertise (Heller & Firestone, 1995); an effort to redesign teacher work with professionalism, autonomy, and career advancement opportunities in order to recruit, retain, and motivate teachers (Smylie, 1994); an attempt to enlist teachers as leaders of reform efforts since their decisions determine the level of innovation implementation (Heller & Firestone, 1995); and the creation of a professional workplace (Little, 1995).

However, reformers have struggled to achieve these purposes and develop strong teacher leadership. Some of the structures reformers have created to support teacher leadership include peer coaching (Joyce & Showers, 1982), mentor teacher programs, teacher centers, or lead teachers (Lieberman, 1988), teacher career ladders (Hart, 1994), site-based management (Robertson et al., 1995), and shared decision making (Conley, Schmidle, & Shedd, 1988). Related research suggests that these initiatives failed to realize the goal of distributing instructional leadership more broadly across the school community due to conditions that worked against the broad exercise of strong instructional leadership (Hart, 1995; Hoerr, 1996; Keedy, 1999; Lieberman, 1988; Little, 1995; Smylie & Denny, 1990). For example, principals may act as an obstacle if they lack the willingness or preparation to support more dispersed leadership in their schools (Hart & Murphy, 1994). Furthermore, teachers typically lack formal authority to exert leadership (Hart, 1995), the additional time required to exercise collegial leadership, the training and capacity for leadership, and the willingness to take on added responsibilities and accountability (Hoerr, 1996). Other researchers point out the trade-offs that may offset the benefits of teacher leadership. For example, as teachers exert greater leadership, they may face role ambiguity, conflict, and work overload (Smylie & Denny, 1990). Increased teacher leadership may violate the egalitarian ethic of the teacher workplace (Lieberman, 1988) and result in reduced teacher collegiality (Little, 1995). Teacher leadership becomes institutionalized and effective in a school only when it is perceived as compatible with the school's prevailing patterns of norms, power, and practice. Without this fit, the leadership is "neutered by dominant socialization cues" (Keedy, 1999, p. 787).

Total, dispersed, and configurational distributions. A more comprehensive perspective—*total* leadership distribution—is advanced by Ogawa and Bossert (1995) who conceptualize leadership as an organizational quality or the total cumulative distribution of leadership in an organization. Ogawa and Bossert explain how the dominant technical-rational conception locates leadership at the highest levels of the hierarchy, in roles that focus on organizational goal attainment. They contrast this perspective with an institutional theory-based view of leadership as an organizational quality whereby individuals throughout organizations lead. Thus leadership is not confined to formal roles; rather it flows through the networks of roles that comprise organizations (Thompson, 1967). Similarly, the medium of leadership is not individual action but rather social interaction. This view aligns with Tannenbaum's (1962) research on organization-wide total leadership.

The remaining two distributions of leadership—*dispersed* and *configurational*—build on the notion of total leadership as it is spread across multiple leaders. Heller and Firestone (1995) examined the pattern of leadership distribution in schools and found that schools that more successfully institutionalized innovations had a set of leadership functions that were performed redundantly by individuals in a variety of roles throughout the organization, including central office staff, principals, teachers, and external consultants. Building on this work, Mayrowetz and Weinstein (1999) described a case study of one district's institutionalization of a special education inclusion innovation. They found that people in a variety of roles performed the leadership functions and that the relative degree of institutionalization was consistent with the level of redundancy. Gronn (2002) has furthered this strand of research on *configurational* leadership distribution by drawing greater attention to the interdependencies among leaders. Gronn argues that particular patterns of leadership role overlap might be more or less effective. Spillane, Halverson, and Diamond (2000, 2001) expand the concept of *configurational* distribution even further, arguing that leadership is constituted in the interactions of leaders, followers, and their situational contexts. This conceptualization moves beyond the notion of leadership as a set of functions performed by multiple persons and draws on ideas of distributed cognition and activity theory to stress the social and situational distribution of task enactment.

Researchers have begun to empirically test the effects of distributed leadership (e.g., Leithwood & Jantzi, 2000; Pounder, Ogawa, & Adams, 1995; Taylor, 2004). However, as these early studies provide initial findings, they also raise new questions as recent treatments reveal the complexity of the construct and the theory of its effects. Consequently, the concept and the effects of distributed leadership remain ambiguous.

Instructional Coaching Versus Other Professional Development

Given that coaching is but one of many forms of instructional leadership and professional development, what is the impetus for its increased popularity? Just as coaching originates from the problematic organizational realities of schools, it is fueled by the inadequacies of existing forms of professional development. Teachers' preservice education is often weak (Levine, 2005), which creates a need for strong in-service professional development. Garet, Porter, Desimone, Birman, & Yoon (2001) argue that well-designed professional development is focused on instructional content, sustained over time, embedded in practice, based in active learning, collaborative, and coherent. However, much of teachers' in-service professional development is made up of brief and incoherent activities (Garet et al., 2001; Kennedy, 1998). Similarly, instructional leadership from principals often consists of rare and brief occasions of instructional guidance, as discussed above. In contrast, instructional coaching extends, embeds, particularizes, brings expertise to, dedicates time for, deprivatizes, connects, and professionalizes professional development.

Professional development sessions are also criticized for being overly generalized. Most professional development sessions take place outside the classroom setting, requiring teachers to transfer new knowledge to the classroom. Coaching, which takes place in the instructional setting, addresses the context-specific nature of teaching. It treats teaching as nonroutine and complex, bringing technical expertise directly into the teacher's classroom. As such, coaching provides learning opportunities that can be adapted to the particular classroom context. Moreover, coaching aids in the transfer and application of new learning to teachers' daily classroom instruction (Joyce & Showers, 1980).

Unlike typical professional development, coaching extends teachers' learning opportunities over a longer span of time and works to connect the practices of teachers within a school. Traditionally, teachers work in isolation, their practice largely unseen by their colleagues. Coaching dedicates extended time to the examination of instructional practice and attempts to connect teachers to create networks that enhance social capital and information flow. As such, coaching develops trust, instills collective responsibility, imparts an innovative orientation, and provides an example of professionalism around instructional practice.

WHY MIGHT INSTRUCTIONAL COACHING WORK?

Because coaching is cited as an effective means to improve teaching and learning, despite the lack of evidence to support such a claim (Russo, 2004), it is critical to examine how and why coaching might improve instruction. Leadership is primarily an indirect process of influence; therefore the influence of leadership/coaching should be examined based on the key mediating outcomes of teachers' thinking, motivation, and knowledge about instructional practice. These intermediary outcomes serve as the basis for teachers' instructional improvement efforts, which ultimately affect students' learning.

Figure 2.1 diagrams the chain of instructional improvement. Beginning on the left, instructional coaching is hypothesized as one factor affecting teachers' cognitive schemata related to instructional improvement. Here, instructional coaching is shown as a single factor but, as shown above in Table 2.2, instructional coaching comes in many types and varies on many dimensions. It stands to reason that some types of instructional coaching are more effective than others, but to date there is insufficient evidence to

Figure 2.1. Chain of instructional improvement.

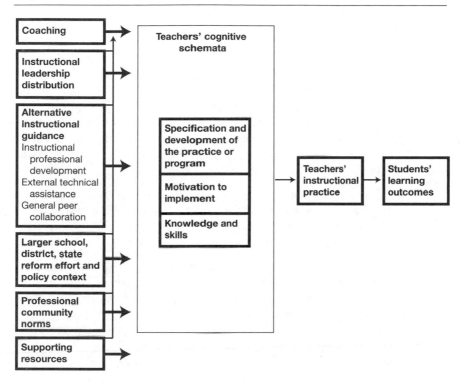

judge which types or dimensions are most effective. The heavy arrows show the main effects and the light arrows show how other factors may interact with and moderate the effect of coaching. The large box in the center represents the intervening role that teachers' cognition plays in mediating the effects of coaching as well as teaching and learning outcomes.

School leaders depend upon teachers' voluntary decisions to enact reform, but school leaders can intervene on the cognitive schemata (i.e., thought structures and processes) that teachers use to think about reform. Three cognitive schemata are necessary for a teacher to improve instruction. First, all instructional improvement efforts are accompanied by some effort to specify and develop an understanding of the desired practice, that is, the effort to define, explain, interpret, and develop their objectives and requirements for action (Cohen & Ball, 1999). Second, teachers' motivation to implement the practice results from their internal motivational calculus of the likelihood that they can make the required changes, that their performances will produce student learning outcomes, and that those outcomes will be valued. This notion draws on expectancy-value theory (e.g., Vroom, 1964) and theories of self-efficacy (e.g., Bandura, 1986). Lastly, enacting instruction requires a fundamental knowledge of the instructional content and pedagogical skills (Cohen & Hill, 1998). Taken together, these theories constitute a comprehensive view of teachers' cognitive basis for instructional decision making.

However, none of these cognitions alone is sufficient for teachers' successful changed instructional practice. Cohen's (1990) portrait of Mrs. Oublier, a teacher motivated to reform her instructional practice but lacking clear understanding of the practices to be implemented, demonstrates that great effort does not necessarily produce the desired practices. Raudenbush, Rowan, and Cheong (1992) argue that

> teachers with high levels of perceived self-efficacy may lack the requisite knowledge or skills to be effective. But low feelings of self-efficacy almost certainly work against effective teaching by decreasing teachers' generative capability to cope with the uncertainties of classrooms. (p. 151)

Thus, having the knowledge and skills to implement reform-type instructional practice does not in itself guarantee effective performance of that practice (Bandura, 1986). Instead, effective practice depends on a clear understanding and the personal expectation that one can mobilize the necessary knowledge and skills to teach effectively under varied and unpredictable circumstances. In this way understanding, motivation, and knowledge are all prerequisites for changed instructional practice.

Shaping Teachers' Thinking About Instruction

Social cognitive theory (Bandura, 1986) provides several insights into why coaching may shape teachers' thinking about instructional reform. Bandura (1986) postulates four sources of information that are used to learn new schemata and reconstruct existing schemata: *Enactive attainment*, or mastery experience, is direct personal experience derived from acting out the performance and experiencing the effects of those actions. *Vicarious experiences* are those where a teacher watches another person's performance and witnesses the outcomes. *Verbal persuasion* is oral or text communication that convinces teachers of their ability to enact the performance and the value of the performance for achieving desired outcomes. *Information about physiological and emotional states* includes personal judgments of the degree of anxiety or stress associated with the performance. Each source provides information that teachers process into new cognitive schemata about the likelihood that they can perform the required tasks, that their performances will produce outcomes, and that those outcomes will be valued.

Coaching functions mirror Bandura's four sources of information in that coaches provide information to teachers about instructional improvement practices and programs. Coaches verbally persuade teachers, create opportunities for teachers to practice and receive performance feedback, provide models of desired practice for teachers to observe, and psychologically support teachers. Moreover, coaching functions can indirectly encourage implementation of instructional improvement practices and programs by increasing teachers' understanding of the effort, efficacy-expectancy-value motivation for the effort, and knowledge and skills needed for the effort. Below, I explore how one coaching function—developing instructional capacity—serves as a source of verbal persuasion, vicarious experience, enactive attainment, and psychological support (see Taylor, 2004, for a discussion of how the other coaching functions shape teachers' instructional decision making).

Developing Instructional Capacity

Coaches develop teachers' instructional capacity through the collective processes of monitoring practice through observation, providing constructive feedback, encouraging self-reflection, modeling within the classroom setting, and providing professional development.

Monitoring through observation is a way to identify when teachers' practice departs from the intended reform efforts. For teachers who resist a reform practice, observations may provide critical enactive experiences to encourage teaching that aligns with the curriculum or reform program. Thus, monitoring through observation provides teachers with an important source of information influencing their thinking about efficacy, instrumentality, and valence. In turn, feedback that focuses on teachers' strengths and areas for improvement can provide teachers with verbal persuasion that they are making progress toward reform. Similarly, when coaches model practices within the classroom, teachers learn vicariously as they observe the kind of teaching they are supposed to implement. Modeling provides evidence that reform practices can be accomplished in the teachers' own context.

Building on the work of Joyce and Showers (1982), recent researchers have explored the importance of developing instructional capacity through coaching (Elmore & Burney, 1997; Neufeld & Roper, 2003; Poglinco et al., 2003; Walsh-Symonds, 2003). Coaching activities include modeling but also involve specific analysis and facilitation that is explicitly tied to teachers' ongoing work. Coaches work with teachers to plan and implement specific lessons, give constructive technical feedback on practice, prompt self-reflection, and provide professional development sessions to individuals and groups. Showers and Joyce (1996) found that teachers who experienced coaching implemented new strategies more appropriately than teachers who were not coached.

Coaching activities develop teachers' understanding of the instructional improvement effort and its practices through ongoing consultation, as well as through the enactive experience of working side by side with an expert. Coaching also provides access to expertise, technical assistance, and socioemotional support that builds teachers' expectations that they can produce the desired performances.

HOW DOES INSTRUCTIONAL COACHING FIT INTO SCHOOLS?

How does school context influence teacher leaders who are performing instructional coaching? These leaders' potential for effectiveness is rooted at the intersection of the work of the school. Accordingly, they are in contact with all elements of the school and subject to the influence of all of the school's contexts. As shown in Figure 2.1 (above), there are at least five key contexts that may moderate the effect of coaching on teachers' instruction: other leadership; alternative instructional guidance; the larger reform effort and policy context; faculty norms; and supporting resources.

First, coaches are not solitary leaders and coaching needs to be considered within the full distribution of leadership. Principal leadership serves as either a supporting or constraining context for coach work (Mangin, 2007). Camburn, Rowan, and Taylor (2003) show that formal instructional leadership is provided by teams of people, rather than individuals. These teams tend to be small, ranging from three to seven formal positions, and heterogeneous with respect to the predominant leadership functions performed by each member. Others have found that informal leadership for instruction can be as significant and even more broadly distributed than formal instructional leadership (see Chapters 6 and 8 of this volume). The configuration of leadership functions across these multiple leaders may generate an enhanced coaching effect through reinforcement and complementary leadership. Alternately, a pattern of incoherent or conflicting leadership functioning may reduce the effect of coaching (e.g., Gronn, 2002; Heller & Firestone, 1995).

Second, other sources of instructional guidance provide another context of competing or complementary instructional guidance. These sources can influence the construction of teachers' understanding of, motivation for, and ability to enact reform efforts. These variables include professional development focused on instruction (Garet et al., 2001; Richardson, 1994;

Sykes, 1996), technical assistance from sources external to the school (Ashton & Webb, 1986; Newmann, Rutter, & Smith, 1989), and general peer collaboration (Bidwell & Yasumoto, 1999; Smylie, 1992; Youngs & King, 2002; Zahorik, 1987). As a point of clarification, I define *general peer collaboration* as collegial activities by teachers with others in the same role (i.e., teacher) that are not focused directly on instruction. Each of these alternative sources of influence on instruction can be replacements for coaching, well-aligned supplements reinforcing coaching, or incoherent influences competing against coaching. These sources of instructional influence may also influence coaching. For example, leaders may supplement their coaching activities with coordinated external assistance or professional development. Coaches may create structures and allocate time for teachers to collaborate, meet, and plan together (Johnson, 1990). Coaches may also shape the professional community norms of the school (e.g., Bryk et al., 1999).

Third, coaching is influenced by other components of a larger reform effort and by educational policy imperatives. Coaching is rarely undertaken as a stand-alone reform effort. More frequently coaching takes place as a part of a comprehensive school reform effort or in connection with another district reform initiative. In this situation coaching may be reinforced by strong complementary efforts or may be frustrated by weak or incompatible efforts (see Chapter 7 of this volume). Similarly, coaching is likely to be affected by the policy environment, including the evolving national, state, and district policy (Stoelinga, Fendt, & Wenzel, 2005). The policy environment is also comprised of a complex historical accumulation of previous reform initiatives; professional development policies; and teacher recruitment, retention, and collective bargaining realities. The role of instructional coach is implemented within this fluctuating policy environment.

Fourth, the norms of a professional community serve as an important resource for school reform (e.g., Louis, Marks, & Kruse, 1996). This leads us to explore whether coaches' influence may be contingent on the faculty norms that characterize a professional community: trust, collective responsibility, academic emphasis, reflective dialogue, and innovative orientation. When such values are normative in a school, they create an informal social means of influence that predisposes teachers toward instructional improvement.

Specifically, trust supports problem solving, social exchange, professional learning, experimentation, and "a moral imperative to take on the difficult work of school improvement" (Bryk & Schneider, 2003, p. 42). Trust promotes open, complete, and credible communication and facilitates problem solving (Tschannen-Moran & Hoy, 2000). Teachers who view their colleagues as trustworthy experts are more comfortable taking risks, like changing practice. Norms of collective responsibility promote accountability while simultaneously easing individual stress and increasing efficacy (Newmann & Wehlage, 1995). An emphasis on academics can provide teachers with a common justification for attempting reform and maintaining high expectations for performance and outcomes. A professional norm of reflective dialogue promotes inquiry leading to greater professional learning and continuous improvement (King, 2002). Similarly, an innovative orientation lends an air of normalcy to change and indicates a predisposition to professional learning and reform.

In a school characterized by professional norms teachers are predisposed to interpret coaches' actions as benevolent, competent, and directed at shared goals and continuous improvement. In contrast, in a context of distrust, individual interests, low expectations, lack of inquiry and stagnation teachers perceive that normal social relations are characterized by malevolence, incompetence, divergent interests, and unfocused purpose. The effect of similar types of instructional leadership in these varied normative contexts is likely to produce different outcomes. Howell, Dorfman, and Kerr (1986) suggest that supportive group norms that foster cooperation with management can enhance the impact of leadership on outcomes, while unaccepting norms can limit leader impact. In an empirical test of this hypothesis, Taylor (2004) found that leadership only had an effect on teachers' motivation to implement instructional improvement when the normative social resources of a cooperative professional community were present.

Fifth, coaching is most likely to be effective when coaches are supported by a series of key resources: time, logistics, training, and expertise. Reform leaders and school administrators must make time for instructional coaching and must deal with logistical constraints to enable instructional coaches and teachers to collaborate (Ackland, 1991; AIR, 2005). Similarly, expert coaches must be recruited and selected or novice coaches must be trained to perform their new roles (see Chapters 4 and 5 of this volume). There are at least two components to the training that coaches require. First, instructional coaches must have adequate knowledge of effective curriculum and instruction (see Chapter 3 of this volume). Second, they must learn how to relate to adult learners, present professional development sessions, use student performance data, develop collegial rapport, and tailor their work to teachers' needs. In essence, they must learn how to coach.

In summary, the promising practice of coaching is most likely to be effective when placed in a context of complementary leadership, coordinated professional development, coherent reform policy, supportive norms, and adequate resources.

WHAT NEXT?

Although a great deal of conceptual work on coaching has been produced, key issues remain unresolved. Despite the definition advanced in this chapter, the meaning of coaching remains unclear. Furthermore, the role and its functions remain vague. This lack of resolution and clarity is due in part to the very diffuse literature on coaching. Coaching research is currently fragmented and needs to be drawn together into one conversation. Coaching research in the educational leadership literature is set within the distributed leadership perspective and is usually conducted by researchers at institutions of higher education. Other coaching research, conducted mainly by providers of professional development (e.g., National Staff Development Council), can be found in the professional development literature. Some of this research and a great deal of practical knowledge is generated by practicing reformers (e.g., Comprehensive School Reform models, Reading First coaches, the International Reading Association, NSF Math and Science Partnerships). There is also an increasing number of coaching proposals or models (see Greene, 2004). However, there is no common arena for debate, classification, and accumulation of knowledge. While this volume marks a significant contribution, a new journal of instructional coaching or special journal issues in existing publications could further this work. Such a common arena would promote a better understanding of the diversity of coaching and perhaps a resolution to the boundaries of coaching (i.e., what is not coaching). The differentiation of coaching from other related phenomena is critical or it will become indistinct and its effectiveness will be difficult to assess.

There is a real need to understand how coaching works. There is a great deal of recent how-to literature on coaching; however, it is rarely informed by research. Yet this how-to literature fills an immediate need for practitioners of coaching and is by far the most influential literature in schools.

These conclusions point to the need for empirical research on instructional coaching and its effects. To construct a useful research base, we need more empirical study of what coaches do, how they fit into the school (e.g., social network analyses), and how they interact with and depend on the rest of the school. But, most critically, we require rigorous empirical evidence of the effects of coaching on teachers' knowledge, teachers' practice, and students' learning.

REFERENCES

Ackland, R. (1991). A review of the peer coaching literature. *The Journal of Staff Development, 12*(1), 22–27.

American Institutes for Research (AIR). (2005). Conceptual overview of the coaching component of the Reading Professional Development Impact Study. Washington, DC: Author.

Ashton, P. T., & Webb, R. B. (1986). *Making a difference: Teachers' sense of efficacy and student achievement.* New York: Longman.

Bandura, A. (1986). *Social foundations of thought and action: A social cognitive theory.* Englewood Cliffs, NJ: Prentice-Hall.

Berman, P., & McLaughlin, M. W. (1978). *Federal programs supporting educational change: Vol. 8. Implementing and sustaining innovations.* Santa Monica, CA: Rand.

Bidwell, C. (1965). The school as a formal organization. In J. G. March (Ed.), *Handbook of organizations.* Chicago: Rand McNally.

Bidwell, C., & Yasumoto, J. (1999). The collegial focus: Teaching fields, collegial relationships, and instructional practice in American high schools. *Sociology of Education, 72*(4), 234–256.

Bird, T., & Little, J. W. (1986). How schools organize the teaching occupation. *Elementary School Journal, 86*(4), 493–511.

Bodily, S. J. (1998). *Lessons from New American Schools' scale-up phase: Prospects for bringing designs to multiple schools* (Report No. MR-942-NAS). Santa Monica, CA: RAND.

Bossert, S. T., Dwyer, D. C., Rowan, B., & Lee, G. V. (1982). The instructional management role of the principal. *Educational Administration Quarterly, 18*(3), 34–64.

Bryk, A. S., Camburn, E., & Louis, K. S. (1999). Professional community in Chicago elementary schools: Facilitating factors and organizational consequences. *Educational Administration Quarterly, 35*(Suppl. S), 751–781.

Bryk, A. S., & Schneider, B. (2003). Trust in schools: A core resource for reform. *Educational Leadership, 60*(6), 40–44.

Camburn, E., Rowan, B., & Taylor, J. E. (2003). Distributed leadership in schools: The case of elementary schools adopting comprehensive school reform models. *Educational Evaluation and Policy Analysis, 25*(4), 347–373.

Carnegie Forum on Education and the Economy Task Force on Teaching. (1986). *A nation prepared: Teachers for the 21st century.* New York: Carnegie Corporation.

Coggins, C., Stoddard, P., & Cutler, E. (2003, April). *Improving instructional capacity through school-based reform coaches.* Paper presented at the annual meeting of the American Educational Research Association, Chicago. (ERIC No. ED 478744)

Cohen, D. K. (1990). A revolution in one classroom. *Educational Evaluation and Policy Analysis, 12,* 327–345.

Cohen, D. K., & Ball, D. L. (1999). *Instruction, capacity, and improvement.* Philadelphia: Consortium for Policy Research in Education, University of Pennsylvania.

Cohen, D. K., & Hill, H. C. (1998). *Instructional policy and classroom performance: The mathematics reform in California*. Philadelphia: Consortium for Policy Research in Education, University of Pennsylvania.

Conley, S. C., Schmidle, T., & Shedd, J. B. (1988). Teacher participation in the management of school systems. *Teachers College Record, 90,* 259–280.

Cox, P. L. (1983). Complementary roles in successful change. *Educational Leadership, 41*(3), 10–13. (ERIC No. EJ 289712)

Edmonds, R. (1979). Effective schools for the urban poor. *Educational Leadership, 37*(1), 15–24. (ERIC No. EJ 208051)

Elmore, R. (2000). *Building a new structure for school leadership*. Washington, DC: Albert Shanker Institute.

Elmore, R., & Burney, D. (1997). *Investing in teacher learning: Staff development and instructional improvement in Community District #2, New York City*. Paper prepared for the National Commission on Teaching and America's Future. Philadelphia, PA: Consortium for Policy Research in Education.

Floden, R. E., Porter, A. C., Alford, L. E., Freeman, D. J., Irwin, S., Schmidt, W. H., & Schwille, J. R. (1988). Instructional leadership at the district level: A closer look at autonomy and control. *Educational Administration Quarterly, 24*(2), 96–124.

Fullan, M. (1991). *The new meaning of educational change*. New York: Teachers College.

Gamoran, A., Porter, A. C., Smithson, J., & White, P. A. (1997). Upgrading high school mathematics instruction: Improving learning opportunities for low-achieving, low-income youth. *Educational Evaluation and Policy Analysis, 19*(4), 325–338.

Garet, M. S., Porter, A. C., Desimone, L., Birman, B. F., Yoon, K. S. (2001). What makes professional development effective? Results from a national sample of teachers. *American Educational Research Journal, 38*(4), 915–945.

Garmston, R. J. (1987). How administrators support peer coaching. *Educational Leadership, 44*(5), 18–26.

Gersten, R., Carnine, D., & Green, S. (1982). The principal as instructional leader—a second look. *Educational Leadership, 40*(3), 47–50.

Goodlad, J. (1984). *A place called school*. New York: McGraw-Hill.

Greene, T. (2004). *Literature review for school-based staff developers and coaches*. Oxford, OH: National Staff Development Council. Retrieved September 29, 2006, from http://nsde.org/library/schoolboardlitreview.pdf

Gronn, P. (2002). Distributed leadership as a unit of analysis. *Leadership Quarterly, 13*(4), 423–451.

Guiney, E. (2001). Coaching isn't just for athletes: The role of teacher leaders. *Phi Delta Kappan, 82*(10), 740–743.

Hallinger, P. (1989). Developing instructional leadership teams in secondary schools: A framework. *NASSP Bulletin, 73*(517), 84–92.

Hallinger, P., & Murphy, J. (1985). Assessing the instructional management behavior of principals. *Elementary School Journal, 86*(2), 217–247.

Hart, A. W. (1994). Creating teacher leadership roles. *Educational Administration Quarterly, 30*(4), 472–497.

Hart, A. W. (1995). Reconceiving school leadership: Emergent views. *Elementary School Journal, 96*(1), 9–28.

Hart, A. W., & Murphy, M. J. (1994). Preparing principals to lead in restructured schools. In P. Thurston & N. Prestine (Eds.), *Advances in educational administration* (Vol. 2, pp. 151–174). Greenwich, CT: JAI Press.

Heller, M. J., & Firestone, W. A. (1995). Who's in charge here? Sources of leadership for change in eight schools. *Elementary School Journal, 96,* 65–86.

Hightower, A. M., Knapp, M., March, J., & McLaughlin, M. (2002). *School districts and instructional renewal.* New York: Teachers College Press.

Hoerr, T. R. (1996). Collegiality: A new way to define instructional leadership. *Phi Delta Kappan, 77*(5), 380–381.

Hord, S. M., & Hall, G. E. (1987). Analyzing instructional leadership behaviors. *Administrator's Notebook, 32*(8), 44–49.

Hord, S. M., & Huling-Austin, L. L. (1986). Effective curriculum implementation: Some promising new insights. *Elementary School Journal, 87*(1), 97–115.

Howell, J. P., Dorfman, P. W., & Kerr, S. (1986). Moderator variables in leadership research. *Academy of Management Review, 11,* 88–102.

Jackson, P. (1986). *Life in classrooms.* New York: Holt, Rhinehart, & Winston.

Johnson, S. M. (1990). *Teachers at work: Achieving success in our schools.* New York: Basic Books.

Joyce, B., & Showers, B. (1980). Improving in-service training: The messages of research. *Educational Leadership, 37,* 379–385.

Joyce, B., & Showers, B. (1982). *The structure of school improvement.* New York: Longman.

Joyce, B., & Showers, B. (1983). *Power in staff development through research on training.* Alexandria, VA: Association for Supervision and Curriculum Development.

Kaplan, L. S., & Owings, W. A. (1999). Assistant principals: The case for shared instructional leadership. *NASSP Bulletin, 83*(605), 80–94.

Keedy, J. L. (1999). Examining teacher instructional leadership within the small-group dynamics of collegial groups. *Teaching and Teacher Education, 15*(7), 785–799.

Kennedy, M. (1998, April). *Form and substance in inservice teacher education.* Paper presented at the annual meeting of the American Educational Research Association, San Diego, CA.

King, M. B. (2002). Professional development to promote schoolwide inquiry. *Teaching and Teacher Education, 18,* 243–257.

Kirby, S. N., Berends, M., & Naftel, S. (2001). *Implementation in a longitudinal sample of New American Schools: Four years into scale-up* (Report No. MR-1413-EDU). Santa Monica, CA: RAND.

Kmetz, J. T., & Willower, D. J. (1982). Elementary school principals' work behavior. *Educational Administration Quarterly, 18*(4), 62–78.

Leithwood, K., & Jantzi, D. (2000). The effects of different sources of leadership on student engagement in school. In K. Riley & K. Seashore Louis (Eds.), *Leadership for change and school reform* (pp. 50–66). London: Routledge/Falmer.

Levine, A. (2005). *Educating school leaders.* New York: The Educating Schools Project.

Lieberman, A. (1988). *Building a professional culture in schools*. New York: Teachers College Press.

Lipham, J. M. (1981). *Effective principal, effective school*. Reston, VA : National Association of Secondary School Principals.

Little, J. W. (1995). Contested ground: The basis for teacher leadership in two restructuring high schools. *Elementary School Journal, 96*, 47–63.

Lortie, D. (1975). *Schoolteacher*. Chicago: University of Chicago Press.

Louis, K. S., Marks, H. M., & Kruse, S. (1996). Teachers' professional community in restructuring schools. *American Educational Research Journal, 33*(4), 757–798.

Mangin, M. M. (2007). Facilitating elementary principals' support for instructional teacher leadership. *Educational Administration Quarterly, 43*(3), 319–357.

Mayrowetz, D., & Weinstein, C. S. (1999). Sources of leadership for inclusive education: Creating schools for all children. *Educational Administration Quarterly, 35*(3), 423–449.

Meyer, J., & Rowan, B. (1978). The structure of educational organizations. In M. W. Meyer (Ed.), *Environments and Organizations*. San Francisco: Jossey-Bass.

Neufeld, B., & Roper, D. (2003). *Coaching: A strategy for developing instructional capacity*. Colorado: Aspen Institute Program on Education.

Newmann, F. M., Rutter, R. A., & Smith, M. S. (1989). Organizational factors that affect school sense of efficacy, community, and expectations. *Sociology of Education, 62*(4), 221–238.

Newmann, F. M., & Wehlage, G. G. (1995). *Successful school restructuring: A report to the public and educators*. Madison, WI: Wisconsin, Center for Education Research, Center on Organization and Restructuring of Schools.

Ogawa, R. T., & Bossert, S. T. (1995). Leadership as an organizational quality. *Educational Administration Quarterly, 31*(2), 224–243.

Osthoff, E., & Cantrell, S. (2005). *LAUSD mathematics teacher and coach focus groups: Views of district instructional guidance from the field*. A SCALE Technical Report. Paper presented at the annual meeting of the American Educational Research Association, Montreal, Canada.

Poglinco, S. M., Bach, A. J., Hovde, K., Rosenblum, S., Saunders, M., & Supovitz, J. A. (2003). *The heart of the matter: The coaching model in America's Choice schools*. Philadelphia: Consortium for Policy Research in Education.

Pounder, D. G., Ogawa, R. T., & Adams, E. A. (1995). Leadership as an organization-wide phenomena: Its impact on school performance. *Educational Administration Quarterly, 31*(4), 564–588.

Purkey, S. C., & Smith, M. S. (1983). Effective schools: A review. *Elementary School Journal, 83*, 427–452.

Rallis, S. F., & Highsmith, M. C. (1986). The myth of the great principal: Questions of school management and instructional leadership. *Phi Delta Kappan, 68*(4), 300–304.

Raudenbush, S. W., Rowan, B., & Cheong, Y. F. (1992). Contextual effects on the self-perceived efficacy of high school teachers. *Sociology of Education, 65*(2), 150–167.

Richardson, V. (Ed.). (1994). *Teacher change and the staff development process: A case of reading instruction*. New York: Teachers College Press.

Robertson, P. J., Wohlsetter, P., & Mohrman, S. A. (1995). Generating curriculum and instructional innovations through school-based management. *Educational Administration Quarterly, 31*(3), 375–404.

Rowan, B. (1990). Commitment and control: Alternative strategies for the organizational design of schools. In C. Cazden (Ed.), *Review of Research in Education* (Vol. 16, pp. 353–389). Washington, DC: American Educational Research Association.

Russo, A. (2004, July/August). School-based coaching: A revolution in professional development—or just the latest fad? *Harvard Education Letter.* Retrieved July 10, 2007, from http://www.edletter.org/past/issues/2004-ja/coaching.shtm

Sanders, W., & Horn, S. (1998). Research findings from the Tennessee Value-Added Assessment System database: Implications for educational evaluation and research. *Journal of Personnel Evaluation in Education, 12,* 138–151.

Sergiovanni, T. J. (1994). Organizations or communities: Changing the metaphor changes the theory. *Educational Administration Quarterly, 30*(2), 214–226.

Shachar, H. (1996). Developing new traditions in secondary schools: A working model for organizational and instructional change. *Teachers College Record, 97*(4), 549–568.

Sheppard, B. (1996). Exploring the transformational nature of instructional leadership. *Alberta Journal of Educational Research, 42*(4), 325–344.

Showers, B., & Joyce, B. (1996). The evolution of peer coaching. *Educational Leadership, 53*(6), 12–16.

Smylie, M. A. (1992). Teacher participation in school decision-making: Assessing willingness to participate. *Educational Evaluation and Policy Analysis, 14*(1), 53–67.

Smylie, M. A. (1994). Redesigning teachers' work: Connections to the classroom. In L. Darling-Hammond (Ed.), *Review of Research in Education* (Vol. 20, pp. 129–177). Washington, DC: American Educational Research Association.

Smylie, M. A., Conley, S., & Marks, H. M. (2002). Exploring new approaches to teacher leadership for school improvement. In J. Murphy (Ed.), *The educational leadership challenge: Redefining leadership for the 21st century: 101st yearbook of the National Society for the Study of Education, Part 1* (pp. 162–188). Chicago, IL: University of Chicago Press.

Smylie, M. A., & Denny, J. W. (1990). Teacher leadership: Tensions and ambiguities in organizational perspective. *Educational Administration Quarterly, 26*(3), 235–259.

Spillane, J. P., Halverson, R., & Diamond, J. B. (2000). *Towards a theory of leadership practice: A distributed perspective.* Evanston, IL: Northwestern University, Institute for Policy Research.

Spillane, J. P., Halverson, R., & Diamond, J. B. (2001). Investigating school leadership practice: A distributed perspective. *Educational Researcher, 30*(3), 23–28.

Stein, M. K. (1998). *High performance learning communities in District 2: Report on year one implementation of school learning communities.* Pittsburgh, PA: Learning Research and Development Center, University of Pittsburgh.

Stoelinga, S. R., Fendt, C. R., & Wenzel, S. A. (2005). *Analysis of schools on probation implementing CMSI curricula.* Chicago: University of Illinois–Chicago, CMSI Evaluation Project.

Sykes, G. (1996). Reform of and as professional development. *Phi Delta Kappan,* 77, 465–467.

Tannenbaum, A. S. (1962). Control in organizations: Individual adjustment and organizational performance. *Administrative Science Quarterly, 7,* 236–257.

Taylor, J. E. (2004). *Distributed instructional leadership and teachers' perceptions of and motivation for instructional improvement.* Unpublished doctoral dissertation: University of Michigan, Ann Arbor.

Thompson, J. D. (1967). *Organizations in action.* New York: McGraw-Hill.

Toll, C. (2006). *Literacy coach's desk reference: The processes and perspectives for effective coaching.* Urbana, IL: National Council of Teachers of English.

Tschannen-Moran, M., & Hoy, W. K. (2000). A multidisciplinary analysis of the nature, meaning and measurement of trust. *Review of Educational Research, 70*(4), 547–593.

Vroom, V. H. (1964). *Work and motivation.* New York: Wiley.

Walsh-Symonds, K. (2003). *Literacy coaching: How school districts can support a long-term strategy in a short-term world.* San Francisco: Bay Area School Reform Collaborative.

Weick, K. (1976). Educational organizations as loosely coupled systems. *Administrative Science Quarterly, 21,* 1–19.

Weise, R., & Murphy, J. (1995). SBM in historical perspective, 1900–1950. In J. Murphy & L. Beck (Eds.), *School-based management as school reform: Taking stock* (pp. 93–115). Thousand Oaks, CA: Corwin Press.

Westbury, I. (1993). Response. *Education Researcher, 22*(3), 21–24.

Wimpelberg, R. K. (1988). Instructional leadership and ignorance: Guidelines for the new studies of district administrators. *Education and Urban Society, 20*(3), 302–310.

Youngs, P., & King, M. B. (2002). Principal leadership for professional development to build school capacity. *Educational Administration Quarterly, 38*(5), 643–670.

Zahorik, J. A. (1987). Teachers' collegial interactions: An exploratory study. *Elementary School Journal, 87,* 385–396.

CHAPTER 3

Content Is the Subject:
How Teacher Leaders with Different Subject Knowledge Interact with Teachers

Christopher M. Manno and William A. Firestone

RECENT CONCEPTIONS of leadership emphasize that it can be a "distributed practice" with multiple people sharing leadership responsibilities and tasks in pursuit of shared goals (Heller & Firestone, 1995; Spillane, Halvorson, & Diamond, 2004). Consistent with a distributed leadership perspective, many scholars and practitioners have asserted that the promotion of school effectiveness, school improvement, morale, teacher retention, and school climate can be enhanced through the development of internal leadership capacity through nurturing and embracing teacher leadership (Harris & Muijs, 2005; York-Barr & Duke, 2004). *Teacher leadership* has a variety of meanings but generally refers to teachers' actions outside the classroom to influence school or district policies or support changing teaching practice (Smylie, Conley, & Marks, 2002).

A reasonable body of evidence suggests that, under appropriate conditions, teacher leaders can contribute to improved teaching (Heller & Firestone, 1995; Smylie et al., 2002; York-Barr & Duke, 2004) but more needs to be known about those conditions. One that has received very little attention is what teacher leaders know, and in particular their understanding of the subjects that they and their colleagues teach (Riordan, 2003). While there has been much discussion of how teachers' knowledge of content contributes to their teaching (Ball & Bass, 2000; Newton & Newton, 2001), less attention has been given to how content knowledge helps teacher leaders in their work.

To learn how content knowledge can help teacher leaders, we studied eight teacher leaders—four who were content experts and four who were not—to learn how the teacher leader's work improved instructional practice. We found that content experts recognized deficiencies in colleagues' content knowledge as a primary problem that they could address in the implementation of math or science reform. Content experts viewed their work as advocacy for teaching of that content to all children. Their specialized knowledge helped content experts develop trust and rapport with colleagues and limited their needs for professional development related to that content.

TEACHER LEADERS' TASKS AND CONTENT KNOWLEDGE

Teacher leadership is not a new idea; variations on the theme go back to at least the beginning of the twentieth century. However, the purposes for introducing teacher leadership have varied. In the 1980s, teacher leadership reforms were primarily role based with the goal of professionalizing the occupation. More recently, the emphasis has been on having teacher leaders help improve practice (Smylie et al., 2002). In the service of this larger goal, teacher leaders typically engaged in seven interrelated tasks, four of which focused directly on promoting change and three of which maintained the organization or facilitated their own roles (Miller, Moon, & Elko, 2000; Silva, Gimbert, & Nolan, 2000; York-Barr & Duke, 2004).

Among the four change tasks, teacher leaders first promoted change by helping colleagues deal with the insecurity that accompanies new practice. To do this, teacher leaders often served more as comforters and helpers rather than strong advocates for practices the district advocated. Silva and colleagues (2000) found that teacher leaders who saw themselves as colearners with their colleagues were more effective at promoting buy-in from those colleagues. Second, teacher leaders promoted professional development. They did this by attending to their own growth and modeling learning (Silva et al., 2000), but also by participating in professional organizations and by leading professional development (Smylie et al., 2002; York-Barr & Duke, 2004). Third, teacher leaders who promoted change advocated for students in several ways. They created learning experiences to meet children's needs; they developed in-class activities that helped students understand how mathematics connected to their futures; and they generally stood up for students with other staff (Crowther, Kaagan, Ferguson, & Hann, 2002). Fourth, they engaged in curriculum work by defining standards and student outcomes and then identifying materials to help achieve those outcomes (Smylie et al., 2002; York-Barr & Duke, 2004).

In addition to supporting change directly, teacher leaders engaged in three tasks that either maintained the organization or facilitated their roles. First, they coordinated and managed, sometimes attending to administrative tasks that involved oversight that might otherwise have been done by administrators. These tasks allowed them to monitor whatever new program they were supposed to be supporting (Heller & Firestone, 1995; York-Barr & Duke, 2004). Second, teacher leaders navigated the school organization to influence policies and find ways around obstacles to change (Silva et al., 2000). For instance, if they handled schedules, they might find ways for teachers to meet together regularly to plan and collaborate. Finally, teacher leaders nurtured relationships necessary to keep people working together during the change process (Hall & Hord, 2001).

Does content knowledge help teacher leaders engage in these tasks more effectively? There is evidence that content knowledge helps teachers teach more effectively. Reviews of quantitative studies of teacher characteristics on student outcomes find that teachers with more courses in the subjects they teach—especially mathematics and science—have students who achieve at higher levels (Darling-Hammond, 1999; Wilson & Floden, 2003). Teachers with deeper content knowledge are more confident in working with their subjects and more fluent when leading discussions. Content knowledge helps teachers respond to questions better, enabling them to hear what students say, to calibrate their answers to promote students' understanding, and to give the information students need. Content knowledge also helps the teacher plan lessons and adjust activities to what the students know because the teacher better understands what is fundamental in the activity being presented (Newton & Newton, 2001; Shulman, 1987). By analogy, we argue that teacher leaders who have a stronger grasp of their content should have similar advantages in working with teachers. However, except for the work of Riordan (2003), there has been little effort to explore this possibility.

RESEARCH ON EIGHT TEACHERS

We studied eight teacher leaders who participated in a professional development program for teacher leaders—the Teacher Leader Institute (TLI)—presented by the New Jersey Math Science Partnership (NJ MSP). The NJ MSP was a consortium of two universities and 11 school districts working together to improve student achievement in mathematics and science through a variety of means. One strategy was to strengthen leadership for change by helping districts to identify and prepare teacher leaders to support other changes being supported by the MSP. TLIs were held in the summers of 2003 and 2004 with follow-up activities during the next year and the following summers. Districts sent cohorts of teacher leaders to develop a vision for improved math and science instruction, improve their content knowledge, and learn how to work with their peers.

A two-person team observed the 2003 TLI for 2 days and interviewed 18 participants. These observations were repeated during the 2004 TLI. In addition, eight teacher leaders were identified to be studied in more detail to learn about several issues, including how their content knowledge influenced their work. Here we briefly describe the sample, methods of data collection, and data analysis strategies.

Study Subjects

We selected participants from the 2004 TLI to vary on two dimensions. The most important was content expertise. A *content expert* was defined as having a minimum of an undergraduate major in the teacher leader's content area and teaching certification in that area. A *nonexpert* was defined to be a teacher leader without a major and certification in the content area, either mathematics or science. Four content experts and four nonexperts were included. Because this study was part of a larger investigation, teacher leaders were also selected to vary the amount of time teacher leaders were able to serve as leaders. Four (two content experts and two nonexperts) were full-time teachers and four (two content experts and two nonexperts) were released full-time to serve as teacher leaders. Table 3.1 provides demographic information on the sample.

Data Collection

Information was collected by interview and observation in the spring of 2005. In every case we interviewed the teacher leader and a district administrator. In seven instances, we interviewed at least two teachers as well; and in six, we were also able to interview a principal with whom the teacher leader worked. These interviews provided further data to triangulate beyond that obtained from the teacher leader (Yin, 1989), thus giving a fuller, more valid picture of that person's work.

The interviews focused on a biographical description of the teacher leader, the teacher leader's overall conception of teacher leadership, and a discussion about the teacher leader's perceptions of his or her role in improving instructional practice in math and/or science and other perceived influences to teacher leadership in the school or district. The interview

Table 3.1. Characteristics of sample.

Classification	Years of Experience	Degree and Certification	Other
Content expert, no release time	5	BS in biology, certified in biology	Taught middle school science, algebra, and geometry
Content expert, no release time	17	BA in chemistry, certified in chemistry	Taught middle school science
Nonexpert, no release time	21	BA in elementary education and psychology, MS in reading	Taught nursery school to college
Nonexpert, no release time	3	BA in business administration	Private sector background
Content expert, release time	2	BA in ceramic engineering, PhD in ceramic science	Ran lab for students
Content expert, release time	12	BA in earth science, MA in education administration	Three years as teacher leader
Nonexpert, release time	2	BA in early childhood education, masters, not specified	Started as substitute, promoted very fast, causing some resentment
Nonexpert, release time	18	BA in education, handicapped certified	Moved from part-time to full-time

protocols ensured that common questions were asked of each teacher leader, teacher, and administrator. Participants were assured anonymity in the reporting of responses. Interviews were taped and ranged from 45–60 minutes long.

Data Analysis

As transcripts were returned, they were entered into a qualitative data analysis program for further processing. A mixture of deductive and inductive reasoning was used to develop a coding scheme (Miles & Huberman, 1994). The main codes included the role of subject content knowledge, coordination and management, school or district curriculum work, professional development of colleagues, participating in school change/improvement, parent and community involvement, contributions to the profession, involvement in preservice, developing own expertise, navigating the organization, nurturing relationships, advocating for children, assisting other teachers, barriers to teacher leadership, and demographic information.

Coded interviews were used to construct eight "cases." Cross-case analysis was then conducted using graphic methods suggested by Miles and Huberman (1994) and others. Throughout these steps, we sought both patterns and themes, disconfirming evidence and alternative explanations (Marshall & Rossman, 1999) until analysis converged on what appeared to be a coherent interpretation of the data.

HELEN THOMAS: PROFILE OF A CONTENT EXPERT

To illustrate how content knowledge helps teacher leaders do their work, we briefly present the case of Helen Thomas, a pseudonym for one of our content experts. (Pseudonyms are used throughout this chapter.) Helen was a middle school science teacher in Shore City, a middle-income school district. She had 17 years of experience and a bachelor's degree in chemistry. She was certified to teach high school chemistry as well as elementary school. Besides running her school's science fair, she coordinated science materials for other teachers in her school, ensuring that they had the wherewithal to carry out the hands-on lessons that were part of the district's curriculum, and regularly led professional development events in the district.

A supervisor in the district saw Helen as someone who contributed to teachers' professional development and helped them with the curriculum:

> I think if there was a complete absence of leadership . . . it would be a lot harder to keep the curriculum more level, more consistent from classroom to classroom. . . . You know having that title kind of affords her reason to go in and share and improve . . . and observe other teachers. Now other teachers come and observe her without playing a favorite or designating one more than the other. I find the position is helpful.

Helen herself describes her role as follows:

> Your mentor, that is what I'd probably say. If you need anything, anything you have questions about. We have a very good e-mail system so even it is just 2 seconds, drop me an e-mail and I'll get right back to you. Pick up the phone and I'll call you. They all have my home phone number so if they have questions at night, just

give me a quick call. It is not just them learning from me, it is me learning from them because they bring in some really good new teaching ideas and some good information. What I can give them in experience, they can give me in excitement and newness. So it is a hand-in-hand [relationship].

Helen's self-description suggests that she saw herself as promoting change by being a colearner more than a top-down leader.

Her capacity to engage in these tasks was strengthened by her content knowledge. Most teachers felt that Helen had helped increase their content knowledge of science through the professional development or coaching she provided. Helen ran a summer institute for new science teachers before they began teaching in the district. She described walking new teachers through the details of curriculum activities, showing how they were aligned with state standards, and helping teachers figure out both the mechanics of those activities, and the science behind them before the teachers would have to do them with students. In addition, she made herself available during the school year to answer questions of new and old teachers alike. Through these activities, she helped teachers understand the content. One teacher explained how Helen helped her:

> [She] helped teach me how to do the formulas last year so she showed me tricks to make the kids remember. . . . She is one of the most knowledgeable science teachers . . . and it just flows out of her. She doesn't have to even think about it. She just gives you the answer.

DIFFERENCES BETWEEN CONTENT EXPERTS AND NONEXPERTS

In examining how teacher leaders played their roles, we identified five differences between content experts and others. The content experts could recognize deficits in content knowledge and work to reduce them, could advocate for their subject areas, could use work around curriculum as entrée for professional development, could use their content expertise as a way to build trust with colleagues, and needed to spend less time engaging in professional development to increase their content knowledge.

Recognizing and Addressing Content Deficits

Content experts were better able than others to diagnose the content knowledge deficits of teachers and help teachers address their knowledge gaps. When colleagues were asked if the nonexperts helped them learn content, the answer was always "No." The nonexperts worked with their colleagues more on general pedagogy and strategies specific to the reform programs being implemented, such as Everyday Math, Math Trailblazers, or the Full Option Science System (FOSS) program. Nonexperts were considered a resource for teaching strategies, planning, modeling, mentoring, but not for the content development of teachers or for answering content questions.

The content experts all recognized that elementary teachers often lacked sufficient content knowledge in math or science and that improved content knowledge would foster better teaching. They described how their knowledge of math or science helped their work. For instance, one teacher leader was only able to identify misinformation a teacher gave students because of her superior knowledge of science:

> I was doing a lesson with a teacher in the first-grade kit, it is called Pebbles, Sand, and Silt. She was trying to say that there were two particular volcanic rocks that both have these little holes in them, but they are different colors. She told them they are the same; they both have the holes. They are totally different rocks; they are not the same. If I didn't know that, I would have just gone right along with it because the lesson was going smoothly and she was doing a wonderful job. Then I had to say nicely, "Well, they are actually a little bit different, not just the color. But this one will sink because it has little holes all over it, but the other one has holes inside, they are little air holes trapped." I had to go into the differences of how they were formed and what makes them so different. She didn't know that, she had no way of knowing that.

Colleagues of teacher leaders recognize the value of working with those who have content knowledge. One of Helen's colleagues stated, "I'll talk to her at least once or twice a week to refresh and talk about some of the activities. Last year it was a lot individually because I was new." Another said, "She basically makes me feel much more comfortable teaching science." Another content expert only had opportunities to work with colleagues in one-on-one situations, but his work was also appreciated by colleagues, one of whom said,

> There were a number of times when I had a question about specific content. . . . I would ask him about that. He would either explain the concept to me specifically, or he would find out the answer. He was good that way.

Advocating for the Subject

The content experts were compelled by a desire for all children to achieve state standards in math and/or science. Their motives were not limited to the successful implementation of a particular program, the focus of the nonexperts.

Lieberman and Miller (2004) described teacher leaders as "innovators in the reconstruction of norms of achievement and expectations for students" (p. 12). While the nonexperts were also concerned with student achievement, the content experts spoke explicitly about improving teachers' understanding in math and science as a vehicle for improving instruction and helping all children achieve standards. Rather than viewing program implementation as the solution to improving teaching and learning, they saw teacher proficiency in the content as the means to develop teacher confidence and willingness to teach more and better math and science.

All of the four content experts viewed themselves as advocating for all children to experience quality standards-based curriculum and instruction. The content experts believed that working to improve the content knowledge of elementary teachers was a form of advocacy for improved math and/or science instruction for all children. This was especially true of science which teacher leaders saw as a subject marginalized in the elementary curriculum and which elementary teachers lacked the confidence and knowledge to teach. As a result, many teachers simply did not teach it or taught it from a literacy and fact-based perspective. The science expert teacher leaders all shared the mission of having more students exposed to science instruction and the standards in science.

Rhonda, another content expert, promoted science in her building through her enthusiasm and excitement about the subject. She said,

> I think the biggest motivation that they see . . . [is] my enthusiasm that I have for science. That's me, I'm all science. . . . when they see that love that I have for it . . . I mean they have jokes around my school building, "Oh there's the science lady. . . . There's the science geek." You know because it's been a subject that they've always neglected.

Similarly, Helen was perceived as an advocate for children. Her principal stated that she was always willing to spend time with students and get involved in a variety of programs to support students and the school. A colleague stated that "she really has a lot of personal interest in helping the students learn science. I feel if she is helping other teachers be better teachers, she feels like she is doing a service to the kids." Mary, another content expert, viewed her role as raising the level of science instruction for all children. When asked about her advocacy for children, Mary described her role as "pushing the science program for all children."

Using Curriculum and Materials Management to Promote Reform

Curriculum and materials management are tasks that facilitate talk between teacher leaders and colleagues that can become opportunities for professional development and can promote change (Harris & Muijs, 2005). Curriculum work provided many opportunities for strong collaboration. These were not limited to simply writing curriculum documents. They also included continual evaluation of textbooks, reform curriculum, and other curricular materials against local, state, and national standards as well as the development and refinement of classroom activities, lessons, and long-range unit planning. Content experts communicated regularly with teachers implementing curriculum to promote consistency and articulation. In addition, curriculum work included teaching teachers the content of the curriculum and modeling how to teach the content. Content experts used the curriculum as a context for their individual mentoring and coaching of colleagues.

Helen engaged colleagues in collaborative curriculum work. Her intimate knowledge of science content allowed her to attend closely to student objectives and standards. Helen worked with teachers to map curriculum objectives to the state science standards. She wrote objectives for each unit and identified standards that students had to meet. She was a discerning consumer of premade curricula and carefully evaluated purchased materials to utilize them as a tool to meet district standards. She worked with teachers to identify the sections in the premade program that would and would not be taught.

Evaluating, developing, coordinating, disseminating, and articulating curriculum with all science teachers in her building were significant components of Helen's work. She met with the teachers in the science department before and throughout the school year to coordinate curriculum, to assure that the curriculum met the state science standards, and to make sure teachers were prepared and comfortable implementing the lessons and using materials in their classrooms. Helen reported "writing objectives for each chapter" and identifying "standards they met for our core curriculum." She worked with the teachers to develop activities for each objective and made sure the teachers knew how to set up all the activities. These curriculum-centered discussions focused solely on teaching and learning. One of Helen's colleagues reported that new teachers really appreciated this level of curriculum articulation and stated, "New teachers coming in think it is wonderful because it gives them pretty well scripted plans day to day." The curriculum supervisor explained that Helen worked with the teachers to develop "binders for each unit" with individual activities for each objective and lesson.

Other content experts in this study engaged in curriculum work in a similar manner, although not to the same extent as Helen. Mary, another expert, worked intensively with teachers to promote curriculum articulation and to help teachers understand and implement the curriculum. She helped teachers with lesson planning and setup. She met with teachers individually and in groups to discuss pacing and coordination. She worked individually with teachers to help them understand the content of the curriculum and the activities. Mary conducted workshops on the use of the FOSS science kits. She facilitated team or grade-level meetings to promote the consistent implementation of the curriculum and to answer questions. Mary conducted demonstration lessons, team taught with teachers, observed and provided feedback to teachers, or just assisted teachers in the classroom. Mary focused heavily on modeling the teaching of content as a primary purpose for the demonstration lessons.

Responsibility for materials management seemed to be an administrative assignment based on time and/or compensation to accomplish the tasks. However, materials management provided an important opportunity for teacher leaders to work with and assist colleagues to promote improved instruction. Three of the four content experts were responsible for materials management, while two of the four nonexperts were responsible for materials management.

Materials management promoted standards-based math and science curriculum and instruction reform. A district that implemented the FOSS inquiry-based science reform program relied on that program to organize its science curriculum. The program was materials intensive and its success relied heavily on the refurbishment and rotation of the kits once they were fully used. The kits generally included materials and curriculum for 8 to 10 weeks of science lessons and then consumable materials were replaced for the next use of a kit. Rhonda, a content expert teacher leader with no released time, was solely responsible for coordinating and managing the FOSS materials for her K–8 building. The district science supervisor highlighted her role in ensuring that the separate kits or modules had all the ingredients needed so teachers could teach with them and for managing schedules:

Teacher leaders have been responsible for making sure that the modules are refurbished. They interface with teachers during the school year to make sure that they have everything. They interface with principals and help to order resources that are needed for the next school year. At the beginning of the school year, Rhonda does all the rotation schedules so Teacher A knows who gets the module after she uses it. Without those teacher leaders, I would really be in a quandary in terms of getting my modules collected.

The content expert teacher leaders viewed the coordination and management of materials as an opportunity to interface with teachers regarding the new curriculum programs and as a way of monitoring teachers' progress with implementation. Rhonda used her materials management responsibility to work with teachers. Going well beyond her responsibility, she helped teachers with the implementation of materials. She welcomed teachers' complaints about the science materials because the complaints indicated that the teachers were teaching science and using the materials. Rhonda felt that her role in coordinating materials allowed her to gauge teachers' progress with the science curriculum. She said, "Because I'm the materials person, all the kits come back to me at the end of the year, so I just sort of assess who used them." Rhonda also used teachers' feedback, questions, concerns, and complaints as a way of assessing teacher progress and proficiency with teaching the curriculum:

They're asking, "When are we rotating the kits?" That means that they have actually been on schedule and they're actually teaching it. The fact that I get a lot of questions from them and they're seeking help tells me that they are doing something. I get a lot of complaints too, but they're doing something with the kits, unlike just leaving them in the classrooms. When they're asking me for graduated cylinders and microscope . . . you know they're attempting to do it.

Carl, a content expert teacher leader with release time, also recognized that materials management was important for the science program. He viewed this responsibility as critical so that teachers had the proper materials available and the necessary support in order to teach science well. Carl was keenly aware of and concerned about elementary teachers' general lack of science content knowledge. He viewed providing materials support as critical to compensating for classroom teachers' lack of science knowledge. Carl thought that if the teachers were not provided with quality science curriculum materials and supported in their use, the teachers would generally choose not to teach science or would teach it from a "language arts perspective."

Building Trust by Demonstrating Expertise

For teacher leaders, a key aspect of navigating relationships in the school is building the trust necessary to establish helping relationships (Crowther et al., 2002; Silva et al., 2000). In this study the content experts built trust by demonstrating expertise in their content areas and leveraging that expertise to assist other teachers. Helen was well regarded by her colleagues as a science expert. Her colleagues had a great deal of respect for her suggestions, direction, and overall work. Each of Helen's colleagues seemed very comfortable working with her. Helen had developed nonthreatening, collegial relationships that promoted productive, positive discussion about curriculum and instruction. The other teachers viewed her as an experienced, knowledgeable teacher who was always willing and able to help them. Her colleagues respected her work with children and her expertise in science content and pedagogy.

Over 2 years Rhonda nurtured trusting relationships with her colleagues, helping them learn the science in the curriculum. Rhonda noticed that trust was built and said that during the 2nd year of the study the elementary teachers were more willing to have her come into their classrooms and were more positive about teaching science:

> Even to let me come in their classrooms and even if it's just to prep a lab ahead of time to get them a little more comfortable, because a lot of the resistance was because they lacked the content. And just going in and helping them and explaining how things work in science and major concepts makes it easier for them to want to do it. Their attitudes are more positive compared to before. I remember when I first started, it was more "Oh, here comes the science person, Oh Lord!" Almost like they weren't receptive at all. But over time, they became more receptive.

Mary was also careful to act in a way that would be perceived as supportive and as a resource. Because she avoided being seen as a supervisor or administrator, she reported good relationships with her colleagues. She did not get involved with mediating between administrators and teachers, nor did she get involved with the cultures or goings on in the building. Rather, Mary focused on working with teachers to help them learn the science of the curriculum and how to implement the curriculum in their classrooms.

Relying on Available Knowledge

None of the content experts discussed developing their own expertise as a major component of their teacher leader work. Instead, they relied on their content background as their primary tool for working with colleagues. All the nonexperts reported participating in extensive professional development to improve their own knowledge of curriculum, instruction, and content. Susan, a nonexpert, participated in lesson study through the MSP for a year prior to bringing it to her school. She felt that working with other teachers has also contributed to her growth. She said, "My understanding of content has increased dramatically because I've been helping other teachers." Beverly, another nonexpert cited extensive training in the Math Trailblazers program and standards-based math reform in general as a major reason for her success in promoting change in math instruction in her building. Harriet, a third nonexpert, developed her knowledge and skills by participating in workshops and conferences. She arranged for a consultant to come to her school to provide professional development in the new programs. Harriet attended these sessions, as well as other workshops through the MSP. She developed her expertise and comfort with the science program through professional development workshops that eventually allowed her to turn-key for other teachers including conducting model lessons.

These teacher leaders' experiences suggest that the initial definition of content expert in this study needs some reconsideration, that there may be "multiple paths" to becoming a content expert in a field. Harriet's supervisor said that she supervised two science teacher leaders in the other middle school, neither of whom were science majors but both were "fabulous." The supervisor said that both of these teacher leaders took measures to develop their science content knowledge on their own: "They took classes and they went to workshops where they learned more about content area knowledge. They read a million books and a million different teachers' editions and did a lot of research on their own."

The nonexperts who developed a fairly high level of proficiency in the content area through workshops or other professional development opportunities worked more with colleagues on content development, but still less than their content expert peers. Moreover, none of the nonexperts were recognized by colleagues or administrators as having developed the content knowledge of colleagues. Both Beverly and Harriet had developed a higher level of subject content knowledge in their areas than the other nonexperts in the study. While the data indicated that neither worked directly with teachers to develop their content knowledge, they did more to promote a change in instruction and professional development in their content areas than the other nonexperts without reaching the level of content experts, even after developing their skills.

CONTENT KNOWLEDGE IS NOT ENOUGH

While content knowledge was an important asset for teacher leaders in their school improvement work, it did not prove to be a magic bullet for making them effective change agents. To explore the consequences of teacher leader content knowledge, we also examined the levels of use of the new programs or curricula in the schools where the teacher leaders worked and that they supported. Hall and Hord (2001) have developed a scale of levels of use ranging from *I* = nonuse, where the observed teacher shows little or no knowledge about the innovation in question, through *IV* = mechanical use, or implementing the innovation step by step with little reflection on use or outcomes, to *VIII* = renewal, where the user researches better ways to accomplish goals and improve the innovation.

With the limited amount of information available to us, we reviewed all the interviews from each school where we observed a teacher leader in order to do a provisional assessment of the levels of use of the curriculum. The placement of schools on the continuum is not meant to be exact, but rather the placements represent a general sense of the status of implementation based on interview data. There may have been, and probably were, significant variations of use within these buildings.

Essentially, four schools scored from levels *I* to *IV* and four scored from levels *V* to *VIII*. Two of the nonexperts worked at schools scoring at levels *I* to *IV*, as did two of the content experts. Similarly two nonexperts worked in schools that scored at levels *V* to *VIII*, as did two of the content experts. Thus there was essentially no relationship between content expertise and level of use.

Rather what seemed to happen was that content experts used their knowledge differently depending on the level of use in the building. For instance, teachers in Carl's and Rhonda's buildings were required by their districts to implement the new reform science program. However, actual implementation was spotty, with some teachers simply not doing it, but levels of use otherwise running from *II* to *IV*. Carl and Rhonda worked with the teachers one-on-one in a nonsystematic fashion to promote the teaching of the curriculum. Emphasis was on encouraging or motivating the teachers to teach the curriculum. Being content experts, Carl and Rhonda did that by trying to improve the content knowledge of colleagues, thereby increasing teacher confidence and comfort with the curriculum. These two teacher leaders reportedly experienced success with teacher colleagues with whom they worked; however, they did not work with all teachers in their buildings. The teachers who were implementing the curriculum in Carl's and Rhonda's schools were reported to be "implementing the program by the book." There was no evidence that teachers were collaborating to reflect upon, refine, and improve the implementation. There was no evidence that Carl or Rhonda promoted collaboration between teachers regarding the reform programs.

Mary, another expert, worked in several schools to promote consistent delivery of a district reform science program but where levels of use tended to be high, generally *V* to *VI*. Mary worked with colleagues to refine their content knowledge and pedagogical skills. She observed teachers and provided feedback to help them reflect upon and improve implementation. She felt that she promoted a change in instructional practice with the teachers with whom she worked. Due to the more diagnostic nature of her position and role, Mary actively worked to help teachers improve their practice and implementation of the program. Because teachers accepted the program, she did not focus solely on program implementation, but worked to develop colleagues' content knowledge as a means of improving science instruction more generally.

Working in the school where levels of use were highest—*V* to *VIII*—Helen worked with all the teachers to nurture a professional learning community in which all teachers appeared to take ownership of the curriculum. It did not appear that the teachers were implementing a prepackaged, commercial product, but rather that they carefully designed the curriculum and corresponding activities to help children achieve standards. She worked with teachers in groups to map the curriculum against state standards and to make modifications to improve the program. The process of analysis was professional development for all teachers, enhancing their understanding of curriculum and practices. Several teachers were involved in meaningful ways in the development of the curriculum. One colleague stated:

> Last year we [all the teachers] put the curriculum together. We started at the curriculum meetings and I was one of the people who helped type it up. So that helped me because I was actually seeing it and writing it and typing it.

In sum, the way content experts used their content knowledge depended at least in part on where teachers were. Where levels of use were low, content experts used their knowledge to support basic use of the curriculum, but where levels of use were higher, teacher leaders could help teachers go beyond basic use and develop deeper knowledge and understanding.

CONCLUSION

This study suffers from some of the limitations of exploratory research, including a small number of cases and limited information on how teacher leaders influenced their colleagues. Another limitation is its focus on mathematics and science. It is not entirely clear how the sequential nature of mathematics and its relative value neutrality as a field when compared to social studies or literature would affect the work of teacher leaders (Stodolsky & Grossman, 1995).

Nevertheless, it suggests some important conclusions about the nature of teacher leadership. Perhaps the most important is that knowledge is power. Teacher leaders bring human capital that has face validity to the teachers with whom they work. While their work benefits from the legitimacy that comes from a position, it benefits even more from their ability to deliver the goods—being able to "teach me how to do the formulas" and "show me tricks to make the kids remember." Moreover, content experts can get right to the work while nonexperts have to spend part of their time developing the human capital that experts already have. With this power, content experts can promote school improvement. This is not to say that nonexperts are unable to promote school improvement so much as that content experts have advantages that nonexperts lack.

Our work suggests two important lessons for the future. First, professional development can be embedded in collaborative curriculum-related tasks rather than formal and more traditional professional development workshops. Professional development activities that were viewed as having the most impact on instructional practice were those that brought teachers together to work on matters directly related to curriculum and content. The richest contexts found in the current study to foster content development and curriculum understanding for teachers were those that involved the evaluation, development, and implementation of curriculum. Moreover, they were not limited to a how-to approach of program implementation. The sharing of ideas to design and refine curriculum promotes a community of learners.

Second, when selecting future teacher leaders, it is important to recruit teacher leaders who already have content expertise. We have seen that content expertise can be replaced to some extent through on-the-job training, but such training does not appear to be as adequate as basic coursework in the subject area.

This work suggests directions for future research. It provides insight into how teacher leaders leverage their content knowledge to promote professional development and instructional reform. Content expertise shapes and guides the tasks in which teacher leaders engage. Teacher leaders promote change along a continuum which is directly related to their content knowledge and the tasks in which they engage. Content knowledge can therefore be viewed as a form of human capital that when leveraged effectively promotes a strong form of distributed practice and shared leadership for improvements in teaching and learning. This research established a connection between content expert teacher leadership and change in instruction. Future research could build upon this study by seeking to establish a relationship between task-focused content expert teacher leadership and teacher understanding of content, observed teaching practice, and/or measured student understanding of curriculum objectives. In addition, differences in perceived changes in instructional practice in this study could not be explained solely by content expertise or teacher leader job structure. Additional investigation could shed light on how personal and organizational factors interact with teacher leader content expertise to promote instructional reform.

NOTE

The work of writing this chapter was supported in part by grant EHR-0226989 from the National Science Foundation. Thanks are due to Nancy Gigante for her help with the fieldwork and collaboration with the data analysis.

REFERENCES

Ball, D. L., & Bass, H. (2000). Interweaving content and pedagogy in teaching and learning to teach: Knowing and using mathematics. In J. Boaler (Ed.), *Multiple perspectives on the teaching and learning of mathematics* (pp. 83–104). Westport, CT: Ablex.

Crowther, F., Kaagan, S. S., Ferguson, M., & Hann, L. (2002). *Developing teacher leaders: How teacher leadership enhances school success.* Thousand Oaks, CA: Corwin Press.

Darling-Hammond, L. (1999). *Teacher quality and student achievement: A review of state policy evidence.* Seattle, WA: Center for the Study of Teaching and Policy.

Hall, G. E., & Hord, S. M. (2001). *Implementing change: Patterns, principles, and potholes.* Needham Heights, MA: Allyn & Bacon.

Harris, A., & Muijs, D. (2005). *Improving schools through teacher leadership.* New York: Open University Press.

Heller, M. F., & Firestone, W. A. (1995). Who's in charge here? Sources of leadership for change in eight schools. *Elementary School Journal, 96*(1), 65–86.

Lieberman, A., & Miller, L. (2004). *Teacher leadership.* San Francisco: Jossey-Bass.

Marshall, C., & Rossman, G. B. (1999). *Designing qualitative research* (3rd ed.). Thousand Oaks, CA: Sage.

Miles, M. B., & Huberman, A. M. (1994). *Qualitative data analysis: An expanded sourcebook*. Thousand Oaks, CA: Sage.

Miller, B., Moon, J., & Elko, S. (2000). *Teacher leadership in mathematics and science: Casebook and facilitator's guide*. Portsmouth, NH: Heinemann.

Newton, D., & Newton, L. (2001). Subject content knowledge and teacher talk in the primary science classroom. *European Journal of Teacher Education, 24*(3), 369–379.

Riordan, K. (2003). *Teacher leadership as a strategy for instructional improvement: The case of the Merck Institute for Science Education* (No. RR-053). Philadelphia: University of Pennsylvania, Consortium for Policy Research in Education.

Shulman, L. (1987). Knowledge and teaching: Foundations of the new reform. *Harvard Educational Review, 57*(1), 1–22.

Silva, D. Y., Gimbert, B., & Nolan, J. (2000). Sliding the doors: Locking and unlocking possibilities for teacher leadership. *Teachers College Record, 102*(4), 779–804.

Smylie, M. A., Conley, S., & Marks, H. M. (2002). Exploring new approaches to teacher leadership for school improvement. In J. Murphy (Ed.), *The educational leadership challenge: Redefining leadership for the 21st century: 101st yearbook of the National Society for the Study of Education*, Part 1 (pp. 162–188). Chicago: University of Chicago Press.

Spillane, J. P., Halverson, R., & Diamond, J. (2004). Theory of leadership practice: A distributed perspective. *Journal of Curriculum Studies, 36*(1), 3–34.

Stodolsky, S. S., & Grossman, P. L. (1995). The impact of subject matter on curricular activity: an analysis of five academic subjects. *American Educational Research Journal, 32*(2), 227–249.

Wilson, S. M., & Floden, R. E. (2003). *Creating effective teachers: Concise answers for hard questions*. Washington, DC: American Association of Colleges for Teacher Education.

Yin, R. K. (1989). *Case study research: Design and methods*. Newbury Park, CA: Sage.

York-Barr, J., & Duke, K. (2004). What do we know about teacher leadership? Findings from two decades of scholarship. *Review of Educational Research, 74*(3), 255–316.

Teacher Leadership in Support of Large-Scale Mathematics and Science Education Reform

Brian Lord, Kate Cress, and Barbara Miller

DISTRICT LEADERS, mathematics and science education policy makers, and education researchers have recognized the promise of teacher leaders in supporting teacher change on a wide scale (Barth, 2001; Carroll & Mumme, 2001; Feiler, Heritage, & Gallimore, 2000; Katzenmeyer & Moller, 1996; Kelly, 2001). The principal appeal and underlying rationale of teacher leaders as change agents is that they are or have been teachers themselves and thus will know best how to help other teachers change (Fullan, 1993; Institute for Educational Leadership [IEL], 2001). In our 3-year study of teacher leadership models in support of mathematics and science education reform, we found that teacher leaders—individuals who are released full-time from their classrooms or other responsibilities to work with their colleagues on a districtwide reform agenda—do indeed draw heavily on their own extensive experience as classroom teachers. While these experiences are often supplemented with additional training (mainly additional math and science content) and on-the-job learning, it is mainly by virtue of who teacher leaders are and what they know *as teachers* that they aim to help their colleagues change instructional practice.

While this reliance on classroom experience provides predictable advantages for teacher leaders, it is also self-limiting in ways that threaten the overall impact of teacher leadership strategies. In this chapter we present findings about the characteristics of teacher leader work (especially about direct classroom support) and about its practical and conceptual foundations. In short, we maintain that teacher leaders essentially "show and tell" teachers how to change. This is consistent with Spillane's (2002) findings about the predominance of behavioral strategies or theories of change among school and district leaders. We use this expression not in a pejorative sense, but as a way of capturing how teacher leaders provide access to their own experiences as a model for how they wish their clients to change. For example, they "show" through direct modeling of instructional practice; they "tell" through planning and advising, sharing details of their own past practice.

Although showing and telling can be powerful tools for providing images of complex instructional practice and for clarifying the connection between these practices and mathematical and scientific ideas, they are seldom sufficient for establishing the kind of collegial critique or reflection that serve as engines for continuous improvement. As we aim to establish, this limit on teacher leaders' work is especially evident in the difficulty they have in providing hard feedback to even their most receptive clients and in the challenges they face in pursuing change on a broad scale. The predominance of show and tell strategies, we argue, is in part a function of the capacities that teacher leaders bring to the job, in part a reflection of their implicit theories-in-action about teacher change, and in part a consequence of the near absence of system supports to create an effective alternative.

THE EVOLVING ROLES OF TEACHER LEADERS

Districts across the country are searching for ways to transform teacher practice through innovative approaches to professional development (Ball & Cohen, 1999; Elmore & Burney, 1999; Loucks-Horsley & Matsumoto, 1999; Thompson & Zeuli, 1999). In many places, teacher leaders are the primary personnel—the change agents—expected to provide these professional development experiences aimed at promoting and supporting change in teachers' classroom practice (Medina & St. John, 1997; Smylie & Denny, 1990). And, not surprisingly, teacher leaders are often charged with implementing these change strategies on the very widest scale (Lord & Miller, 2000).

In practice, the work of teacher leaders can be quite varied (Lieberman, 1992; Loucks-Horsley, Hewson, Love, & Stiles, 1998). Recent studies have begun to unpack the nature of teacher leadership work, the various "moves" employed by teacher leaders as they work with their colleagues (Lord & Miller, 2000; National Board for Professional Teaching Standards [NBPTS], 2001; Silva, Gimbert, & Nolan, 2000). Yet few studies have set out to understand and describe the nature of the work undertaken by teacher leaders in classrooms or to determine how well it contributes to achieving broader goals of instructional change.

We do know, however, that teacher leaders' work focuses predominantly on classroom-level support of teachers. Because they spend so much time in one-on-one coaching, teacher leaders are generally expected to have firm content knowledge (Carroll & Mumme, 2001; Feiler et al., 2000; Snell & Swanson, 2000), familiarity with new or proposed curricula, and facility in using new technologies or classroom materials that often present problems to teachers. Noting the important combination of knowledge and ability for successful leadership, Zimpher argues that "teacher leadership must be an outgrowth of expert practice and expert knowledge" (1988, p. 54).

There is emerging evidence, however, that more than content knowledge and teaching expertise is required. Teacher leaders need "an array of skills [including] . . . facilitation skills, the ability to work with adult learners, and knowledge of the change process" (Horizon Research, Inc. [HRI], 2000, p. 8). They need political acumen, an ability to "go into a school and pick up clues as to what's important" (p. 9). Lemlech and Hertzog (1998) maintain that teacher leaders are commonly expected to be able to "build trust and respect in colleagues; understand and deal with school culture; work collaboratively with others while managing conflict; use resources to help others; manage time, work and priorities; and build skill and confidence in others" (p. 3). Bryk and Schneider (2002) find that the capacity to build trust is a strong predictor for successful reform at the school level. Rogers (1995) emphasizes that individuals adopt innovations as a consequence of their interpersonal connections with other people (e.g., empathy and homophily—a fundamental alikeness between change agent and client).

Even if teacher leaders bring content knowledge and years of classroom experience, and possess the political acumen and trust-building skills necessary to gain acceptance in schools, there is a further set of skills required. These are the skills necessary to actually transform teacher practice. Chief among these skills, as we will later discuss, is the ability to offer hard feedback. By *hard feedback* we refer to instances where a teacher leader's honest critique of classroom practice is issued even though the critique actively challenges the teacher's preferred practice and may lead the teacher to experience some level of professional discomfort. The importance of this kind of feedback can be seen in the stress some authors put on organized, methodical, and incisive coaching techniques (Joyce & Showers, 1988; Staub, Mahon, & Miller, 1998; Wasley, 1991; West & Staub, 2003).

Joyce and Showers (1988) observe that "coaching develops the shared language and common understandings necessary for the collegial study of new knowledge and skills" (p. 84). They affirm that teachers who are coached "practice new strategies more frequently . . . exhibit greater long-term retention of knowledge about and skill with strategies in which they had been coached . . . [and] exhibit clearer cognitions with regard to the purposes and uses of the new strategies" (pp. 88–89). Coaching and collaboration thus encourage teachers to embrace reform over time and promote support for reform by helping teachers understand the purposes and benefits of reform.

As we will discuss, teacher leadership that supported self-sustaining collegial critique was rare in the sites we studied. While NSF-supported math and science teacher leaders in these sites focused on working one-on-one with classroom teachers, this work often stopped at the show-and-tell stage, rather than moving on toward a more mutual engagement around strategies for instructional improvement.

STUDYING TEACHER LEADERSHIP IN NSF PROGRAMS

We use data from a 3-year research study that posed the following central question: How does teacher leadership help to develop and sustain science/mathematics/technology education reform on scale? Our study was set in the context of the National Science Foundation's efforts to foster systemic reform in mathematics and science education in urban school districts. These efforts included the Urban Systemic Initiatives (USI) and the Urban Systemic Program (USP), which, together, supported 40 school districts in initiating and sustaining bold changes in curriculum and instruction across all K–12 classrooms and among all teachers charged with teaching mathematics, science, or both. We focused on full-time release teacher leaders in six of these USI/USP sites. These professional staff worked in various schools, but they served primarily as district or USI/USP program agents and were generally housed in district or other central office space.

Site Selection

Three criteria influenced our site selection. First, we selected two sites from each of the three cohorts of the USI program, resulting in sites that were at various points in their NSF-funded reform work. At the start of our data collection, there were 19 active or recently completed USI programs, from which we selected our six sites. We speculated that the longevity of reform efforts in a site (as indicated by duration of USI/USP programs) would inform the work and understanding of teacher leaders. Second, we selected sites where we could reasonably anticipate some variation in the configuration of the teacher leader role, such as variation in the number of teacher leaders, their deployment across participating schools (including grade levels served), and their official relationship to their districts. And finally, we looked for variation in the organization of the wider USI/USP programs within which the teacher leader programs were seated. Three of the programs were single district initiatives, while three involved multiple districts. The number of students served by USI/USP in the six sites ranged from 100,000 to more than 200,000.

Data Collection and Analysis

We gathered data through interviews, a teacher leader survey, document review, on-site job shadows, and focus groups with teacher leaders.

In the first year of the study, we conducted 60-minute phone interviews with 99 individuals across the six sites. Approximately half of these interviews were with full-time release teacher leaders (approximately 30% of the total of 165 teacher leaders in the six sites). The remaining interviews were conducted with USI/USP program staff, district staff, principals, or teachers at the school level with leadership responsibilities. The aim of these interviews was to collect information about the characteristics of teacher leaders' work, teacher leaders' background and leadership capacity, and the contribution of teacher leaders to the overall USI/USP effort. Interview data were coded with attention to these dimensions of teacher leaders' work and cross-coded to determine interrater reliability. Cross-coding of key items yielded reliability rates of roughly 0.75.

In Year 1, we administered a questionnaire to all 165 teacher leaders in the six sites and achieved a 96% return rate. The instrument was designed to elicit information about the type, frequency, and perceived impact of teacher leader work and about teacher leaders' professional development and background. Data from the questionnaires were analyzed for descriptive statistics (central tendency and variability) as well as inferential statistics (chi-square analysis) to test hypotheses about the effects of training, prior experience, and motivation on the characteristics of teacher leader work.

We conducted site visits in the 1st and 2nd years of the study, consisting of focus group interviews with teacher leaders, job shadows with a small number of teacher leaders in each site, and individual interviews with USI/USP program staff and district staff. In the Year 1 focus group, we tested our emerging understanding of the nature and intended purpose of teacher leader work, patterns of teacher leader deployment in schools and across districts, the "clients" targeted in teacher leader work, and the integration of this work in a larger, systemwide effort. The Year 2 focus group relied on a pathway and sequence analysis tool that provided teacher leaders with a chance to identify strategic moves in their work.

Job shadows in both years provided observers with a firsthand look at teacher leaders' classroom support work. Follow-up interviews during Year 1 and Year 2 site visits provided a chance to confirm initial findings and to create a better picture of the system supports that enabled or constrained teacher leaders' work.

A PROFILE OF TEACHER LEADER WORK

An overall profile of teacher leaders emerges from our data. Teacher leaders in these sites were, on the whole, quite experienced as classroom teachers. Both the mean and median years of teaching experience was fifteen. Most (73%) were actively recruited into their jobs. Despite their extensive prior experience, however, teacher leaders had little time on the job. The median time on the job was 29 months, the mean was 33 months. In other words, the teacher leader position was itself quite new, so there were few "old hands" to define the job or set its standards. Many of the teacher leaders in our study were still figuring out how to shape the work, and 72% acknowledged classroom experience as the prior experience that most enhanced their work. Teacher leaders in these sites reflected the teaching demographics of their districts: across the six sites, 23% were African American, 20% were Hispanic, and 56% were White. Teacher leaders were well educated with 73% having a master's degree or higher.

Teacher Leader Work in Classrooms

Across our research sites, several features of teacher leaders' work stood out, notably their focus on one-on-one support for classroom teachers, their commitment to improving mathematics and science education for underserved students, and their strong collegial ties to other teacher leaders. In this chapter we concentrate largely on the characteristics and underlying rationale for their one-on-one support for classroom teachers.

Teacher leaders spent the majority of their time in school buildings, and often classrooms, working directly with classroom teachers to promote change. Ninety percent of teacher leaders in our sample worked with individual teachers in their classrooms at least once a week; 38% are in classrooms every day.

Teacher leaders' classroom support focused on sharing their own exemplary experience with teachers. In our study, we identified six discrete (though frequently interrelated) activities at the heart of teacher leaders' work. These included: classroom observation, demonstration teaching, coteaching, planning, advising, and providing feedback. Though each of these is important in its own right, for purposes of the argument in this chapter we concentrate on three: demonstration teaching, coteaching, and providing feedback. (For a more complete descriptive account of teacher leaders' work, see Lord, Cress, & Miller, 2003.)

Demonstration teaching. Teacher leaders demonstrate lessons that highlight important features of instruction, such as the management of materials, the organization of student discourse, the informal assessment of student understanding, and the facilitation of student work. These lessons frequently focus on the introduction of challenging new curriculum materials and are often aimed at novice teachers or at veterans who harbor low expectations of student work.

With novices, teacher leaders offer visual images of how standards-based instruction should look, in the hope that new teachers will then attempt such lessons themselves. One teacher leader explained how she sought permission to offer a demonstration:

> And actually, you can say "Let me teach for today." I've done that. Say "Let me do this next period." For a very new teacher, not for an experienced teacher, of course. I say "Let me show you what I would do with this Algebra 2 class this period." And we actually teach them.

And with more experienced teachers, teacher leaders turned to demonstration teaching to show the skeptics that their students were indeed capable of undertaking challenging work. A teacher leader from another site observed that

> teachers, a lot of times, will say, "Some of my students can't do this." And they're always referring to the historically underserved students, be it the bilingual or resource student. And I guess we've been able to help them, to show them that those students can do it. And I guess it's been because we've done so much model teaching and coteaching.

Demonstration teaching can serve as an existence proof, a way teacher leaders can convince teachers that students and teacher alike will benefit from standards-based instruction.

Coteaching. Coteaching, unlike demonstration teaching, requires active participation by the teacher. Typically the teacher leader and the classroom teacher divide a particular lesson, or series of lessons, and pursue the work together. Usually the teacher leader begins by modeling desired strategies; then the teacher begins to try things out incrementally. An experienced teacher leader describes this relationship:

> If they're not comfortable, I'll instruct the first hour. The second hour, we'll team teach it. And the third hour, they're on their own, but they can come and get me if they get in trouble.

The importance of coteaching lies in its aim to link teacher leader demonstrations more directly to teachers' experimentation with new instructional moves. The presence of the teacher leader provides a safety net in this evolutionary stage on the way to improved instruction.

Providing feedback. Providing feedback offers teacher leaders a chance to respond to what they're seeing in teachers' classrooms and to offer recommendations based on their own knowledge and experience. It generally involves debriefing after some kind of work with a classroom teacher (e.g., an observation, an occasion of coteaching, or a study group meeting) and takes this activity or practice as the basis for a professional exchange. Not surprisingly, providing feedback appears in the conceptual mapping of almost all (roughly 90%) of our study's focus group participants. Teacher leaders recognize that providing classroom teachers with some kind of commentary on their practice is an essential part of the teacher leader's job, though, as we argue in more detail later in this chapter, they generally provide *soft feedback*—noncontroversial comments calculated to preserve the quality of carefully constructed relationships with their client teachers.

In summary, then, we found that teacher leaders spent the majority of their time providing one-on-one support to classroom teachers, especially in the form of demonstration teaching, coteaching, and providing feedback. Taken together, these various moves provided the main pathway for engaging teachers in new work and supporting their progress toward instructional change, though they offered little chance of reaching all or even most teachers in the large or midsized districts we studied. The crux of the one-on-one work appears to lie in the structure of teacher leaders' feedback to classroom teachers, and here the overreliance on soft feedback can be crippling when bold changes are envisioned.

These initial findings leave us with two pressing and interrelated curiosities. First, given that one of the primary objectives of the NSF's USI and USP initiatives has been to achieve change in instructional practice on a very broad scale, why did teacher leaders spend so much time providing one-on-one support to a relatively small number of classroom teachers, the seeming antithesis of any larger-scale change strategy? And second, why did teacher leaders find it so difficult to provide hard feedback to the classroom teachers with whom they work, even those whose instructional practice is noticeably deficient? In the following sections we will discuss additional findings in light of these questions and try to develop plausible accounts for why the work looks the way it does.

TEACHING, TEACHER LEADERSHIP, AND THE PROBLEM OF SCALE

The teacher leaders in our study were recruited for their capacity as teachers, trained to enhance this capacity (especially around curriculum and standards-based instruction), and deployed in settings where on-the-job learning further supplemented their skills. Yet, taken together, recruitment, training, and on-the-job learning often failed to build the capacity of teacher leaders to do more than share their prior classroom experience with other teachers. Little in teacher leaders' backgrounds or training equipped them for challenges of leadership outside of direct classroom support, and little prepares them to critically examine a teachers' classroom practice or to give substantive feedback. As we suggested earlier, they often retreated to the default position of showing and telling teachers how to change. In the following sections, we review teacher leaders' recruitment, training, and on-the-job learning for the light they shed on teacher leaders' propensity for one-on-one work.

Recruitment

Teacher leaders were hired from the ranks of the teaching profession because they were perceived to be strong, "super" math and science teachers. As one USI/USP leader put it, recruitment efforts involved "going after" and "surfacing" terrific teachers. A closer look at the recruitment process shows that the teachers hired to be teacher leaders possessed three notable qualities: extensive classroom teaching experience, a propensity for instructional innovation, and distinctive personality characteristics including a high level of motivation and unswerving commitment to teachers and their students.

When asked to pinpoint the primary skill they drew on in the work, teacher leaders identified their previous classroom experience. Survey results show that 72% of teacher leaders in our study strongly agreed that their own teaching experience enhanced their work as teacher leaders. No other prior experience was close. Only 44% strongly agreed that prior leadership experiences were significant in their teacher leader work. As a

USI/USP program leader in one site explained, she avoided recruiting new teachers who were still "figuring out" many issues; she worried that the teacher leadership role might "burn them out." Instead, she looked for the "well-respected" and "experienced teacher . . . who does a great job with kids" and "someone who is influential and can communicate well with their colleagues." She described the teacher leader role as a "career path" for more veteran teachers, where they can draw on their past experiences but be reenergized in a new kind of role.

Teacher leaders with many years of teaching experience can call on an extensive repertoire of moves that help them advise and support other teachers in the classroom. One teacher leader described this repository of practical knowledge: "You can see how after 24 years of experience I can just share a lot of other things that are not a written strategy somewhere, but just from experience." Experienced teacher leaders know how to demonstrate a lesson using standards-based curriculum, show a teacher how to bring to order a chaotic class, or work with a teacher and plan an innovative lesson for the next day; and these proved to be critical factors in their recruitment.

Propensity for innovation. Even when they came to the job with few years of classroom teaching experience, however, the teacher leaders in our study tended to be innovators, the early adopters of reform in their schools. One of the less experienced teacher leaders explained:

> I had to go through the change myself. Even though I had only taught a short time, I was getting in that traditional, "Okay, we're on page 36 and we're going to do these problems, and this is how we're going to do it." And I had to go through that change. I didn't like what I was doing. So I started looking for alternative ways to do it. . . . I started looking at new programs, and started doing new things, and went through the things I am asking people to do now.

Many of the teacher leaders in our study had significant experience with standards-based materials while still classroom teachers. Yet, even among those who did not, there was a general predisposition to experiment with standards-based instructional strategies. Because standards-based approaches had "worked" for them as teachers, or were consistent with their overall instructional philosophy, teacher leaders' work featured a process of alerting and converting fellow teachers to a standards-based approach.

Personal characteristics. In addition to their classroom experience and propensity for innovation, teacher leaders were often recruited because they were highly motivated individuals who found it easy to work with others. One teacher leader emphasized her ability to cope with conflict: "I got put in a couple of not really comfortable positions, but I just let [it] roll off my back like [water off] a duck." And another stressed the importance of patience and good listening skills:

> [I rely on] my ability to listen to them, to listen to their stories, and to validate where they were, and to not be critical and not to put [them] down. And [I] realize that, for some people, what I might think is a small change for them is a big change.

Program leaders in our sites sought out individuals who displayed these skills, realizing that the quality of teacher leaders' relationships with classroom teachers was critical to success.

Because teacher leaders were recruited largely on the basis of their teaching experience, their propensity for innovation, and a set of personal characteristics that tied them closely to their commitments to students and teachers, they were likely to gravitate toward classroom support work, a series of one-on-one interventions with classroom teachers. They viewed the problem of reform—and the challenge of scale—as changing one teacher at a time. Thus they were less likely to see their primary task as one of cultivating or supporting school-based or districtwide structures that might broaden the reach or accelerate the pace of change. And even where they participated in such structures (e.g., study groups, school reform teams, lesson study teams, and the like), there was little evidence of strategic calculations about how to turn them toward broader ends.

Training

Teacher leaders in these NSF-funded sites were provided with extensive and generous training once they became teacher leaders. The majority of this training was aimed at boosting their content knowledge in mathematics and science, yet most sites provided a broad spectrum of learning experiences on the assumption that the more teacher leaders know, the more they will be able to help teachers change. The question, of course, is whether this training (in its constitutive parts or taken together) prepared teacher leaders for the jobs they actually assumed. Just as so much of professional development for classroom teachers fails to make a substantive connection with the real work of classrooms, so it seems that much of the training provided to teacher leaders made little connection with the novel and politically charged work they were being asked to do. For example, it had little to do with helping them gain access to a school or classroom where there was no investment in math/science reform. Moreover, it did not help them challenge poor practice when they saw it. What, then, did this training look like in the sites we studied?

Increasing teacher leader knowledge and skills. The most prevalent training teacher leaders received was in math and science content. One teacher leader describes the training:

> We often had the high school math and science teacher [leaders] do content, all day Friday sessions with us. And those were extremely powerful.

The operative assumption seems to be that you can't lead what you don't know and that, despite their early commitment to innovative math/science education, most teacher leaders had spotty knowledge of the relevant math/science content.

A tour of reform. Training for teacher leaders was especially plentiful in the early years of the USI/USPs because these initiatives had the goal of preparing the initial cohort in a uniform way. These were powerful initiation experiences for teacher leaders, who, in interviews, talked about how much they learned from this "tour" of important school reform strategies and initiatives. Indeed, these experiences were so prominent among the first cohort of teacher leaders, that they spawned envy among subsequent cohorts. One teacher leader captured the heady nature of the early training in this way:

> [We received training on] how to work with teachers. We got cooperative learning. We've been trained in equity. We've been trained [in] brain theory and how that works. We've gone through observation training, how to go in and observe, what kinds of things to look for, what's a good lesson look like. . . . [W]e had ESL training. I mean if I probably pulled out my notes, I don't know what we haven't been trained in. It's been wonderful. Absolutely wonderful, the experience.

Yet, as with most tours, there were real questions about what individuals took away from the experience and whether or how well it helped participants grasp important concepts, or, more to the point, how well it prepared them to assist others in grasping them. While teacher leaders appreciated training and believed it helped them improve their skills as teachers (78% were satisfied or extremely satisfied with the professional development they received), these early training experiences did not anticipate the very real challenges teacher leaders would face on the job.

A review of content and a tour of the key elements of reform succeeded in helping teacher leaders "place" themselves in the reform landscape. But the day-to-day work of teacher leaders also involved a more complex engagement with strategic considerations—when, where, with whom, how long, and toward what end they should work. Knowing what they wanted teachers to know and do is not the same as knowing how to help them learn or do it, much less how to achieve these changes on a broad scale.

On-the-Job Learning

Teacher leaders increased their knowledge and skills not only through formal training but through on-the-job learning as well. Because the work of teacher leadership was new in most sites and because there was no good map for professional practice, teacher leaders found themselves piecing together the needed skills as they went along. They learned on the job in two important ways: (1) by visiting many classrooms to confirm what they knew and what they needed to know about math and science reform, and (2) by supporting one another and supplementing each other's knowledge base. In both cases, on-the-job learning contributed significantly to teacher leaders' overall store of knowledge about the work of teaching, yet less to their knowledge about how to translate their one-on-one efforts into schoolwide or districtwide capacity for change.

Exposure to many classrooms. Teacher leaders used words like *awakening* and *enlightening* to describe their exposure to the work of teachers across many classrooms. As we noted earlier, most teacher leaders came out of the classroom and, as classroom teachers, were likely to have had little opportunity to observe their colleagues at work (Little, 1990). Yet, as teacher leaders, they moved from classroom to classroom, seeing the challenges of reform play out before their eyes. One teacher leader captured the process of learning by exposure, saying that she began with "a lot of ideas in my head," but because of experiences on the job, "now I really understand what the whole thing [reform] is about." Seeing many teachers in many classrooms helped her translate her own personal teaching knowledge into a wider, more generic understanding of teachers' needs. Such exposure helped teacher leaders reflect on how to use what they knew to intervene in support of individual teachers. Yet, life inside these classrooms provided little insight into how to propel changes on any larger scale.

Learning from other teacher leaders.   Teacher leaders also learned from one another. They learned together when they met, brainstormed, and planned how to work with teachers, and when they helped each other enact these plans. In three of our sites teacher leaders devoted at least one day per week to organized meetings with their peers. These meetings were sometimes organized by grade level, sometimes by subject area, and sometimes focused on particular professional development themes. The aim was to provide teacher leaders with an environment for exchanging ideas and information and for participating in formal or informal professional development. In addition, in most of our sites teacher leaders spent at least some of their time working in pairs as they visited schools and classrooms. This time spent working together increased morale and a shared sense of identity as teacher leaders. As one teacher leader observed:

> We never would have made it if we hadn't had each other, because this is a job that no one else knows, because it's never existed before. You don't have anyone to say, "Oh yes, I know how that is. It's really bad." Principals have each other, and teachers have each other, but . . . we're neither administrators nor teachers anymore, so we just needed each other.

These opportunities to work and meet together provided a space for mutual encouragement and a forum for processing the challenges of the work.

Our findings about on-the-job learning reinforce our findings about classroom experience and training, that is, that teacher leaders approached the work of teacher leadership as teachers. Exposure to many classrooms helped them understand the needs of many teachers, which in turn helped them tailor their assistance as they worked with individuals. The support teacher leaders' gained from other teacher leaders helped to fill in some of the gaps in their own knowledge and provided emotional support as they pursued the often difficult work of instructional change together.

The insights, perspective, and skills teacher leaders gained—from many classrooms and each other—supplemented their skills as teachers. Yet our data yield little evidence that teacher leaders' on-the-job learning provided guidance on how to develop leadership capacity outside the classroom, how to build learning communities that could be sustained over time, or how to orchestrate teacher leader effort to serve large numbers of teachers in urban districts. For example, little of what teacher leaders gleaned from on-the-job learning had to do with negotiating with principals about the terms of access to schools and classrooms and even less to do with negotiating the terms of accountability (for what teachers taught and how they taught it). In other words, their on-the-job learning had more to do with increasing their capabilities to help individual teachers improve their instruction and much less to do with figuring out how to engage a larger number of teachers in self-sustaining systemic change.

In fairness to the teacher leaders, at least some of this guidance and the supporting infrastructure had to come from the reform program (USI or USP in this case) and its directors and/or from district leaders with a commitment to mathematics and science education reform. Yet, this kind of strategic design of teacher leader programs was largely missing in the sites we studied. In the absence of system supports (e.g., coherent and interrelated systems of curriculum, assessment, and accountability), teacher leaders fought an uphill battle to gain entry into schools and classrooms, to develop a long-term focus for the work they were asked to do, and to create structures that cut across classrooms and enlarged the community of participants. The fact that on-the-job learning did little to equip teacher leaders with skills they needed to play a wider role in the change process pushed them, by default, back to those skills with which they were most familiar, the skills of a successful classroom teacher.

THE CHALLENGE OF PROVIDING FEEDBACK

The second curiosity that emerges from our findings concerns whether and in what ways teacher leaders provided feedback to teachers. In particular, we ask, why did teacher leaders find it so difficult to provide hard feedback to the classroom teachers with whom they worked, even those whose instructional practice was noticeably deficient?

Part of the answer to this question is that teacher leaders' prior experience, recruitment, training, and on-the-job learning did little to prepare them for roles that fell outside of the ordinary experience of teaching. Providing feedback, especially hard feedback, to other classroom teachers is something that most teachers never do. In some cases, contractual rules forbid teachers from playing evaluative roles vis-à-vis their colleagues. In other cases, it's simply a matter of time and scheduling. But, whatever the reason, the fact remains that, in their prior work as classroom teachers, teacher leaders were unlikely to have observed or participated in giving hard feedback to other teachers or to have received hard feedback themselves. Therefore, they had little to turn to in the way of experience and little to alleviate the reticence they felt at playing such an untried and potentially uninvited role.

Another part of the answer to our question lies in the privacy of practice and the norms of noninterference (Hargreaves, 1993; Little, 1993) that so often influence the shape of teachers' professional interactions and that were evident in the districts we studied. There were few, if any, structures in the school systems or the individual schools we studied that supported the critical review of practice (formally or informally) and thus no point at which teacher leaders could easily or naturally have intersected with teachers on the hard issues. Teacher leaders described department meetings and grade level meetings as forums for exchanging information, but seldom as settings for critically analyzing practice. Both cross-classroom and cross-site visitation were rare, and study groups generally avoided close analysis of student performance data or instructional practice. Instead, these groups turned to readings from educational periodicals (seldom from peer-reviewed research) that provided noncontroversial recommendations for change. Thus, if teacher leaders hoped to work within structures that fostered the critical review of practice, they were faced with creating these structures themselves. This was a task for which they had little preparation and even less authority. In consequence, they often got stuck on providing soft feedback, offering help and encouragement, but ignoring bad practice. While preserving tact was critical to building strong relationships with classroom teachers, teacher leaders often lacked the skill or the will to move beyond the relationship-building phase.

Providing powerful feedback requires that teacher leaders move beyond mere sharing of expertise and toward a more complicated engagement around the work. In effect, it requires that teacher leaders challenge teachers to change their practice. Yet, because most teacher leaders lacked authority to evaluate teacher performance or to directly request changes in classroom practice, they delivered feedback that was suggestive, not directive, and that was couched in terms calculated not to offend. One teacher leader described this balancing act:

> It requires a little bit more patience to work with adults than it does with the children. You have more authority with children. . . . You have to develop a rapport with [adults], and a level of respect where they will listen to what you're saying, and value what you say. And you have to do that in such a way that it's palatable.

These more tactful formulations involved asking questions, making suggestions, and acknowledging that "we're all in this together." As one of our focus group participants commented,

> We try to find the answers together, whether it's through . . . an informal little ministudy—"We did this. This worked. This didn't work"—to something very formal—"Let's write this up, and let's keep track of our data."

We came across very little evidence that teacher leaders, or the directors of teacher leadership programs, were pushing beyond the idea of sharing elements of practice with teachers as a model for change. And seeing so little evidence of attempted critical feedback led us to conclude that substantive feedback did not hold a significant place in the theory of change informing the work of teacher leaders in these USI/USP sites. As we argued earlier, the theory of change implied in the teacher leader work we studied was that teachers changed by exposing them to images of successful practice, images that these teachers then incorporated into their own instruction. Yet, this theory of showing and telling did little to build the reflective capability of the individual classroom teacher. It placed the responsibility for change and the knowledge about change in external agents, whose numbers were limited. An alternative theory of change would have placed greater weight on a culture of critical feedback, on the creation of structures in which the teachers' own practice would have been the most important data in the relationship with teacher leaders.

SUMMARY AND CONCLUSION

District leaders in mathematics and science education have turned to teacher leadership as a core strategy for achieving instructional improvement on a wide scale. On the surface, the strategy is quite appealing—it begins the hard work of mediating between change in systemwide policies and change in instructional practice. Teacher leaders, former teachers themselves, are well positioned to command the respect of their peers in the classroom. Yet, in most urban districts, the role of teacher leader is still under construction. The nature of the work is only loosely defined, and often teacher leaders are left to their own devices to establish the focus and the means for accomplishing broad goals. Not surprisingly, they rely heavily on their past experience as teachers to guide their day-to-day decision making as leaders. As we've argued, this fosters one-on-one interventions that emphasize demonstration teaching and coteaching (i.e., showing and telling).

Little in their prior experience or training provides teacher leaders with a workable alternative to this one-on-one, classroom support model of instructional change. In the absence of a clear picture of how to orchestrate their efforts to intersect with districtwide or schoolwide learning structures, teacher leaders push ahead with what they know best, relinquishing those parts of the job that are unfamiliar or politically charged. Consequently, there is a notable gap (perhaps even a chasm) between the work that teacher leaders are able (and willing) to do and the expectations for systemic change in instructional practice at the heart of current math/science reform. Working with teachers one by one is an unlikely strategy for achieving math/science education reform on scale in large urban districts.

This is not to argue that one-on-one classroom support provided by teacher leaders has no benefit. Indeed, in our study we witnessed many classroom teachers who benefited enormously from the assistance provided by teacher leaders—support for the implementation of new curricula, the introduction of new instructional strategies, and the integration of new technologies into math and science classrooms. For many classroom teachers, the teacher leader is a critical bridge between traditional practice and new, more robust approaches to instruction. Teacher leaders provide images, models, advice, and encouragement and can serve as sounding boards and advocates while teachers navigate unfamiliar terrain. Yet, even here in the more comfortable circumstance of one-on-one work, teacher leaders' influence may be limited. In order to preserve trust and strengthen relationships with their clients, teacher leaders often avoid giving hard feedback. Instead, they opt for less direct, tactful commentary that, while easier and less threatening to deliver, may leave difficult issues unaddressed and unresolved. That teacher leaders pursue a more diplomatic course with their clients should come as no surprise. In circumstances where their responsibilities often exceed their authority and where they often have limited experience or exposure to models for delivering critical feedback, teacher leaders once again fall back on their familiar experience as teachers, electing a less confrontational path.

Teacher leadership, as crafted in the USI and USP initiatives in our study, represents an important step toward new roles for large-scale instructional change. Teacher leaders are in the vanguard of a national effort to create a more visible, more public, and more empirically grounded approach to teaching practice. We cannot emphasize enough that these roles are in their infancy and that much remains to be learned about how best to recruit, train, deploy, and support teacher leaders in efforts to achieve change on scale. That said, our findings in this chapter suggest several important directions for consideration by teacher leader program staff and education researchers.

First, getting beyond show and tell approaches to teacher leadership is critical if the aim is to support teachers in a more reflective and critical engagement with their own practice. In the best case, teacher leaders' work would help foster school- and district-based structures that encourage greater visibility and collegial scrutiny of instructional practice. Teachers are able to accelerate and deepen their understanding of instruction when they have opportunities to observe one another teach and critically review what they see. Teacher leaders' work might have greater strategic impact if it focused on the organization and facilitation of groups that support this goal. This suggests that teacher leaders' prior work as teachers, though necessary, may not be sufficient to achieve broader aims. They will need much more skill at facilitating groups of adults focused on candid critique of practice as well as savvy in navigating the political landscape of schools, departments, and classrooms. Researchers might wish to study the characteristics and efficacy of these approaches.

Second, expectations for teacher leaders' work with teachers should be made explicit—for teacher leaders and for teachers. Demonstration teaching, coteaching, and other elements of a show and tell approach are default strategies because they often present the path of least resistance for both parties. The teacher leader isn't challenged to go beyond one-on-one support, and the teachers with whom they work are seldom held accountable and can easily opt out. Teacher leaders need to work closely with principals, department heads, and other school leaders to craft a clear set of expectations to guide the teacher leader's work and insure the classroom teacher's full involvement. A well-defined plan governing teacher leaders' work with classroom teachers has the added advantage of establishing the conditions and limits of their involvement. Teacher leaders will have a clearer rationale for determining with whom, how long, and toward what end they work. And teachers, too, will know what they can expect and can shape their requests accordingly.

Third and finally, teacher leaders' work needs to be viewed as one part of a larger, districtwide effort to achieve instructional change across schools and classrooms. Where such an effort is clearly articulated, teacher leaders are able to focus their work and make more sense of their support of classroom teachers, whether through one-on-one modeling or through support of collegial learning. In a significant number of urban districts the introduction of new curricula in mathematics or science has provided this focus. Researchers might wish to study teacher leader programs that are clearly tied to a district focus. The picture that emerges would likely be quite different than the one of teacher leader as solo agent, lacking authority and clear direction.

Teacher leadership, as a strategy for instructional improvement in mathematics and science education, represents a substantial investment of national and local resources. Developing a better understanding of how teacher leaders are recruited, trained, deployed, and supported and crafting a more detailed account of the work they actually do will help education leaders achieve higher returns on this investment.

NOTE

This research was funded by the National Science Foundation under Grant No. 9970830, *Teacher Leadership for Systemic Reform.* The authors gratefully acknowledge the Foundation's support through all phases of our work and wish to offer special thanks to our program officer, Dr. Bernice Anderson, for her advice and guidance throughout the study.

REFERENCES

Ball, D., & Cohen, D. (1999). Developing practice, developing practitioners: Toward a practice-based theory of professional education. In L. Darling-Hammond & G. Sykes (Eds.), *Teaching as the learning profession: Handbook of policy and practice* (pp. 3–32). San Francisco: Jossey-Bass.

Barth, R. S. (2001). Teachers at the helm. *Education Week, 20*(24), 32–33, 48.

Bryk, A. S., & Schneider, B. (2002). *Trust in Schools.* New York: Russell Sage Foundation.

Carroll, C., & Mumme, J. (2001). *Leadership for change: Supporting and developing teacher leaders in mathematics renaissance K–12.* Unpublished manuscript.

Elmore, R., & Burney, D. (1999). Investing in teacher learning: Staff development and instructional improvement. In L. Darling-Hammond & G. Sykes (Eds.), *Teaching as the learning profession: Handbook of policy and practice* (pp. 263–291). San Francisco: Jossey-Bass.

Feiler, R., Heritage, M., & Gallimore, R. (2000). Teachers leading teachers. *Educational Leadership, 57*(7), 66–69.

Fullan, M. G. (1993). Why teachers must become change agents. *Educational Leadership, 50*(6), 12–17.

Hargreaves, A. (1993). Individualism and individuality: Reinterpreting the teacher culture. In J. W. Little & M. W. McLaughlin (Eds.), *Teachers' work: Individuals, colleagues, and contexts.* New York: Teachers College Press.

Horizon Research, Inc. (HRI). (2000). *What have we learned? Local systemic change initiatives share lessons from the field.* Retrieved September 1, 2003, from the Horizon Research, Inc. Web site at http://www.horizon-research.com/LSC/news/learned.pdf

Institute for Educational Leadership (IEL). (2001). *Leadership for student learning: Redefining the teacher as leader.* Retrieved on September 1, 2003, from the Institute for Educational Leadership Web site at http://www.iel.org/programs/21st/reports/teachlearn.pdf

Joyce, B. R., & Showers, B. (1988). *Student achievement through staff development.* New York: Longman.

Katzenmeyer, M., & Moller, G. (1996). *Awakening the sleeping giant: Leadership development for teachers.* Thousand Oaks, CA: Corwin Press.

Kelly, K. (2001). Teachers helping teachers. *Harvard Education Letter, 17*(3), 5–7.

Lemlech, J. K., & Hertzog, H. (1998). *Preparing for leadership roles.* Paper presented at the annual meeting of the American Educational Research Association, San Diego, CA.

Lieberman, A. (1992). Teacher leadership: What are we learning? In C. Livingston (Ed.), *Teachers as leaders: Evolving roles* (pp. 159–165). Washington, DC: National Education Association.

Little, J. W. (1990). The persistence of privacy: Autonomy and initiative in teachers' professional relations. *Teachers College Record, 91*(4), 508–536.

Little, J. W. (1993). Teachers' professional development in a climate of educational reform. *Educational Evaluation and Policy Analysis, 15*(2), 129–151.

Lord, B., Cress, K., & Miller, B. (2003). *Teacher leadership as classroom support: The challenge of scale and feedback in mathematics and science education reform.* Retrieved May 30, 2007, from the Education Development Center Web site at http://cllc.edc.org/docs/TeacherLeadershipClassroomSupport_1005.pdf

Lord, B., & Miller, B. (2000). *Teacher leadership: An appealing and inescapable force in school reform?* Retrieved September 1, 2003, from the U.S. Department of Education Web site at http://www.ed.gov/inits/Math/glenn/LordMiller.doc

Loucks-Horsley, S., Hewson, P., Love, N., & Stiles, K. (1998). *Designing professional development for teachers of science and mathematics.* Thousand Oaks, CA: Corwin Press.

Loucks-Horsley, S., & Matsumoto, C. (1999). Research on professional development for teachers of mathematics and science: The state of the scene. *School Science and Mathematics, 99*(5), 258–271.

Medina, K., & St. John, M. (1997). *The nature of teacher leadership: Lessons learned from the California subject matter projects.* Inverness, CA: Inverness Research Associates.

National Board for Professional Teaching Standards (NBPTS). (2001). *The impact of National Board certification on teachers: A survey of National Board certified teachers and assessors.* Arlington, VA: National Board for Professional Teaching Standards.

Rogers, E. M. (1995). *Diffusion of innovations* (4th ed.). New York: Free Press.

Silva, D., Gimbert, B., & Nolan, J. (2000). Sliding the doors: Locking and unlocking possibilities for teacher leadership. *Teachers College Record, 102*(4), 779–804.

Smylie, M., & Denny, J. (1990). Teacher leadership: Tensions and ambiguities in organizational perspective. *Educational Administration Quarterly, 26*(3), 235–259.

Snell, J., & Swanson, J. (2000). *The essential knowledge and skills of teacher leaders: A search for a conceptual framework.* Paper presented at the annual meeting of the American Educational Research Association, New Orleans, LA.

Spillane, J. (2002). Local theories of teacher change: The pedagogy of district policies and programs. *Teachers College Record, 104*(3), 377–420.

Staub, F. C., Mahon, L. K., & Miller, A. (1998). *Content-focused coaching: Scaffolding teaching and reflection on core issues of instructional practice.* Paper presented at the annual meeting of the American Educational Research Association, San Diego, CA.

Thompson, C., & Zeuli, J. (1999). The frame and the tapestry: Standards-based reform and professional development. In L. Darling-Hammond & G. Sykes

(Eds.), *Teaching as a learning profession: Handbook of policy and practice* (pp. 341–375). San Francisco, CA: Jossey-Bass.

Wasley, P. (1991). *Teachers who lead: The rhetoric of reform and the realities of practice*. New York: Teachers College Press.

West, L., & Staub, F. (2003). *Content-focused coaching: Transforming mathematics lessons*. Portsmouth, NH: Heinemann.

Zimpher, N. L. (1988). A design for the professional development of teacher leaders. *Journal of Teacher Education, 39*(1), 53–60.

CHAPTER 5

The Influence of Organizational Design on Instructional Teacher Leadership

Melinda M. Mangin

INSTRUCTIONAL TEACHER LEADERSHIP positions are intended to build collective instructional capacity by providing teachers with effective professional development. Scholars indicate that professional development is most effective when it contains three main components: a focus on instructional matters, collaborative interaction that is sustained over time, and a school-embedded context (Hawley & Valli, 1999). The outcomes of such professional development may include increased instructional capacity, changed practice, and overall school reform (Chrispeels, 1997; Cohen & Hill, 2001). Instructional teacher leaders may be one way to promote this kind of ongoing, collective instructional improvement.

Despite the potential benefits of instructional teacher leadership, multiple challenges have surfaced including the ambiguity of the roles (Smylie & Denny, 1990), the need for legitimacy to serve as leaders (Firestone & Bader, 1992), the potential for leadership positions to divert teachers' attention from instructional matters (Smylie, 1997), and the tendency for teacher leadership roles to focus on individual job enhancement rather than collective instructional improvement (Hart, 1990; Pounder, 1999; Silva, Gimbert, & Nolan, 2000). Moreover, the strategies teacher leaders have used to gain access to resistant teachers deemphasized instructional change in an effort to gain teachers' trust (Mangin, 2005).

Given this conflicting set of challenges and benefits, one potentially useful avenue of research is to examine how the design of teacher leadership initiatives can ameliorate or exacerbate the challenges that teacher leaders face. The design of teacher leadership initiatives sets the stage for how the positions will be enacted. Existing research on instructional teacher leaders does not sufficiently examine variations in role designs or subsequent differences in outcomes (York-Barr & Duke, 2004). The need for such information may be greatest in districts that develop localized teacher leader positions outside the context of comprehensive school reform models, which frequently include guidelines on how to develop leadership positions for teachers.

This chapter therefore examines variations in the design of teacher leadership initiatives and the effect of design on enactment. Five school districts were reviewed, each with formal teacher leadership positions intended to improve elementary-level math instruction. Despite this commonality, the five districts exhibited sometimes radically different designs. The investigation included interviews with 63 participants, including math teacher leaders, district-level supervisors, principals, and elementary teachers. The findings highlight the design constraints that districts experienced, trade-offs inherent in different designs, and designs that offer greater potential for advancing instructional teacher leadership.

ORGANIZATIONAL DESIGN THEORY

This examination of teacher leadership design draws on organizational design theories to help make sense of variations across districts. Organizational design refers to structural and cultural aspects of the organization, including the formal system of task and authority relationships, the use of resources, and the coordination of motivation and behavior (Jones, 2001). Much of the literature on organizational design comes from the field of business management. Traditionally, this literature has advanced a rational model of thought. As such, organizations are seen as setting goals and objectively identifying and implementing strategies appropriate for achieving those goals (Mintzberg, 1990). Organizations that optimize the alignment of strategies with goals, their strategic fit, are believed to have the greatest competitive advantage or level of effectiveness.

A rational model of organizational design has a number of limitations. Foremost, it assumes "clear goals, complete information, and the cognitive capacity to analyze the problem" (Tarter & Hoy, 1998, p. 213). Faced with a more complex and ambiguous reality, the ability of organizations to engage in rational thought and optimize the best possible design choice is constrained. Instead, the decision-making process more closely replicates a system of bounded rationality whereby choices are made within the context of what is believed feasible and what is satisfactory (Simon, 1993).

As such, organizations make the best possible design choices within a narrowed range of alternatives.

When districts design teacher leadership initiatives they make choices about the use of valuable human resources. Of particular importance are (1) teacher leader selection and professional development, (2) teacher leader distribution, and (3) communications management. These human resource–related design components affect how the positions will be enacted and perceived. A rational view suggests that districts can best optimize the goal of instructional teacher leadership—improved teaching practice—by selecting the design that yields the highest results. At the same time, a bounded view recognizes that contextual factors threaten design optimization and cause organizations to deviate from the optimal choice. Here I discuss each design component as it relates to the implementation of instructional teacher leadership roles.

Teacher Leader Selection and Professional Development

A rational model of organizational design suggests that an organization needs to hire the right people to maximize its goals. According to Bolman and Deal (2003) successful organizations select employees based on their people skills (Pfeffer, 1998), intelligence (Stross, 1996), and level of motivation (Simon, 1996). When organizations know what kinds of employees they need and when they exercise selectivity in hiring, they promote strategic fit and increase the likelihood of success.

Within the context of instructional teacher leadership, the goal of math instructional improvement suggests that teacher leaders should have mathematics knowledge. This notion is supported by nascent research indicating that content knowledge contributes to teacher leaders' effectiveness (see Chapter 3 of this volume). Moreover, research shows that teachers view other teachers as leaders based on their level of knowledge and skill, or human capital (Spillane, Hallett, & Diamond, 2003). At the same time, advocates of teacher leadership have indicated the importance of personality for earning teachers' trust (Crowther, Kaagan, Ferguson, & Hann, 2002; Harris & Muijs, 2005; Lieberman & Miller, 2004). To date, there is little systematic evidence linking teacher leader qualifications to teacher leadership outcomes (York-Barr & Duke, 2004).

Regardless of the desired qualifications, employee selection is highly dependent on the availability of both human and financial resources. That is, districts must have access to qualified people and sufficient funds to hire them. Without adequate resources, a district's intentions to optimize the teacher leadership design are constrained to a limited set of options.

One way for districts to increase the knowledge and skills of their teacher leaders is to create learning opportunities (Elmore, 2002). Research points to the importance of professional development as a means for building capacity and facilitating successful school improvement initiatives (Cohen & Hill, 2001; McDonnell & Elmore, 1987). For example, a district that hires teacher leaders with limited math content knowledge may dedicate funds for additional math training. As such, inadequacies in the available human resources may be compensated for through other design strategies.

Teacher Leader Distribution

Another aspect of design is the organization's distribution of human resources. Decisions about teacher leader distribution focus on who should have access to teacher leaders and for what purpose (see Chapter 2 of this volume). A rational view of human resource distribution suggests that the best distribution takes into account organizational goals, needs, and priorities (Hatch, 1997). As such, decisions about how to distribute teacher leaders should be linked to the goal of instructional improvement; that is, those teachers in need of the greatest improvement would have the greatest access.

This rational formula of matching needy teachers to qualified instructional teacher leaders is bounded by several challenges. Teachers who are identified as needing assistance may not desire assistance and, moreover, there may be insufficient teacher leader resources to adequately address the needs (Mangin, 2005). The challenge then is determining how to prioritize teachers' needs. Some possibilities include newly hired teachers, teachers implementing new curriculum, or teachers working at grade levels where student achievement is assessed for accountability purposes. Such targeting of teachers circumscribes efforts at collective improvement to the improvement of a limited group of teachers.

Communications Management

A third aspect of teacher leadership design is the management of formal communication. Communication structures can be used to facilitate the exchange of information and the coordination of tasks, promoting effective organizational functioning (Hatch, 1997). Organizations with complex technologies or nonroutine tasks have a greater level of complexity, which creates a need for increased coordination across positions and, subsequently, more complex communication structures (Galbraith, 1973; Perrow, 1986). Educational organizations are inherently complex given the level of variability in the core technologies of teaching and learning. Teacher leader positions have been introduced, in part, to help in the coordination of these complex technologies. Yet, the addition of another educational role creates a need for increased coordination and communication.

A rational view suggests the importance of managing formal communication systems, particularly when informal communication could potentially undermine organizational intentions (see Chapter 6 of this volume). A more bounded perspective points to numerous challenges associated with coordinating communication including schools' culture of autonomy (Lortie, 2002), teachers' concern that teacher leaders may act as administrative "spies" (Mangin, 2005), administrators' heavy workload (Spillane & Louis, 2002), and the sheer ambiguity of what to communicate (Hart, 1990; Smylie & Denny, 1990). Such challenges inhibit effective communication.

The organizational design components discussed in this chapter relate to the management of human resources—arguably the most important resource a school can possess (Darling-Hammond, 1999). How schools design teacher leadership initiatives likely affects the extent to which this new resource can be optimized.

DISTRICT CONTEXT

In this study, each of the five school districts (see Table 5.1 for demographics) employed math teacher leaders whose formal job titles included specialist, helper, lead teacher, coordinator, and trainer. In all the districts, the math teacher leaders were released from teaching responsibilities to assist elementary-level colleagues with mathematics professional development. At the same time, the districts exhibited variation in the design of their teacher leadership roles (see Table 5.2).

To learn about the relationship between design and enactment, interviews were conducted with 63 participants. First, a representative sample of 12 math teacher leaders was drawn from across the five districts. These teacher leaders worked with 21 principals, 15 of whom were interviewed. In addition, 6 district-level supervisors—administrators responsible for the development and oversight of the teacher leader position—were also interviewed. Finally, a purposive sample of 30 elementary classroom teachers was selected for participation, 2 from each of the schools that had participating principals. These teachers were selected with the assistance of math teacher leaders and their school principals based on their divergent viewpoints: one teacher who was more receptive to the work of the math teacher leader and one who was more resistant.

The data reported here come predominantly from interviews with these participants, which were audiotaped and transcribed. The analytic procedures included both deductive and inductive reasoning (Miles &

Table 5.1. Demographic characteristics of participating districts, 2001–02.

	District				
	A	B	C	D	E
District Factor Group[a]	B	C/D	B	G/H	B
Total enrollment (*n*)	7,526	2,202	5,898	6,052	3,332
White (%)	1	41	37	31	85
Black (%)	71	45	37	44	6
Hispanic (%)	28	10	22	11	7
Passing rate on high school proficiency test[b] (%)	29.4	42	47.4	59	63.9
Students on free or reduced-price lunch (%)	64	50	45	27	35
Ratio of 9th to 12th grade enrollment[c]	1.79:1		1.33:1	1.64:1	1.40:1
High school attendance (%)	90.5	90.4	92.8	87.2	93.2

Note: From "Facilitating Elementary Principals' Support for Instructional Leadership," by M. M. Mangin, 2007, *Educational Administration Quarterly, 43,* pp. 319–357. Copyright © 2007 by Sage Publications, Inc. Reprinted with minor editorial changes with permission.

[a] The District Factor Grouping (DFG) system was created in 1975 and uses seven indices to reflect socioeconomic status: (1) percent of population with no high school diploma, (2) percent with some college, (3) occupation, (4) population density, (5) income, (6) unemployment, and (7) poverty. Category intervals reflect a distance of one tenth between the lowest and highest scores. Intervals are represented by a letter-based scale that ranges from A to J, with A being the lowest socioeconomic category. The DFG rankings presented here are based on 2001–2002 data derived from the New Jersey Department of Education District Factor Grouping (DFG) System (http://www.state.nj.us/njded/finance/sf/dfgdesc.shtml).

[b] In District E, the high school enrolled students from surrounding townships that were better off socioeconomically, which probably accounts for its higher passing rate on the high school proficiency test.

[c] No 12th-grade class in District B.

Table 5.2. Teacher leadership variation: Distribution and instructional context by district.

	District				
	A	*B*	*C*	*D*	*E*
Distribution (*n*)					
Math teacher leaders	3[a]	2	2	2[b]	3
Elementary schools	3	2	8	4	4
Schools per teacher leader	1[c]	1	8	3[d]	1[e]
Subjects covered	Math	Math	Math Soc. studies Lang. arts	Math	Math
Instructional Context					
Math program/text	Math Investigations	Everyday Math	Everyday Math	Harcourt Brace text	Math Trailblazers
School reform model	America's Choice	—	—	—	—
Year position created	Fall 2001	Fall 2002	Fall 2000, new design in Fall 2002	Fall 2000, expanded in Fall 2002	Fall 2002

Note: From "Facilitating Elementary Principals' Support for Instructional Leadership," by M. M. Mangin, 2007, *Educational Administration Quarterly, 43,* pp. 319–357. Copyright © 2007 by Sage Publications, Inc. Reprinted with minor editorial changes with permission.

[a] The total population of teacher leaders in District A was 11. Three teacher leaders were sampled randomly for participation in this study. In the other four districts, the entire population of elementary math teacher leaders was included in the study.

[b] A third position was added in March 2003. That teacher leader is not included in this study.

[c] One large school has two math teacher leaders. Thus, the total population of 11 teacher leaders was spread across 10 schools.

[d] This unusual configuration of schools to teacher leaders was the result of targeting some grade levels at some schools.

[e] The two K–2 schools were shared by one math teacher leader. The two upper elementary schools, which were larger, had one teacher leader each.

Huberman, 1994) as well as extensive use of memos and data matrices (Patton, 2001). A computer software program facilitated the identification of broad themes, which were refined over time as new data were assimilated and patterns emerged across respondents and contexts.

TEACHER LEADER SELECTION
AND PROFESSIONAL DEVELOPMENT

All five of the districts were challenged to hire highly qualified teacher leaders. How they responded to teacher leaders' professional development needs differed across districts.

Selection

In seeking to fill the teacher leadership positions, supervisors in all five districts indicated a desire to hire teachers with math knowledge and evidence of leadership expertise. Yet, the recruitment process yielded few candidates with such qualifications. One supervisor reported, "There were hardly any resumes. There aren't that many people out there who understand what this job entails. We got very few that we felt were even eligible for an interview." As a result, supervisors considered other qualifications including personality, years of teaching experience, and willingness to learn. In the process, all five districts eliminated math certification (or a formal degree in mathematics) from their requirements. According to one supervisor, "A job description was created, but it was things like demonstrated leadership, ability to facilitate workshops, understanding of mathematical concepts, and interest in promoting standards-based mathematics. So, they were very generic requirements." More than anything, a "willingness to learn and grow" became the foremost qualification. As a result, only 5 of the 12 teacher leaders described themselves as having high levels of math expertise when they were hired.

In addition to a lack of qualified candidates, the selection process was also constrained by a desire to hire from within the district. Of the 12 participating teacher leaders, 8 were internal hires—from their school or district—and 4 were hired from outside the district. In some instances, the preference for internal hires reflected a cultural belief about the unique needs of districts and schools. As summarized by one teacher, "If they're not fully aware of the district that we're teaching in, the particular needs of the school then [they're] useless." At the same time, there were trade-offs to hiring internally. Teachers expressed reservations about their classroom colleagues taking on positions that inferred greater knowledge and higher status. One teacher speculated that her school's teacher leader might have been more successful if she had been hired from outside the district. She explained, "If someone is from the outside it's almost like a clean slate."

Internal hiring was also a way to prevent teacher layoffs. Two of the internal hires assumed teacher leader positions when their jobs as "enrichment teachers" (working with pull-out groups of students) were discontinued. One principal described the situation:

> In all sincerity, the decision was kind of arbitrary . . . we had to find something for this person to do if they weren't enrichment [teachers] anymore. It was a district-level [decision] that the math coach would be much more relevant than an enrichment person. So those duties were just transferred over.

Thus, instead of conducting a search for the most qualified people, 8 of the 12 teacher leader searches were constrained by a preference to hire from within.

According to both teachers and teacher leaders, the issue of qualifications and expertise often became a stumbling block that could limit teachers' perception of the teacher leaders as a useful resource. Teachers questioned their teacher leaders' years of teaching experience, knowledge of a particular math program, ability to understand all grade levels, and decreased time spent in classrooms. Alternately, those teacher leaders with high levels of math knowledge indicated that teachers more readily accepted them as experts and leaders regardless of whether they were hired internally or externally. One District D teacher leader with nearly three decades of math experience explained:

> I've only taught only math. I taught first in a small private school where I did different levels in the classroom and then an enrichment program for every grade in the school. . . . Then, in another school I was teaching different levels of math and also I worked with the Math Counts program—a nationwide competition for seventh and eighth graders.

Such extensive math knowledge earned this teacher leader her position and also made her more readily accepted by teachers.

Development

One way that teacher leaders who lacked expertise stayed one step ahead of their teachers was to participate in professional development. Four of the five districts provided professional development to their teacher leaders, which typically came from the textbook companies or math programs contracted by the district. This training tended to be geared toward classroom teachers or building administrators and seldom addressed the needs of teacher leaders who worked across multiple grade levels. Hence, teacher leaders received the bulk of their training side by side with teachers. This delivery strategy compromised teachers' perception of the teacher leader as experts since they perceived little differentiation in the level of teachers' and teacher leaders' knowledge.

Two districts provided additional professional development beyond the math textbook or math program. Teacher leaders in District E received professional development in leadership skills in addition to math content. Both kinds of sessions were offered by a local state university. District E teacher leaders received at least 4 days of training beyond what teachers received. In District A, teacher leaders participated in weekly half-day sessions conducted by the district-level math supervisor and with regular assistance from a math education professor from the nearby state university. These sessions were intended to deepen the teacher leaders' math content knowledge. One of the teacher leaders described the sessions as "very helpful—to share ideas and strategies. I may internalize something from [the math program] one way, and talking to someone else, they may internalize it one way, so it gives us a chance to just debrief." Such comments point to the potential usefulness of professional development, both for gaining new knowledge and also for developing status as experts.

Finally, in an unusual approach, District D provided no professional development to their two teacher leaders. The impetus for this decision was twofold. First, the district's math texts lacked the kind of constructivist approach that the teacher leaders were hired to promote, making training from the textbook company antithetical to the goals of the position. Second, the district hired teacher leaders with high levels of math expertise and prior experience in the math teacher leader position. Thus, by hiring highly qualified teacher leaders, the district ostensibly eliminated their need to provide professional development.

TEACHER LEADER DISTRIBUTION

The five districts exhibited great variation in how they distributed math teacher leaders. They had to make two primary choices with regard to distribution: how to distribute teacher leaders (1) across schools and (2) across teachers.

Distribution Across Schools

District supervisors agreed that the optimal design would place one math teacher leader in each elementary school, which would greatly increase the availability of instructional support and expertise. At the same time, lack of funds and qualified people meant that only one of the five districts, District A, truly implemented a one-teacher-leader-per-school design (see Table 5.2). Districts B and E came close to such a design with some slight variations. In District B each of the two teacher leaders worked in a single school but they spent part of their day working with children rather than teachers. In District E one of the three teacher leaders was divided between two small lower elementary schools. The designs in Districts C and D had even wider teacher leader distribution. The two teacher leaders in District D traveled to three of the district's four schools and District C's two teacher leaders were stretched across eight schools.

Designs that spread teacher leaders across schools created logistical challenges for teachers, principals, and teacher leaders alike. Teachers noted the difficulty of gaining access to teacher leaders, as described by one District D teacher: "It would be nice if the teacher trainer was in this school. That way, it'd be much easier to do scheduling, talk with them at lunch and in the hallway." Another potential problem was an increase in the size of the teacher population. As one District C principal explained, "We need more [teacher leaders] . . . there are eight schools. . . . It's a lot of kids . . . a lot of kids means a lot of teachers and a lot of classrooms—a lot of problems to solve." The additional time spent traveling between schools also complicated the teacher leaders' work. Not only did they have less time to focus on instructional matters, traveling made it difficult for teacher leaders to keep track of individual teachers' needs. A District C teacher explained, "It's really difficult for them because they don't know what they're walking into all of the time."

Being stretched across schools created other challenges as well. Even when the teacher leader didn't work with larger populations of teachers, working in multiple schools gave teachers the impression of decreased teacher leader availability. The teachers in District E who shared a teacher leader frequently reported that she spent more time in the "other" school, suggesting that being distributed between schools was as much a symbolic obstacle as it was a true impediment. Finally, working across schools left teacher leaders "homeless." One District D principal expressed how teacher leaders would benefit from being located in one school: "Having that person as part of the faculty meeting or part of the party for the teacher that just found out she's going to be leaving on maternity, having that person be part of the whole picture, makes that person more a part of the team and not an intruder." Taken together, these challenges suggest that a one school–one teacher leader model is more likely to optimize the value of the teacher leadership position.

At the same time, the participants did point to some benefits associated with multisite distribution. Foremost, working in more than one school afforded the teacher leader greater knowledge of the math program and insight into its districtwide implementation. As one District E teacher stated, "She's had experience in other people's classrooms with the lesson . . . she has experience with the lesson ten times more than I do because there are ten first-grade classes." Similarly, a teacher from District C explained, "Even though we can't get to [the other school], she'll tell us how it's working there."

Teacher leaders also reported benefits to "homelessness." For example, the District D teacher leaders shared an office in the district's administrative building. They expressed appreciation for quiet work space, a telephone and a computer, and freedom from school duties. One District D teacher leader described some of the trade-offs:

> When you're in one school you're more aware of the social interactions in the school, you have more of a group that you're involved with and so you have ways of either finding out things or people are more involved with you personally. That's a difference, but [being in multiple schools] you're also asked to do fewer extra chores that people are always asked to do in schools. So it works both ways.

Thus, although the participants generally preferred teacher leaders to be located in one school, there were some identifiable benefits to being stretched across school contexts.

Distribution Across Teachers

When teacher leaders were stretched across schools they commonly targeted subsets of teachers, thus narrowing the population of teachers with whom they worked. One targeting strategy was to identify those teachers with the highest instructional improvement needs. Although none of the districts explicitly targeted low-performing teachers, Districts C and D and one school in District B intentionally targeted subsets of teachers identified as needing assistance: new teachers and teachers working at grade levels where student achievement was assessed for accountability purposes. For example, the District C supervisor instructed teacher leaders to work with new teachers explaining, "They're covering teachers who were not in traditional training programs and teaching them how to be teachers [rather] than taking a curriculum and trying to introduce it to all teachers." An added benefit of working with new teachers was their greater receptivity to receiving assistance from the teacher leader.

In addition to new teachers, teacher leaders frequently targeted teachers working at grade levels where students took state standardized tests. The purpose was twofold: to increase standardized test scores, which would subsequently justify the work of the teacher leader. Even when the position was intended as a resource for all teachers, teacher leaders tended to target tested grades. One teacher from District A reported, "[Teacher leaders] are preoccupied with the grade levels that are testing grades, third and fourth grades, which I've noticed receive a lot of the support." Teacher leaders explained that not only was more at stake for teachers at tested grade levels, but those teachers displayed greater willingness to receive assistance from the teacher leader, presumably because of the accountability pressures they experienced. Thus new teachers and teachers at tested grade levels were targeted because they were perceived as having greater needs but also because of their increased receptivity. What is unclear is the extent to which other high-need teachers might be overlooked as a result of this targeting strategy.

A second way of distributing teacher leaders was across all teachers in a school. Districts A and E, and one teacher leader in District B used this design as a way to facilitate even implementation of new math programs. These teacher leaders reported two main challenges: finding time to meet with all teachers and having sufficient content knowledge for all grades. As one District B teacher explained, "They have her stretched to the limit. [Maybe] two people would be better for the building." In addition to time pressures, these teacher leaders lacked sufficient expertise across all grade levels. This challenge was somewhat diminished in District E where the schools were limited to either upper or lower elementary. Toward the end of this study, District A decided that the following school year they would increase teacher leaders' expertise by assigning them to a particular grade level and having them travel across 5 of the district's 10 schools. Unfortunately, this study concluded before the new design could be implemented and studied. Still, one might hypothesize that the increase in grade-level expertise might be offset by a decrease in time spent working with teachers due to increased travel time.

COMMUNICATIONS MANAGEMENT

Communication is an important part of coordinating tasks and roles. Examining how organizational design contributes to the formal communication of teacher leadership goals can inform the future development of teacher leadership positions. The management of communication differed greatly in the five districts. Only District A developed formal structures intended to maximize communication and implementation. Communication structures in the other four districts were more limited, adding to the challenge of teacher leadership implementation.

Extensive Communication

District A created formal structures intended to maximize the coordination of tasks and the exchange of information across a range of positions. The District A supervisor stated, "We all try to be on the same page. There's constant articulation between administrators, myself, my director, principals, me, math coordinators, me, principals, math coordinators." As such, the communication structure in District A included formal meetings between the supervisor and principals, the supervisor and teacher leaders, and between principals and teacher leaders.

The District A supervisor held monthly meetings with the principals to set expectations about the teacher leadership role and to increase the fidelity of implementation. The supervisor explained that originally some principals utilized the position for noninstructional tasks: "[Teacher leaders] had been pulled for great lengths of time to do the budget, to do the school's accountability plan, things like that. But that doesn't seem to be happening as much anymore." Hence, formal opportunities for communication appeared to maximize principals' support for the position and facilitate appropriate implementation.

The District A supervisor also conducted weekly, half-day training sessions where teacher leaders could learn about math content knowledge and the supervisor could provide information, clarify directives, and reiterate goals. These group meetings were augmented by individualized sessions that took place within the context of the teacher leaders' schools. The supervisor explained, "I met with them individually. Sometimes I followed them around to see what they were doing and we talked about their practice and issues that they were having on a one-on-one basis."

The District A teacher leaders met with their principals in regularly scheduled, weekly meetings. One of the teacher leaders described a typical session: "It's me saying 'these are the things that are being done and these are the things I have planned to do.' And then she might say, 'I went in this class or this class and I've been seeing this,' and she and I can talk about the things that maybe we could do." These formal meetings provided opportunities to clarify the teacher leaders' work. One District A teacher leader provided an example of how these formal communication structures facilitated his work:

> Our principal is very hands-on, she follows through, she reads plans, and everything's black or white. So we don't have the issue of people trying to skirt [math coordinator visits] . . . they're gonna do it, it's the way it is, so we don't have to deal with that issue and I think that makes my life a lot easier. . . . The guidelines are clear, the expectations are clear, and there's follow-through.

As articulated by this teacher leader, communication structures provided a mechanism for clarifying expectations and made the teacher leader's work easier.

Finally, information about the teacher leadership role was formally communicated to teachers through various mechanisms and sources. In staff meetings and in daily interactions, principals repeatedly communicated the expectation that teachers should seek instructional assistance from the math teacher leaders (see Mangin, 2007). The district supervisor visited teachers in their classrooms to conduct "walk-throughs" with the math teacher leaders. And teacher leaders met regularly with teachers in grade-level meetings where they discussed math content as well as the kinds of instructional assistance teachers might expect from the math teacher leader.

Limited Communication

In the other districts, the development of formal communication structures was bounded by competing concerns and constraints. For example, in Districts C and D, the supervisors' desire to facilitate the teachers' trust and the teacher leaders' autonomy led district supervisors to intentionally limit communication. Limited communication resulted in decreased knowledge of the position, diminished support, and reduced receptivity.

The District C supervisor actively discouraged the teacher leaders from communicating with him or with principals, explaining that decreased communication would promote trust and reduce teachers' perception of teacher leaders as administrative spies:

> I purposely said . . . "I don't want anybody to think you're over here a lot because then they'll think you're talking about them." . . . I really don't want to see [the teacher leaders] simply because the tendency would be, the more I see them, the more I might find out something that I really shouldn't know.

Moreover, the District C supervisor made little effort to communicate with principals, who reported knowing little about the teacher leaders' work. The only open line of communication was between teacher leaders and teachers but even this was limited due to the lack of information from superiors and the teacher leaders' distribution across eight schools.

In District D, the supervisor prioritized autonomy over communication, indicating that her two highly skilled math teacher leaders required little guidance. She explained, "I let [them] run with it for the most part. Every once in a while we had to meet to kind of make sure that we were still on the same track." Communication between the supervisor and principals was similarly infrequent although conversations occasionally occurred at the principals' monthly meeting with the assistant superintendent if there were "specific concerns or questions." One teacher leader explained how the lack of communication structures affected both principal involvement and teachers' receptivity:

> It would be nice if the principals indicated to all staff that this is a priority and [teachers] should take advantage of the services. That would be a wonderful way to start the year . . . to say, "we have these people on staff and they will be available. We'll arrange for you to meet them and if there's anything you need them to do, feel free to contact them." That would be good. That would be very good.

Like District C, the teacher leaders became the primary source for teachers' information. As such, only targeted teachers—those at tested grade levels—were knowledgeable about the teacher leaders' work.

In Districts B and E, the communication structures were bounded by time limitations and ambiguity about the teacher leader role, which compromised implementation. In District B, the supervisor met monthly with teacher leaders and quarterly with teachers from each grade level; yet, principals generally declined to participate in these meetings due to time constraints. In the words of one principal, "Sometimes I go, sometimes I don't—generally not because it's a time issue." Despite having limited communication with the supervisor and vague knowledge of her vision, District B principals were responsible for overseeing the teacher leaders' work. One principal asked her teacher leader to work with all teachers equally while the other principal asked the teacher leader to target willing teachers and to work part-time with groups of students. Thus the gaps in the communication structure resulted in divergent implementation of the teacher leader position.

In the case of District E, the supervisors' well-intentioned efforts to communicate were undercut by an overemphasis on learning about the new curriculum and a lack of attention to the teacher leader roles themselves. One principal described the impact of this oversight: "There was a lot of gray area when the positions were created and we're still trying to combat that confusion . . . to have a full year ingrained under that confusion—it's sort of difficult to re-create [the position]." Confusion about the position limited the ability of principals, teacher leaders, and teachers alike to implement it. In response, the supervisors renewed their efforts at communication. This same principal explained: "The two district-level people have much more input than they had last year . . . [and] they've made a really good attempt to corral those skills and reinvestigate what the central focus needs to be." So the supervisors' initial failure to communicate limited implementation, but led to renewed communication efforts.

SUMMARY AND DISCUSSION

These cases present new evidence of the organizational complexity of teacher leadership initiatives. Not only is teacher leadership design difficult to optimize, it requires careful consideration of the various design trade-offs and attention to key design components. Participants described ways in which teacher leadership design affected its enactment. These findings enable a deeper understanding of the importance of organizational design and may contribute to the creation of a set of design principles that facilitate more effective design of teacher leadership roles.

Selection and Development: Investing in Teacher Leadership

Two primary factors constrained supervisors' ability to optimize the selection of teacher leaders: a lack of applicants with strong content knowledge and a preference for internal hires. Faced with few qualified applicants, supervisors selected teacher leaders on the basis of their willingness to take on the position. According to both teachers and teacher leaders, the resulting lack of content expertise made teachers less likely to use the teacher leader as a resource. Thus willingness to do the work of the teacher leader is not enough; rather, teacher leaders must have the skills and knowledge necessary to be recognized as a valuable resource. These results align with research indicating the importance of school leaders' knowledge and expertise (see Chapter 3 of this volume; Spillane et al., 2003).

One way to increase teacher leaders' level of expertise may be to broaden the search for teacher leaders beyond internal employees. As such, supervisors may increase the likelihood of receiving qualified applicants. When lacking qualified candidates, school districts need to commit sufficient funds for additional professional development. Two districts, Districts A and E, bolstered teacher leaders' expertise through professional development that went beyond the development provided to classroom teachers. These additional opportunities increased the teacher leaders' skills while simultaneously raising their status as experts and teachers' perception of them as a useful resource. These findings point to organizational designs that can optimize teacher leadership resources despite a shortage of highly qualified applicants.

At the same time, designs that incorporate professional development for teacher leaders increase the cost of the initiative beyond the already steep costs associated with hiring additional staff and moving successful teachers out of the classroom. As such, teacher leadership initiatives could face even greater pressure to demonstrate teaching and learning benefits commensurate to their costs. Ironically, a lack of sufficient financial investment to cover professional development may make it even more difficult for teacher leadership initiatives to substantiate their worth.

Distribution: Balancing Trade-offs

Only District A was able to fully optimize teacher leader distribution by placing one full-time release teacher leader in each of its elementary schools. In the other districts, distribution was constrained by a lack of resources—both human and financial—needed to hire and train sufficient numbers of qualified teacher leaders. Instead, districts made choices within the parameters of what was feasible and satisfactory, as described by Simon's theory of "satisficing" in decision making (1993). The choices that districts made regarding teacher leader distribution involved trade-offs. For example, distributing teacher leaders across multiple schools gave them a broader perspective of instructional practice and contributed to their skill development but it also tended to increase the teacher population and decreased overall availability. Similarly, targeting subsets of teachers focused the teacher leaders' instructional improvement efforts but did not necessarily ensure that the teachers with the highest needs would be reached.

Barring the extraordinary infusion of financial and human resources needed to optimize distribution, it seems likely that districts will continue to be confronted with difficult choices regarding the placement of teacher leaders across schools and teachers. The findings presented here can enable district administrators to better understand the inevitable trade-offs in various design options. As a result, districts can make more informed, albeit imperfect, decisions about teacher leadership role design. Evidence of design trade-offs may be especially useful for districts that develop instructional teacher leadership positions outside the context of large-scale, comprehensive school reform models. Such homegrown teacher leadership initiatives are more likely to lack the financial capital associated with large-scale reform, forcing them to make consequential choices about the use of resources and design of teacher leadership roles.

Although this study presents new evidence of the specific trade-offs involved in teacher leader distribution, the effect of these choices on teacher and student learning remains unknown. Thus district administrators face an array of design options with no clear evidence of their long-term outcomes. Will differing distributions of teacher leadership resources yield divergent results or are they merely different paths that lead to the same place? In the absence of outcome data, it seems likely that administrators' choices will hinge on local contexts and goals. Thus there is a continued need for research on the relationship between local contexts, teacher leader designs, and learning outcomes.

Communication: Maximizing Potential

Organizational design theorists state the need for extensive communication management in complex organizations such as schools (Galbraith, 1973; Perrow, 1986). Nevertheless, the districts in this study faced numerous constraints that limited their ability to maximize communication, including a desire to build trust, concern for autonomy, lack of time, and ambiguity about the teacher leadership position. As such, communication in four of the five districts was limited. Predictably, limited communication hindered the exchange of information and the coordination of roles (Hatch, 1997). Specifically, participants reported a lack of information about teacher leadership, low levels of principal involvement, reduced teacher receptivity, inconsistent implementation, and confusion. These findings provide new evidence of the impact that communication structures can have on teacher leadership role implementation.

The findings also demonstrate how communication structures facilitated teacher leadership. In District A, communication management involved complex structures that promoted task coordination and the exchange of information. As a result, principals and teacher leaders had access to information, expectations were clear, and the accuracy of implementation increased. It is worth noting that for all three design components discussed here—selection and professional development, distribution, and communication—District A consistently demonstrated designs that most closely approximated the optimal structure. This observation raises questions about the interrelatedness of these components, suggesting the possibility that some design aspects may influence or predetermine others.

CONCLUSION

Given the enduring trend toward educational accountability it seems likely that school districts will continue to advance instructional teacher leadership positions as a way to improve teaching and learning. At the same time, the high financial and human resource costs associated with formal teacher leaders will likely increase the pressure to demonstrate results. As such, district administrators will need to carefully consider the design of teacher leadership initiatives, keeping in mind that design influences implementation. Moreover, there is a clear need for continued investigation into possible outcome variability associated with different designs.

Equally important, design optimization may be dependent on the presence of supportive organizational contexts. Teacher leadership initiatives build on notions of instructional improvement, organizational learning, and effective professional development. Without genuinely embracing such concepts, it seems unlikely that schools will be able to maximize teacher leadership designs.

REFERENCES

Bolman, L., & Deal, T. (2003). *Reframing organizations: Artistry, choice, and leadership* (3rd ed.). San Francisco: Jossey-Bass.

Chrispeels, J. H. (1997). Educational policy implementation in a shifting political climate: The California experience. *American Educational Research Journal, 34*(3), 453–481.

Cohen, D. K., & Hill, H. C. (2001). *Learning policy: When state education reform works.* New Haven, CT: Yale University Press.

Crowther, F., Kaagan, S. S., Ferguson, M., & Hann, L. (2002). *Developing teacher leaders: How teacher leadership enhances school success.* Thousand Oaks, CA: Corwin Press.

Darling-Hammond, L. (1999). *Teacher quality and student achievement: A review of state policy evidence.* Seattle, WA: Center for the Study of Teaching and Policy.

Elmore, R. F. (2002). *Bridging the gap between standards and achievement.* Washington, DC: Albert Shanker Institute.

Firestone, W. A., & Bader, B. D. (1992). *Redesigning teaching: Professionalism or bureaucracy?* Albany, NY: State University New York Press.

Galbraith, J. (1973). *Designing complex organizations.* Reading, MA: Addison-Wesley.

Harris, A., & Muijs, D. (2005). *Improving schools through teacher leadership*. New York: Open University Press.

Hart, A. W. (1990). Work redesign: A review of literature for education reform. In S. B. Bacharach (Ed.), *Advances in research and theories of school management and educational policy* (Vol. 1, pp. 31–69). Greenwich, CT: JAI Press.

Hatch, M. J. (1997). *Organization theory: Modern symbolic and postmodern perspectives*. New York: Oxford University Press.

Hawley, W. D., & Valli, L. (1999). The essentials of effective professional development. In L. Darling-Hammond & G. Sykes (Eds.), *Teaching as the learning profession: Handbook of policy and practice* (pp. 127–150). San Francisco: Jossey-Bass.

Jones, G. R. (2001). *Organizational theory: Text and cases* (3rd ed.). Upper Saddle River, NJ: Prentice Hall.

Lieberman, A., & Miller, L. (2004). *Teacher leadership*. San Francisco: Jossey-Bass.

Lortie, D. C. (2002). *Schoolteacher: A sociological study* (2nd ed.). Chicago: University of Chicago Press.

Mangin, M. M. (2005). Distributed leadership and the culture of schools: Teacher leaders' strategies for gaining access to classrooms. *Journal of School Leadership, 15*(4), 456–484.

Mangin, M. M. (2007). Facilitating elementary principals' support for instructional teacher leadership. *Educational Administration Quarterly, 43*(3), 319–357.

McDonnell, L. M., & Elmore, R. F. (1987). Getting the job done: Alternative policy instruments. *Educational Evaluation and Policy Analysis, 9*(2), 133–152.

Miles, M. B., & Huberman, A. M. (1994). *Qualitative data analysis: An expanded sourcebook*. Thousand Oaks, CA: Sage.

Mintzberg, H. (1990). The design school: Reconsidering the basic premises of strategic management. *Strategic Management Journal, 11*, 171–195.

Patton, M. Q. (2001). *Qualitative evaluation and research methods*. Newbury Park, CA: Sage.

Perrow, C. (1986). *Complex organizations: A critical essay* (3rd ed.). New York: Random House.

Pfeffer, J. (1998). *The human equation: Building profits by putting people first*. Boston, MA: Harvard Business School Press.

Pounder, D. G. (1999). Teacher teams: Exploring job characteristics and work related outcomes of work group enhancement. *Educational Administration Quarterly, 35*(3), 317–348.

Silva, D. Y., Gimbert, B., & Nolan, J. (2000). Sliding the doors: Locking and unlocking possibilities for teacher leadership. *Teachers College Record, 102*(4), 779–804.

Simon, H. A. (1993). Decision making: Rational, nonrational, and irrational. *Educational Administration Quarterly, 29*(3), 392–411.

Simon, H. A. (1996). *Hidden champions: Lessons from 500 of the world's best unknown companies*. Boston, MA: Harvard Business School Press.

Smylie, M. A. (1997). Research on teacher leadership: Assessing the state of the art. In B. J. Biddle (Ed.), *International handbook of teachers and teaching* (pp. 521–592). Dordrecht, The Netherlands: Kluwer.

Smylie, M. A., & Denny, J. W. (1990). Teacher leadership: Tensions and ambiguities in organizational perspective. *Educational Administration Quarterly, 26*(3), 235–259.

Spillane, J. P., Hallett, T., & Diamond, J. B. (2003). Forms of capital and the construction of leadership: Instructional leadership in urban elementary schools. *Sociology of Education, 76*(1), 1–17.

Spillane, J., & Louis, K. S. (2002). School improvement processes and practices: Professional learning for building instructional capacity. In J. Murphy (Ed.), *The educational leadership challenge: Redefining leadership for the 21st century: 101st yearbook of the National Society for the Study of Education,* Part 1 (pp. 83–104). Chicago: University of Chicago Press.

Stross, R. E. (1996, November 25). Microsoft's big advantage—hiring only the supersmart. *Fortune, 134*(10), 159–162.

Tarter, C. J., & Hoy, W. K. (1998). Toward a contingency theory of decision making. *Journal of Educational Administration, 36*(3), 212–228.

York-Barr, J., & Duke, K. (2004). What do we know about teacher leadership? Findings from two decades of scholarship. *Review of Educational Research, 74*(3), 255–316.

CHAPTER 6

Leading from Above and Below:
Formal and Informal Teacher Leadership

Sara Ray Stoelinga

THERE IS a soft buzz of activity in Hope Elementary's Room 304 as 26 second graders move in groups of four and five through learning centers on "Becoming a Thoughtful Reader." (All names of schools and individuals are pseudonyms.) At Station 1, four students pretend they are journalists, working through a set of interview questions in pairs from which they will write the story of each other's lives. At Station 2, five students work together to read a story and think through the comprehension questions that follow. A teaching assistant patiently works with the four boys at Station 3 to piece together the sequence of a story using sentences on strips of paper. The atmosphere is electric. Children are on task and working well together. The teaching assistant circulates, mostly functioning as a timekeeper, softly blowing a whistle every few minutes for students to move in groups through the activities.

As the students are involved in learning activities with the teaching assistant, the two adults sitting in the reading corner at a round table do not immediately attract attention. Here Mrs. Macintosh, the classroom teacher, sits with Carla Avery, the school's literacy coordinator, a teacher freed from classroom responsibilities to function as an instructional teacher leader, softly debriefing the lesson she just taught on reading comprehension. "I still think I am not giving them enough time to think through questions before calling on someone," Mrs. Macintosh reflects. The two talk through classroom management options and Ms. Avery gives suggestions of ways to reorganize the lesson to bring out the ideas and input of the lower achieving students in the class. The conversation then shifts to content. The pair works through Mrs. Macintosh's lesson plans for the coming week, talking about the long-term instructional plan for the class and how to tailor this to the individual needs of her students. The debriefing session is an intense 25 minutes. Ms. Avery schedules a time to come in to present a demonstration lesson that Mrs. Macintosh will observe. She is then off to first-grade Room 102. "My biggest challenge," she tells me as we walk together to the next classroom, "is simply being able to keep up with all the teachers who want to work with me this way."

In Aspen Elementary, only a few miles from Hope, literacy coordinator Mary Sampson hands the sixth-grade teacher a book on turtles. "I was thinking this might be useful for the class science fair unit you have coming up," Ms. Sampson says hopefully. The sixth-grade teacher stands in the doorway, and in one swift motion takes the book from Mary, nods, and closes the classroom door, leaving the two of us in silence as the echo of the closing door bounces down the empty hallway. It is not until we are safely behind the closed door of her office several minutes later that either of us speaks. "I don't know what else to do except to keep bringing them materials and taking an interest," she says, shaking her head. "Eventually I hope someone will invite me into a classroom."

How are we to understand the variation in the implementation of this instructional teacher leader position? What about the initiation of the literacy coordinator position at Hope School allowed the deep penetration into school life for Carla Avery that Mary Sampson struggled to attain at Aspen? What factors determine the extent to which, and the manner in which, an instructional teacher leader position is stabilized into school life?

This inquiry will focus on the institutionalization of teacher leader positions into the informal school organization. The current literature on enactment of teacher leader positions focuses largely on their introduction into the *formal* school organization, the allocation of staff, division of knowledge, allotment of time and uses of physical space. This inquiry, in contrast, will situate teacher leaders in the *informal* organization, among the day-to-day interactions of school staff and within the organizational values of a school.

Through the analysis of three school case studies, four main findings emerge. First, the alignment between formal and informal organizational structures and the extent to which pathways of communication exist between them is a critical factor in the enactment of teacher leader positions. Second, informal teacher leaders can be extremely powerful, in either supporting or opposing instructional teacher leader positions. Third, the positionality of teacher leaders within the school influence the character of role enactment. Fourth, widening the scope of teacher leadership studies to consider the informal school organization deepens our understanding of why such reforms succeed or fail.

TEACHER LEADERSHIP AND THE SCHOOL ORGANIZATION

The formal organization of a school leads to the allocation of leadership across formal positions, the division of knowledge into subject matters, the allotment of time into designated schedules, the division of students into age or ability groups, the grouping of students into classrooms, and so on (Barr & Dreeben, 1988). Job descriptions, time schedules, grade-level arrangements and spatial organization, and other properties of the physical plant of schools influence the implementation of teacher leader positions.

Research on teacher leadership often focuses on implementation in the formal school organization. For instance, researchers focus on the interaction of teacher leaders with those in other formal leadership positions demonstrating how the insertion of a new position into a school can lead to role change or conflict (Mangin, 2005; Smylie & Brownlee-Conyers, 1992; Trachtman, 1991). These disagreements about the definition of position components can lead to role ambiguity (Wasley, 1991).

Other studies of the implementation of teacher leader positions in the formal structure of schools focus on aspects of the physical and structural organization of schools that support or impede the instructional influence of teacher leaders (Hart, 1990a; Hart, 1990b; Smylie & Denny, 1990; Trachtman, 1991). The hierarchical ordering of the traditional school (Donaldson, 2001; Lieberman & Miller, 1999), and the lack of natural support structures for teacher leader work (Katzenmeyer & Moller, 2001) are also identified as influencing the character and effectiveness of the positions.

What we gain from education literature on teacher leadership is insight into the formal functioning of the role of the teacher leader. Role development is largely focused on the translation of the position into the formal operations of the school, in terms of time schedules, space, and distribution of resources. We emerge from teacher leadership literature with rich descriptions of teacher leaders in action, and a better understanding of the many challenges to their functioning. What about the implementation of these positions in relation to the informal interactions of teachers in the school?

Beside the formal organization of day-to-day life in a school are the informal understandings and relations of school staff. In a profession prone to uncertainty, teachers turn to informal networks of teacher colleagues to solve problems (Bidwell, 1965; Meyer & Rowan, 1977; Meyer & Rowan,

1978). Scholars stress the importance of teacher networks in the success of planned change efforts and in reducing isolation and uncertainty in the work of teaching (Bidwell, 2001; Little, 1990a; Little, 1990b; Talbert & McLaughlin, 1994). Also important are individuals who are "opinion leaders" in a school's communication structure, influencing other staff members (Rogers, 1995). In contrast to formal organizational arrangements, these colleague networks are

> more differentiated with respect to problem-solving skill than the formal grade- or subject-specialized teacher roles, more responsive to daily instructional problems than the formal curriculum, and more capable of coordinating the work of colleagues than the formal administrative hierarchy. (Bidwell, 2001, p. 105)

Additional insights into understanding the informal structure in an organization can be found in the application of these theoretical constructs discussed above to case studies undertaken by sociologists. Understanding the internal life of organizations to be interactive and open systems, Selznick described them as "adaptive social structures" (Selznick, 1949, p. 10). To Selznick, this implied the need to pay attention to the informal communication patterns to understand the functioning of the organization. Durkheim (1977) referred to this informal organizational structure as the "inner life" of institutions, and believed that identifying "how they are motivated and what goals they are trying to achieve" was essential to understanding their past, present and future organizational form (p. 10).

Understanding the institutionalization of teacher leaders is dependent upon situating the position within these informal networks and relationships. How can we study this? What data and analysis tools are appropriate?

DATA AND ANALYSIS TECHNIQUES

The case study data analyzed here were collected as a part of the longitudinal evaluation of the Chicago Annenberg Research Project in Chicago Public Schools at the Consortium on Chicago School Research (CCSR). Data consisted of interviews, observations, field notes, school documents, student work samples, and survey data. Interviews, observations, case studies, and vignettes were coded for information about literacy coordinators. Additional data were collected on time, role development, and supports and barriers to role enactment.

Calendar data were collected through a two-stage process. In the first two months of the study, coordinators were given blank calendars with time periods marked for them to write in descriptions of how they spent their day. These first calendars were then coded by type of task. A new calendar was given to the coordinators from 3 months forward with the emergent categories included.

Collection of network data was restricted to teachers, administration, and school services staff that worked at least 50% time in the school. Respondents were asked: "Please list the *three* staff members in your school that you talk to most frequently about issues related to the teaching and learning of students in literacy."

Two network analysis techniques are used in the case studies: degree centrality and CONCOR (convergence of iterated correlations) block modeling. *Degree centrality* is a calculation of the number of ties an individual has to all other staff in the network. It is based on the idea that central individuals have the most ties to others in the network (Wasserman & Faust, 1994). *CONCOR block modeling* is a technique of positional analysis used to cluster individuals to create subgroups of school staff that report interacting most frequently with one another. Additional details of these analyses can be found in Hallman (2004).

THREE PORTRAITS OF LITERACY COORDINATORS

In this section, three school case studies are presented, illustrating the varied relationship between teacher leaders and the informal school organization. A section that analyzes these cases comparatively follows.

Hope Elementary

Hope Elementary is a Chicago public elementary school located on the southwest side of the city. The school serves kindergarten through fifth grade with an enrollment of approximately 1,000 students. Nearly all of the students are Hispanic (97%) and the vast majority is designated as low-income (98%).

Hope school organization: Formal and informal. Leadership is allocated across school staff in three respects at Hope. The division of labor across the long-time principal, assistant principal, literacy coordinator, and bilingual coordinator is one aspect of distribution. They, along with the school counselor and social worker, are the Leadership Team. Principal Elizabeth Mitchell also relies on leadership from her teachers. Grade-level chairs conduct grade-level meetings weekly and meet once a month with other chairs and the Leadership Team to discuss grade-level issues. Mitchell organized school schedules and room assignments so that grade-level teachers had the same preparation periods and were clustered near one another to facilitate working and meeting together. Weekly grade-level meeting time is protected and honored, led by teacher leaders, and attended by Leadership Team members as observers or presenters.

The final component of the distributed leadership structure at Hope is the School Improvement Planning Committee. One teacher per grade level works to design and monitor the annual School Improvement Plan (SIP) that is required for Chicago Public Schools. Principal Mitchell makes it a requirement that the teachers on the SIP monitoring committee cannot also serve as grade-level chair at the same time, promoting different leaders in the school. The SIP committee meets weekly during the writing of the SIP document in the late winter and monthly throughout the rest of the year to monitor implementation. The committee collects information from grade-level teachers about their needs through the grade-level meeting structure, and crafts the draft document. This document is then circulated for revisions to the rest of the faculty and the Leadership Team.

Network analysis provides information about the role formal leaders play in the informal organization at Hope. The literacy coordinator, the bilingual coordinator, and the principal are connected to the most staff members in the network and thus have the highest degree centrality (see Table 6.1). The centrality of these formal leaders shows the strong representation of the Leadership Team in informal communication about literacy instruction at Hope.

The network core schematic for Hope (Figure 6.1), which summarizes the CONCOR block-modeling results, shows the three most central staff members and their subgroups. This provides a sense of the staff members operating at the "core" of the school. It is important to note that the core schematic, while picturing the three most central individuals within their subgroups and the ties between the 3 central staff members, does not illustrate the ties that exist between the subgroups, the ties between these subgroups and those in the outer layers of the school network, nor the strength of the ties among subgroup members themselves. The purpose of the schematic is merely to identify the staff members most frequently identified as central in teaching and learning in literacy and to compare formal and informal leadership.

The literacy coordinator has a subgroup of six other teachers, primarily the teachers who teach the English-speaking classrooms. Complemen-

Table 6.1. Degree centrality of central staff in three schools.

School	Position	Extent Chosen (centrality in school)	Degree Centrality
Hope Elementary	Literacy coordinator	First	40.0
	Principal	Second	24.4
	Bilingual coordinator	Third	24.4
Aspen Elementary	3rd-grade teacher	First	53.3
	8th-grade teacher	Second	26.7
	Principal	Third	26.7
Spruce Elementary	Principal	First	62.5
	Literacy coordinator	Second	27.5
	6th-grade teacher	Third	20.0

tarily, in the bilingual coordinator's subgroup are teachers from bilingual classrooms. The principal is at the center of a subgroup of four other administrative staff members.

The most critical feature of the Hope informal network around literacy is the high degree of overlap between the formal and informal enactment of leadership. The literacy coordinator, bilingual coordinator and the principal are all members of the school Leadership Team and thus are functioning as formal leaders in the building. The teachers who appear in the core subgroups around these three most central staff members were all formal leaders at the time of data collection. Four of these teachers were functioning as grade-level chairs; the other six were part of the School Improvement Planning Committee. When asked about whom they speak to about issues of teaching and learning in literacy, school staff at Hope identified staff members in formal leadership positions, suggesting a high consistency between formal and informal leaders.

The second notable fact is that, almost without exception, the English-speaking teachers rely upon the literacy coordinator for assistance in literacy while the bilingual education teachers utilize the bilingual coordinator for those services. The emergence of this informal leadership structure is no accident, it is a result of explicit design of the bilingual and literacy coordinator positions.

Figure 6.1. The Hope school network.

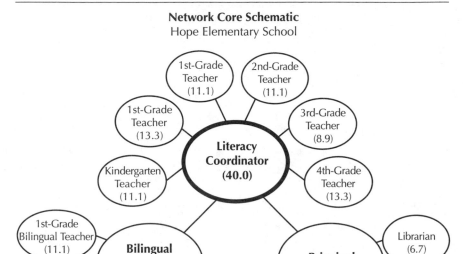

Network Core Schematic
Hope Elementary School

The principal, literacy coordinator, and bilingual coordinator strategically utilized the bilingual coordinator to tie the school together. The leadership of the bilingual coordinator was inserted intentionally into the school to provide Hispanic teachers with a connection to an instructional mentor and to connect the work of teachers together. The literacy coordinator and bilingual coordinator share an office; in a sense they have parallel roles. In a joint interview of the literacy coordinator and bilingual coordinator, the literacy coordinator stated, "The longer we have worked together, the more we see our roles as interchangeable. As long as teachers are connected to one of us, we feel they are connected."

Finally, it is important to note that the three most central staff members in the network are also connected to one another. This indirectly links together the staff members tied to each of them, tightening the connectedness of the core network as a whole.

The literacy coordinator role at Hope. The high degree of overlap between formal and informal leadership leads to a literacy coordinator role that is tightly focused on literacy instruction. Through strategic planning by the principal and the literacy coordinator, the coordinator primarily focuses on teacher mentoring and assessment. "We realized early that we had to prioritize this role or nothing would get done," stated Principal Mitchell. The literacy coordinator's schedule is notable for a complete lack of involvement in materials, social services, parent initiatives, and new teacher training (see Table 6.2). "There are certain roles and activities that we have purposely just given to others," commented Literacy Coordinator Avery.

Carla Avery believes that defining her role as literacy coordinator has been facilitated by her relationship with the Leadership Team. Avery and Mitchell both talked about the ways in which their longtime work together made it possible to define the role of the literacy coordinator.

Mitchell pointed to Carla's ongoing challenge of role definition and how they worked together to solve it:

> Carla came to me and told me that she just was struggling to make her schedule work right and to find the right way to organize classroom visits and debriefing. And so I suggested that I spend a few days shadowing her and working with her.

Characterized by a high amount of overlap of formal and informal leadership, the Hope network around literacy largely consists of those in formal leadership positions. The literacy coordinator role definition within this highly aligned formal and informal structure is tightly and deliberately focused on instruction.

Table 6.2. Literacy coordinator's time allocation in three schools (percent).

Activity	Hope	Aspen	Spruce
Individual teacher mentoring	25	13	18
New teacher training	0	0	10
Group teacher mentoring	15	3	8
Assessment	35	30	20
Meetings	8	8	13
Materials	0	7	12
Work time	10	5	5
Social services/parent programs	0	0	10
Other	7	34	4

Aspen Elementary

Aspen Elementary is a Chicago public school located on the south side of the city. Aspen serves approximately 650 students, kindergarten through eighth grade. Nearly all of Aspen's students are African American (99%). The vast majority (99%) of Aspen's students are specified as low-income.

Aspen school organization: Formal and informal. Leadership at Aspen is distributed across an eight-person Leadership Committee. This committee consists of the principal, assistant principal, disciplinarian, counselor, social worker and three elected teachers. While this structure exists, the influence of these leaders is not strong or central in the school. The emphasis on teacher autonomy, rather than committee leadership, is clear in the allocation of human, time, and monetary resources. Teachers are given individual materials budgets by the principal in order to be able to choose their own instructional materials. This high level of autonomy is valued by Aspen staff, and teachers describe a "respectful distance" to pursue "the art of teaching."

In contrast with the structured, formalized role of teachers in school decision making and leadership at Hope, Aspen teachers engage in school governance voluntarily. When asked about grade-level meeting structures, a fourth-grade teacher responded, "You know, it just isn't really the culture here to get together regularly. We are encouraged to be the expert in our classroom and that is seen as our primary role in this school."

Analysis of the informal organization of Aspen shows the extent of teacher autonomy at the school and some resulting tension with the role of the literacy coordinator. Network analysis reveals a lack of centrality of the literacy coordinator in the informal school structure, and the centrality of school faculty members most resistant to the literacy program (see Table 6.1).

The network core schematic for Aspen (Figure 6.2), which summarizes the CONCOR block-modeling results, shows the three most central staff members, again in terms of degree centrality. The three most frequently listed by colleagues as someone spoken to about literacy instruction are third-grade teacher Amy Smith, the principal, and eighth-grade teacher Iris Campbell. The literacy coordinator is not one of the three most central staff members in literacy but rather appears as part of the principal's subgroup.

Three important observations can be made about the informal school organization at Aspen: (a) a lack of centrality of formal leaders in the informal leadership structure; (b) the centrality of informal leaders most resistant to the literacy coordinator; and (c) a lack of connection between

Figure 6.2. The Aspen school network.

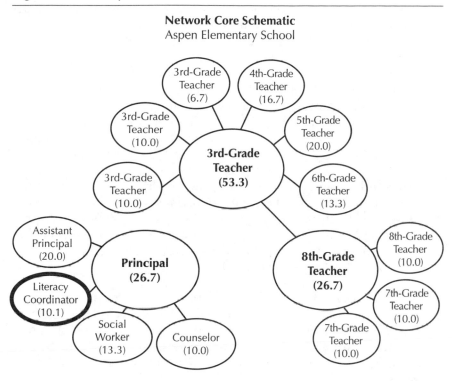

Network Core Schematic
Aspen Elementary School

the three most central staff members. On the first point, it is clear in look-ing at the network core schematic that in contrast to Hope Elementary, there is a low degree of overlap between the formal and informal leaders in the building. The third- and eighth-grade teachers who appear as two of the three most central individuals in the network do not sit on the Lead-ership Committee and neither has been involved in the school improve-ment process or other formal inroads to leadership.

Second, the centrality of third-grade teacher Amy Smith is notable. She is individually connected to all second-, third-, fourth-, fifth-, and sixth-grade teachers. In addition, she has ties to many members of the admin-istrative staff such as the librarian, social worker, counselor, and case manager. In stark contrast, the literacy coordinator only has ties to the librarian, the psychologist, the principal, and assistant principal. Not a single teacher chose her as someone they talk with most frequently about teach-ing and learning in literacy.

The third- and eighth-grade teachers who appear as among the most central individuals in the school, are at the center of resistance to literacy coordinator Mary Sampson and the implementation of the literacy program more generally. Third-grade teacher Amy Smith stated:

> I didn't want the literacy coordinator position. Had I wanted it, I would have had it. Had I said I wanted it and someone else had been given it, I could have rallied the staff behind me to get it back. But that doesn't mean I need any help in my room, either. Mary has plenty of other people to work with besides a teacher with my seniority.

The third notable aspect of the Aspen network is the lack of connection between the three most central staff members in the network. While the third- and eighth-grade teachers are linked to one another, the principal is not linked to them directly. This illustrates the lack of connection between formal school leaders in the principal's subgroup and the informal resistance leaders very clearly.

The literacy coordinator role at Aspen. Despite her formal job description provided by the university literacy organization, Mary spends relatively little time mentoring teachers in their classrooms (see Table 6.2). A high level of resistance from teachers to her work because of the high value placed on autonomy has always made it difficult to get into classrooms to do mentoring work.

Seniority and union issues are at the root of informal leader resistance to the literacy coordinator. Mary Sampson was selected as the literacy coordinator after her fourth year of teaching. In a school with many teachers who had been there for more than 20 years, this was problematic. Every teacher in third-grade teacher Amy Smith's subgroup raised the issue of seniority as one of the reasons they did not want literacy coordinator Mary Sampson's mentoring services.

Also important in the Aspen story are union issues. Iris Campbell, the eighth-grade teacher who is among the three most central staff members, is the union representative. Her centrality in the school reveals the importance of union issues to teachers. Mrs. Campbell sees herself as a protector of teacher rights, and in some ways this put her in direct opposition to the work of the literacy coordinator:

> I can see Mrs. Sampson providing materials and supporting teachers, but when I hear them pushing for a longer school day [for

meetings and professional development], I see it as my obligation as union representative to resist that.

The Aspen informal school organization is characterized by a lack of significant overlap with the formal school leadership positions. At the same time, analysis of the informal communication patterns reveal issues of importance to teachers, such as seniority and union rights, that are taking priority over the formal goals of the school represented in school improvement initiatives like the literacy coordinator position. As a result, the role of literacy coordinator is characterized by a lack of penetration into instructional practice.

Spruce Elementary

Spruce Elementary is a Chicago public school located on the south side of Chicago. Spruce serves 600 students, kindergarten through eighth grade. The students are 75% African American and 23% Hispanic with a small White population. Nearly all of Spruce's students (98%) are specified as low-income.

Spruce school organization: Formal and informal. Leadership at Spruce occurs both formally and informally. The formal leadership is distributed across the principal, the assistant principal, and the literacy coordinator, although there is no formal structure that ties them all together. In general, the principal functions as the figurehead. "My role is to keep the pulse of the various teachers, staff members, partners, etc., to ensure harmony around here," he stated. The assistant principal primarily focuses on disciplinary issues. He also takes care of the budgeting and the teacher evaluation process. The role of the literacy coordinator is to tie together the many programs and approaches that the principal has welcomed into the school. Grade-level meetings occur regularly and the charge of teachers is to "share issues that emerge in these meetings with the principal, assistant principal, or literacy coordinator." However, no formal structure exists for teachers' input into school governance.

Analysis of the use of money and time reveals a pattern of spreading resources widely to many diverse programs and approaches. According to the 1997–2001 SIP documents for the school, there are four distinct reading programs and three different approaches to math simultaneously being undertaken in the school. In each case, the school was approached by partners and a subgroup of teachers were interested so the principal allowed them to implement the program.

The blending of formal and informal leadership at Spruce reveals a sort of midpoint between the highly formalized structure at Hope and the dominance of informal leaders at Aspen, as can be seen in its network core schematic (Figure 6.3), which summarizes the CONCOR block-modeling results. At Spruce, the principal maintains a relatively small number of formal leadership positions. However, he openly embraces the emergence of informal teacher leadership around their interests and passions. This approach is facilitated by Principal Dale's general approach to running the school, which is based upon his belief that adopting a wide range of programs enriches students' education. He maintained the formal literacy coordinator position because "the accountability comes down to literacy." At the same time, he understood the other subjects to be open to "use of a wide range of materials and approaches to reach the many learning styles of our diverse students." As a result, the principal welcomes informal leadership around a variety of initiatives. "When a teacher comes to me with

Figure 6.3. The Spruce school network.

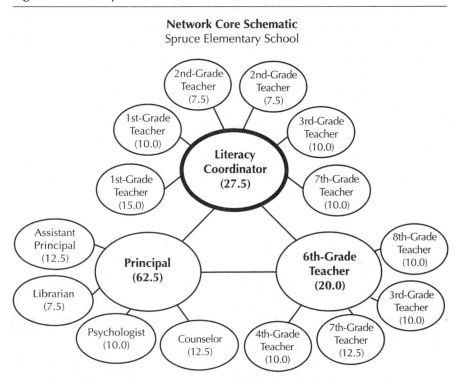

an idea of how to improve the school, I embrace them," Dale stated. "I then ask them, wouldn't they like to act as the lead on that exciting new idea?"

The network analysis at the time of the study reveals one such informal leader, sixth-grade teacher Evan Blaine. Mr. Blaine approached Principal Dale with the idea of implementing a single math program at Spruce. "He had done his homework and really knew the program," Dale explained. "He convinced me, the assistant principal, and the literacy coordinator that this was a good idea." Mr. Blaine became the informal leader of getting the teachers on board with implementing a single math program. This was happening when the network analysis data were collected. Thus the three most central leaders in the network (those most often designated by colleagues as someone spoken to about literacy instruction) at the time were the literacy coordinator, the principal, and Mr. Blaine (see Table 6.1). Notable is the connection between these three central staff members, represented in the Spruce network core schematic by the lines between them.

Mr. Blaine convinced Principal Dale of the need for the school to focus on math education and was given the nod to be an informal leader on bringing the program to the school. In his subgroup are four teachers who were all endorsed in math education and believed that literacy had long taken the focus away from math. While at Aspen these divisions became a source of resistance to formal leadership and the literacy coordinator, at Spruce this led instead to shared leadership between formal and informal leaders. Informal communication between school leadership and the group of teachers most in favor of the math program led all involved to believe that the goals of improving literacy and math were not mutually exclusive. "Mr. Dale made it clear right away that I, too, was to be a part of paving the way for the math program," literacy coordinator Lucy Campbell explained. "We are a team first and foremost, both literacy and math," stated sixth-grade teacher Evan Blaine.

Conflicting interpretations of this situation were evident. While the principal saw the literacy coordinator and Mr. Blaine working together as a victory for the school, the external literacy partner saw the approach as incoherent. "Bringing in program after program, unrelated with different school leaders may make for [better relations among staff members] but not school improvement," one staff member from the university literacy organization stated. Mrs. Campbell and Mr. Blaine both expressed their own uncertainty about whether the principal's approach was what was best for kids. "I never question that Mr. Dale makes staff relations really good," the literacy coordinator explained. "But I am not sure that my role actually improves literacy instruction. We are all over the place."

The literacy coordinator role at Spruce. "The best way to describe what I do is a little of this and a little of that," stated Spruce literacy coordinator Lucy Campbell. The literacy coordinator position at Spruce is characterized by the way time is sprinkled across a variety of role components (see Table 6.2). Campbell is in charge of the training of all teachers and the parent programs for the school. She sits on the committee that refers students to special education services. She attends all faculty and grade-level meetings. She coordinates the school's local assessment system. She leads the professional development workshops on system in-service days. "In between the concrete committees and functions I spend as much time in classrooms working with teachers as I possibly can," Lucy Campbell stated.

Two difficulties stem from the organization of the literacy coordinator position around such a wide range of activities. First, there is the problem of being stretched across so many activities that none gets sufficient attention. "I see that if more people were doing each of these little roles I am taking on, things would be done more thoroughly," Lucy stated. At the same time, the literacy partner worried that Lucy did not have time to focus on the instructional practices of teachers: "There is a real problem when the teacher mentor doesn't have time to mentor. This is the reason reforms never reach the classroom."

Characterized by a blend of formal and informal leadership and a rotation of new programs and approaches, Spruce presents an interesting midpoint between the dominance of formal leadership at Hope and that of informal leaders at Aspen. The role of the literacy coordinator—while welcomed by informal leaders—is spread across a large number of components, lacking instructional focus.

COMPARATIVE ANALYSIS OF THE CASES

The analysis of the intersection of formal and informal leadership in three schools provides insight into the influence of school organizational culture on teacher leader role enactment. What can we learn from the comparison of Hope, Aspen, and Spruce?

Table 6.3 provides a summary of the comparative analysis of the cases. Hope Elementary is characterized by the existence of multiple, formal, distributed leadership structures that incorporate large numbers of school staff members. These structures are interlocking, ensuring that communication occurs between the groups and that work is coordinated with school goals. At Hope, the central staff members in the informal school organization are the formal leaders from the Leadership Team, grade-level chairs, and School Improvement Planning Committee.

Table 6.3. Influence of school organizational factors on the literacy coordinator role in three schools.

School	Central Staff Members	Literacy Coordinator Role
Hope Elementary	Central staff are the formal leaders from the Leadership Team, grade-level chairs, and School Improvement Planning Committee.	Role is focused strategically on teacher mentoring and assessment. Formal roles are well-defined and linked to governance structures and school goals.
Aspen Elementary	Central staff are largely informal leaders. Central staff are protective of dominant organizational values (teacher autonomy, seniority, union issues).	Difficulty gaining access to teachers' classrooms and lack of well-defined role lead to large percentage (34%) of time being spent in tasks outside role description. Some teacher mentoring, assessment, and work with materials.
Spruce Elementary	Central staff are a mix of those in formal leadership positions and informal leaders. Principal supports rotation of informal leaders on teacher-identified initiatives and programs.	Role is to tie together many diverse programs in the school. Little time is spent in direct mentoring of teachers; most time is spent attending meetings and coordinating programs and services across the school.

In contrast, at Aspen the leadership is formally invested in a Leadership Committee. However, the roles of those in leadership positions are relatively loose and undefined. Analysis of school culture at Aspen reveals a high value placed on teacher autonomy, seniority, and union rights. The central staff members identified in network analysis are largely informal leaders not included in the Leadership Committee. By appointing a literacy coordinator who was a junior teacher, the principal violated norms of seniority. The literacy coordinator, in trying to gain access to classrooms to mentor teachers, violated norms of autonomy. And the coordinator and the principal, in pushing the school staff to vote to extend the school day, violated important norms of loyalty to the union. Aspen is characterized by the strength of informal leadership, more powerful than formal leadership positions.

Finally, at Spruce the leadership is stretched over fewer leaders with formal positions, blended with a variety of informal teacher leaders. As at Hope, there is a commitment to certain formal leadership positions, like that of the literacy coordinator, demonstrating the importance of the subject that determined school ranking in district and state accountability systems. As at Aspen, school leadership is mixed between formal and informal leaders. However, the principal encourages the emergence of informal teacher leadership around specific programs and initiatives and works to smooth potential rifts between formal and informal leaders. Representing a wide-range of ever-changing programmatic and instructional approaches, informal teacher leaders move in and out of positions of centrality in the informal school organization.

The extent of harmony between the values represented in instructional teacher leader positions and existing organizational values influences the character of role enactment. The role of the literacy coordinator at Hope was consciously defined narrowly. Without competing demands from conflicting values in the informal school organization, the role of the teacher leader was more easily focused on teacher mentoring and assessment. At Aspen, a lack of harmony between the assumptions behind the teacher leader position and the existing values in the informal organization made it very difficult for the literacy coordinator to gain access to teachers' classrooms, resulting in a role that often focused on activities unrelated to supporting literacy instruction. At Spruce, the principal embraced the emergence of new instructional approaches and informal leadership. As a result, the role of the literacy coordinator was stretched thin to accommodate a quickly shifting landscape of changing instructional foci.

Role enactment of formal teacher leader positions is shaped by informal leadership, both directly—as when teachers did not allow the literacy coordinator in their classrooms at Aspen—and indirectly—as when the value of embracing a wide range of approaches stretched the literacy coordinator across many role components at Spruce. The influence of informal leaders and the values they represent have a critical influence on role enactment, as illustrated in the case studies of Hope, Aspen, and Spruce.

CONCLUSION

Four conclusions follow from this analysis. First, the alignment between formal and informal leadership positions, the values they represent, and the extent to which pathways of communication exist between them are critical factors in the enactment of teacher leader positions. The role of teacher leaders is influenced by the extent of alignment of formal reform goals with the existing understandings in the school. The connection between the formal and informal leaders allows school administration to understand issues important to staff, tweaking reform initiatives to fit with existing organizational priorities. The lack of an understanding of the values represented in the informal school organization can lead to the inability of school staff in formal leadership positions to take into account the interests of powerful individuals and subgroups. This was the case in Aspen, where the school administration underestimated the importance of seniority, autonomy, and commitment to the union to teachers in the school and expressed surprise that informal leadership around these issues was so strong.

Second, analysis of these case studies demonstrates that informal teacher leaders can be extremely powerful and, if applied to school goals, they can be a strong force in school improvement efforts. At the same time, if informal power is wielded against the reform approach of formal leaders, it is an impediment indeed. At Spruce, the principal was able to balance informal and formal leaders largely because the school had such a wide range of programmatic and instructional approaches. Priorities that emerged informally, as Mr. Blaine's drive to adopt a single math program at Spruce, were recognized by the principal, and teachers were allowed to lead based on their passions and interests. This was much more difficult at Aspen, where the issues that came to the surface were in direct conflict with the literacy coordinator position. In a school where organizational values on autonomy and seniority were already supported in other parts of the school organization, for example through granting teachers their own materials budgets, the teacher leader position was perceived as being in direct violation of these norms. As a result, the literacy coordinator was rejected through informal channels.

Third, this study demonstrates the influence of teacher leader positionality within the school communication structure on role enactment. Harmony between existing organizational values and the values underlying the literacy coordinator position led to high centrality of the Hope coordinator in the school's informal network. In turn, this centrality allowed the Hope literacy coordinator to continue to expand her work to include additional teachers as the teachers she was working with were willing to encourage their colleagues to draw on her expertise. At the same time, her position of centrality also gave her access to teachers' hopes and concerns, placing her in a position to make necessary changes in her approach, taking into account evolving teacher needs. Centrality also allowed the Hope coordinator to connect the work of teachers, allowing them to learn from one another and allowing the literacy coordinator to rely upon the expertise of teachers in areas where she was weaker. In short, while factors in the existing organizational culture made it possible for the Hope coordinator to gain centrality in the school early in the enactment of the position, her centrality in turn made her work increasingly more useful and relevant to teachers' needs.

Finally, the findings in this chapter challenge understandings of the reasons why school reform efforts that rely upon teacher leaders succeed or fail by acknowledging the influence of school context. In 2001 the literacy program at Aspen was discontinued and the literacy coordinator position with it. Representatives from the literacy external partner associated with

Aspen Elementary, in an official report stated that implementation of the program had failed "because of a lack of commitment on the part of school leaders [and] a lack of skills and knowledge on the part of the [literacy coordinator]." In no place in the report do the representatives write about the lack of harmony between the ideals behind the reform policy and those of the autonomously oriented teachers. Instead, the failure of institutionalization of the teacher leader position was written off as a human resource deficit.

Widening the scope of teacher leadership studies to consider the informal school organization builds some sense of the complexity of the change proposed in the introduction of teacher leadership positions. Far from being the simple implementation of a position, these teacher leadership roles imply a change in the roles, approaches, and values of other school staff. Without the careful consideration of informal school organizational factors, this type of teacher leadership approach will fail to be deeply institutionalized and effective, regardless of whether teacher leadership is an appropriate tool for school improvement in general.

The institutionalization of a value is dependent on the extent to which it aligns well with existing beliefs—the extent of its legitimacy to staff within an organization (Selznick, 1949; Stinchcombe, 1968). Institutionalization represents a harmony between existing organizational values and the new value that is introduced. Without that harmony or without some way of influencing organizational culture to align the values of the organization and those underlying the teacher leader position, institutionalization cannot occur. This study presents one way to explore existing organizational values, represented in informal leaders and informal communication networks, to identify their influence on teacher leader role enactment. Continuing to increase our understandings of the informal school organization—a representation of school "culture"—is an important step in designing teacher leader positions that take into account existing culture and to assessing strengths and weaknesses of teacher leader positions as a tool for school reform.

REFERENCES

Barr, R., & Dreeben, R. (1988). *How schools work.* Chicago: University of Chicago Press.
Bidwell, C. E. (1965). The school as a formal organization. In J. G. March (Ed.), *Handbook of organizations* (pp. 972–1022). Chicago: Rand McNally.
Bidwell, C. E. (2001). Analyzing schools as organizations: Long-term permanence and short-term change. *Sociology of Education, 74,* 100–114.
Donaldson, G. A. (2001). *Cultivating leadership in schools: Connecting people, purpose, and practice.* New York: Teachers College Press.

Durkheim, E. (1977). *The evolution of educational thought.* Boston: Routledge & Kegan Paul.

Hallman, S. (2004). *Knitting the right sweater: Institutionalization of teacher leaders in the school fabric.* Unpublished doctoral dissertation, University of Chicago.

Hart, A. W. (1990a). A career ladder's effect on teacher career and work attitudes. *American Educational Research Journal, 24,* 479–503.

Hart, A. W. (1990b). Work redesign: A review of literature for education reform. In S. B. Bacharach (Ed.), *Advances in research and theories of school management and educational policy* (Vol. 1, pp. 31–69). Greenwich, CT: JAI Press.

Katzenmeyer, M., & Moller, G. (2001). *Awakening the sleeping giant: Helping teachers develop as leaders.* Newbury Park, CA: Corwin Press.

Lieberman, A., & Miller, L. (1999). *Teachers—transforming their world and their work.* New York: Teachers College Press.

Little, J. W. (1990a). The "mentor" phenomenon and the social organization of teaching. *Review of Research in Education, 16,* 345–369.

Little, J. W. (1990b). The persistence of privacy: Autonomy and initiative in teachers' professional relations. *Teachers College Record, 91,* 509–536.

Mangin, M. M. (2005). Distributed leadership and the culture of schools: Teacher leaders' strategies for gaining access to classrooms. *Journal of School Leadership, 15*(4), 456–484.

Meyer, J. W., & Rowan, B. (1977). Institutional organizations: Formal structure as myth and ceremony. *American Journal of Sociology, 83,* 340–363.

Meyer, J. W., & Rowan, B. (1978). The structure of educational organizations. In M. Meyer (Ed.), *Environments and organizations* (pp. 78–109). San Francisco: Jossey-Bass.

Rogers, E. M. (1995). *Diffusion of innovations* (4th ed.). New York: Free Press.

Selznick, P. (1949). *TVA and the grass roots: A study in the sociology of the formal organization.* Berkeley: University of California Press.

Smylie, M. A., & Brownlee-Conyers, J. (1992). Teacher leaders and their principals: Exploring the development of new working relationships. *Educational Administration Quarterly, 28,* 150–184.

Smylie, M. A., & Denny, J. W. (1990). Teacher leadership: Tensions and ambiguities in organizational perspective. *Educational Administration Quarterly, 26,* 235–259.

Stinchcombe, A. (1968). *Constructing social theories.* Chicago: University of Chicago Press.

Talbert, J. E., & McLaughlin, M. W. (1994). Teacher professionalism in local school contexts. *American Journal of Education, 102,* 123–153.

Trachtman, R. (1991). Voices of empowerment: Teachers talk about leadership. In S. C. Conley & B. S. Cooper (Eds.), *The school as a work environment: Implications for reform* (pp. 222–235). Boston: Allyn & Bacon.

Wasley, P. A. (1991). *Teachers who lead: The rhetoric of reform and the realities of practice.* New York: Teachers College Press.

Wasserman, S., & Faust, K. (1994). *Social network analysis.* New York: Cambridge University Press.

CHAPTER 7

Going to Scale with Teacher Leadership: Lessons Learned from a Districtwide Literacy Coach Initiative

Eric M. Camburn, Steven M. Kimball,
and Rebecca Lowenhaupt

THIS CHAPTER presents a case study of a literacy coach initiative that was implemented in a large, decentralized urban district. When viewed in light of research on literacy coaching, adult learning, and district support for instructional improvement, the design of the initiative holds great promise. Our findings show that a series of developments at the district level, as well as competing demands at school sites, served to dilute the potential effectiveness of the initiative. The case study provides an illustration of the possibilities and challenges of implementing formal teacher leadership strategies on a large scale.

We assessed the promise of the initiative by viewing it through three lenses: literature on instructional coaching, social and situative learning theories, and arguments about instructional improvement in decentralized contexts. Empirical results from a mixed-method evaluation of the initiative describe the history and implementation of the initiative, detail the enactment of the literacy coach role in two schools, describe variation in coaching across the district, and document factors that supported and challenged instructional coaching.

THE DAVIS LITERACY COACH INITIATIVE:
A PROMISING STRATEGY FOR LEVERAGING
TEACHER LEADERSHIP ON A LARGE SCALE

The Davis Public School district (DPS) serves a city with over 500,000 residents and enrolls over 90,000 students in approximately 200 schools. (Davis and all other names used in this chapter are pseudonyms.) The student population is diverse with approximately 60% African American, 20% Hispanic, 14% White, and 4% Asian students. In 2001, the district made a commitment to use literacy coaches to support instructional improvement. The initiative was part of a larger district decentralization movement in the 1990s and early 2000s. Efforts to decentralize during this period included a change to school site-based budgeting, school discretion in hiring staff, and a new requirement for educational planning at the school level. Resources provided by the district to support decentralization included instructional guidance through new district learning benchmarks, new curriculum frameworks for literacy and mathematics, and training for school leadership teams. Like similar decentralization movements, the DPS reforms were intended to encourage better school performance by empowering local communities to shape educational programs that more effectively met local needs.

Significant human resources were committed to the literacy coach initiative. Initially, the program was fully funded with federal Title I funding and district resources. After the first year of the program, the district used Title I and Title II funds to support 75% of a literacy coach position for each elementary school, with schools providing the remaining 25% for the position. Middle and high schools had to provide 50% matching funds. Of the nearly 200 schools within Davis, 55 opted to not fund a literacy coach position.

The district also provided funding for a cadre of literacy specialists whose primary responsibility was to train and support literacy coaches. Initially, the district funded six literacy specialist positions. At the time of this study, the program was operating with only four specialists who were responsible for about 40–50 schools each. The district also funded a Direct Instruction specialist to support schools adopting that program, but this person operated independently from the literacy coach program. Direct Instruction is a highly structured curriculum that uses a "systematic, explicit, and aural" approach to teaching through "teacher modeling and leading, unison reading, and systematic review and practice" and leveled student grouping (Ashworth, 1999).

The Literacy Coach Role

Developers of the initiative envisioned coaches as key members of formal school leadership teams whose purpose was to provide direct assistance to teachers to help improve literacy instruction. The expectations of the coach role were delineated as follows:

a. Demonstrate teaching, provide model lessons, and engage in collaborative teaching with classroom teachers
b. Deliver professional development and facilitate teacher work groups
c. Hold conferences that help teachers set goals and provide feedback to teachers based on observations
d. Engage in strategic planning using student data
e. Serve on the school leadership team
f. Attend district-provided professional development

As this list of expectations makes clear, direct work with teachers in their classrooms was the primary vehicle for delivering embedded professional development. In addition to providing direct support to teachers, literacy coaches were expected to document their activities through weekly reports.

While the district spelled out expectations for the coach role, it did not develop a separate evaluation instrument for the role. Instead, principals evaluated literacy coaches using the teacher evaluation instrument, which focused on classroom instruction. This lack of alignment between the intended coaching role and the tool used to evaluate coaches left an opening for literacy coaches to be used in ways unintended by the district.

Guidance and Support for Coaches

Developers of the initiative intended for the instructional practices promoted by literacy coaches to focus on district standards. Two kinds of standards were in effect at the time of our study: the DPS Literacy Framework, which outlined six major content areas for literacy instruction, and the DPS Learning Benchmarks, which described grade-by-grade student performance objectives in literacy as well as other major subject areas. Even though there was considerable leeway provided for local schools to decide how to achieve district literacy standards, the developers made clear that teaching practices promoted by coaches should reflect the district's literacy framework and should help students achieve district performance standards.

Coaches were to be supported by district literacy specialists. The specialists were initially intended to play a developmental role, primarily by providing professional development to coaches through district-level training and school-level support. In particular, specialists were to provide professional development on a range of topics including adult learning, cognitive coaching, assessment, and research-based instructional practices. Literacy specialists were also to monitor coaches' activities through meetings and written logs. As members of the collective bargaining unit, however, specialists had a nonevaluative role.

Potential of the DPS Initiative

Viewed from the perspective of research on instructional coaching and professional learning, the initiative demonstrates the potential to support improved literacy instruction through the direct coaching of teachers. The model advocated by the DPS reflects current thinking about appropriate roles for literacy coaches.

DPS coach roles reflect current professional standards. The International Reading Association (IRA) recently published a statement on the role and qualifications of reading coaches (IRA, 2004) and standards for middle and high school literacy coaches (IRA, 2006). These guidelines make clear that the primary activity for coaches should be collaborative work with teachers focused on instruction. Common activities that appear in the IRA's and other published compendia include the following:

- Providing professional development
- Modeling lessons in classrooms
- Observing teachers
- Providing instructional materials
- Sharing current research results
- Assisting with planning

The IRA guidelines stress that these activities are likely to be more effective if they involve frequent, individual conversations between coaches and teachers in a nonsupervisory, peer relationship. In addition to interactive coaching activities, the IRA guidelines also indicate that coaches are often expected to provide administrative support for instructional programs, to act as liaisons between teachers and administrators, and to use assessment data to identify the instructional needs of students. The definition of the literacy coach role in DPS reflects both the general principles and the specific responsibilities outlined in the IRA guidelines.

The DPS coach role reflects characteristics of effective adult education. Peer coaching models like the DPS literacy coach initiative also reflect trends in professional education and the learning sciences about the factors that support effective adult learning. From the earliest writings on the subject, peer coaching for teachers has been considered a form of professional learning (Joyce & Showers, 1980; Showers & Joyce, 1996). Recent reforms of professional education in other fields such as medicine, law, and the ministry, have brought about a greater use of group learning, peer learning, and mentorships (Sykes, King, & Patrick, 2002). The notion that peer interaction can be an effective vehicle for professional learning finds justification in social learning theory (Bandura, 1977) and more recent cognitive learning theories that take a situative perspective (Putnam & Borko, 2000). These theories argue that learning is an inherently social act and that learning through social interaction can result in the acquisition of abstract knowledge and knowledge of how to engage in discourse and practice within a particular community (Lave & Wenger, 1991). Social and situative learning theories also posit that the social context within which learning occurs is an important determinant of the effectiveness of learning experiences. One implication of this idea is that knowledge transfer is expected to be greater when knowledge is encountered within a realistic, practice-based context, rather than presented in an abstract, decontextualized fashion (Brown, Collins, & Duguid, 1989).

Viewed in light of these learning theories, the peer learning advocated by the DPS coach initiative has the potential to support significant changes in teachers' literacy instruction throughout the district. The design of the DPS initiative may also provide a similar sort of peer scaffolding for literacy coaches. The design of the DPS initiative stipulated that literacy specialists should collaborate with—rather than supervise—literacy coaches, provide direct support and guidance to coaches through regular interactions, and model coaching.

Decentralization may pose special challenges to the coach initiative. The promise of the DPS literacy coach initiative is tempered by a substantial body of evidence on the failure of large-scale instructional improvement initiatives in decentralized districts (Corcoran & Christman, 2002; Elmore, 1993). In the case of Philadelphia decentralization reforms, for example, authority for a range of functions was rapidly shifted to individual schools and clusters of schools. Local implementation was hampered due to lack of central office guidelines and contradictions in the district policies (Corcoran & Christman, 2002). A number of researchers have argued for the critical importance of providing coherent, understandable guidance that clearly communicates expectations for the implementation of an initiative to practitioners (Cohen & Ball, 1999; Mazmanian & Sabatier, 1981; Newmann, Smith, Allensworth, & Bryk, 2001). Others have emphasized that decentralizing authority does not mean an abdication of direction and guidance from the central office. Instead, district initiatives in decentralized settings require clear communication of performance standards and goals, with accountability systems to motivate performance (Odden, 1998; Smylie, Lazarus, & Brownlee-Conyers, 1996). In the case of the DPS literacy coach initiative, requiring that instructional changes be focused on district standards may impose a degree of coherence by "tuning out" competing messages. However, given the autonomy afforded to local schools to approach instructional improvement as they see fit, there is ample room for schools to either subjectively interpret central guidance or to seek out alternative sources of guidance. Further, given demands on school principals to respond to increasing management and accountability requirements, teacher leaders released from classroom responsibilities may be tasked with new administrative functions that interfere with their instructional support roles.

POTENTIAL PUT TO THE TEST:
IMPLEMENTATION OF THE COACH INITIATIVE

Clearly the Davis Literacy Coach initiative held substantial promise to support improved literacy instruction in the district through coaching. But to what degree was that potential realized? At the behest of the DPS, we conducted a mixed-method evaluation that was guided by three questions: (1) What was the history of the development of the literacy coach initiative? (2) How was the initiative implemented in schools? and (3) What factors served as supports and impediments to implementation?

We attempted to develop an understanding of the history and development of the literacy coach initiative by interviewing key district staff members. We were particularly interested in gaining an understanding of the district's intended purposes in supporting the coach initiative as well as the outcomes expected by district leadership. Our understanding of the district's perspective on the coach initiative was formed through discussions with current and former district-level managers in curriculum and instruction and professional development, current and former literacy specialists, and individuals involved in the program design.

We examined how the DPS coach initiative was implemented in schools using data from a survey of literacy coaches. Coaches in 58 elementary schools answered detailed questions about their work with teachers, their work with literacy specialists, and their professional development opportunities. Analyses of the survey data revealed the practices of a "typical" coach in the district and also showed how coaching practices varied from school to school. We also gained an understanding of the implementation of the coach initiative through in-depth case studies of eight elementary schools, two of which are featured in this chapter. In each of the schools, evidence about the initiative was gathered through interviews with principals, literacy coaches, and classroom teachers.

Our third objective in examining the implementation of the coach initiative in Davis was to gain an understanding of factors that served as supports and barriers to the implementation of coaching responsibilities. Multivariate analyses of survey data examined districtwide patterns of support for literacy coaching. In these analyses the quality of professional development and the degree to which coaches understood role expectations emerged as factors that supported the implementation of coaching practices advocated by the Davis initiative. The school case studies yielded a more detailed and nuanced picture of how the work of coaches was impacted by a range of school- and district-level factors.

EVOLUTION OF THE DPS LITERACY COACH INITIATIVE

Literacy specialists figured prominently in the evolution of the literacy coach initiative during its first four years. As the link between the district and local schools, the literacy specialists not only trained literacy coaches, but also acted as a conduit through which policy guidance flowed from the district to local schools. Our interviews provided several examples of literacy specialists working with coaches in collaborative, supportive ways that were sensitive to the needs of individual schools. There were some cases, however, where coaches rarely interacted with their specialists. In addition, our interviews identified a number of challenges to collaborative, locally sensitive interactions between coaches and specialists. These challenges included inadequate numbers of specialists, a shift from locally driven to district-driven professional development, internal dissent among literacy specialists, and school-level barriers to getting time with coaches. Ultimately, these challenges might have lessened the impact of specialists.

Both current and former literacy specialists provided examples of how they supported coaches in ways that were consistent with the initiative's design. The provision of district-level training and school-based professional development were commonly mentioned activities. Literacy specialists clearly dedicated a large amount of time to their roles, often going beyond their contracted hours. This hard work appears to have impacted some coaches who provided examples of positive support they received from literacy specialists.

Despite the positive impact of some literacy specialists, their reach was limited at the time of this study due to a staffing shortage. At that point, two of the six specialist positions were not filled, and two of the positions that were filled were temporary. This staffing shortage resulted in specialists supporting 40–50 schools each. Specialists compensated by focusing direct support on newer coaches or schools that were struggling academically.

Our interviews indicated that over the first four years of the initiative, responsibility for the design of coach trainings shifted from the literacy specialists to central office staff. The specialists were initially housed in the professional development division and granted full discretion over coach training and school-level support. In the 1st year, they primarily provided support to coaches on literacy instruction. During the 2nd year of the initiative, the district eliminated the professional development division and moved the coaching program to the curriculum and instruction division. When this occurred, specialists were no longer in charge of district training, but were increasingly asked to support training created by district-level program managers. Although the specialists had input, some believed training was designed to meet district priorities at the expense of school-specific needs. Due to a loss of autonomy in developing training programs, internal dissent, and the feeling of inadequate support from the district, four of the six original literacy specialists left their positions in the 3rd year of the initiative.

The change in training was accompanied by a revision of role expectations for specialists. A major part of the revised specialist role was to keep schools focused on district initiatives. There was a perception among district leaders of the literacy coach program that previously specialists were not coordinating activities as a team and instead were providing professional development on a case by case basis. The leaders wanted a more centralized structure that concentrated on overarching district strategies. These strategies included implementing the district literacy framework, designing school improvement plans, organizing curriculum around district learning benchmarks, using student assessment data, and providing general training that might apply to all schools.

As a result, specialists increasingly focused coaches' attention on district priorities through trainings and by monitoring their activities through the coach logs. However, some coaches chose not to complete the logs, and literacy specialists could not require compliance. Specialists also could not require coaches to attend district training. One coach in our sample indicated that she stopped attending trainings because they were not supportive of her school's literacy program, which was based on Direct

Instruction. Instead, this coach relied on training provided by the district Direct Instruction specialist. Another coach also indicated that former literacy specialists did not support Direct Instruction. Subsequently, a specialist with experience using Direct Instruction was added to the literacy specialist team.

One district supervisor summed up the changes to the specialist role by stating that "coaches are [the] delivery mechanism for everything the district wants to take to the school level." Coaches also confirmed this notion. In interviews, coaches indicated that literacy specialists emphasized the monitoring of coaches' work and the communication of district priorities more than collaborative work to develop teachers' literacy instruction. Specialists also confirmed that this was a primary focus area for them. When describing the role of specialist, one explained that it was "to oversee the professional development in the building concerning the district initiatives."

While the central office attempted to exercise greater control over the literacy coach initiative, principals had a large impact on how the coach role was carried out. In fact, coaches and specialists reported that a primary challenge was the demands placed on coaches by principals. Specialists expressed frustration that principals did not ensure coach attendance at required training or the completion of logs. They also believed that principals were not held accountable when they used coaches for activities unrelated to literacy coaching (e.g., substitute teaching and monitoring the cafeteria or playground). As one specialist said, "Coaches are very happy once they get permission from principals to support them in what they've been asked to do by the district." Similarly, a former literacy specialist stated, "They have to fight to do anything related to literacy coaching."

The tension between teacher leadership and administrative functions was also evident among coaches. Several coaches in our study expressed concerns about their limited impact because they felt they had to wait for a teacher invitation to visit classrooms or could only make suggestions to teachers about their instruction after observations. When teachers did not incorporate the suggested changes, coaches felt informing principals might be seen as evaluative.

Specialists also reported difficulties getting access to coaches in their schools. As a result, one specialist explained that her strategy was to first meet with the principal and school leadership team before visiting a coach. Only after securing this support could the work with coaches consistently occur. As this specialist indicated, "My interactions with the literacy coaches are [only] as effective as my interactions with their administrators."

Our district-level interviews highlight a critical tension in decentralized districts between local autonomy and central control. Constraining the content of coach trainings to district standards could serve the purpose of building coherence in the instructional guidance provided through the training by making it more focused. However, shifting control over the content of professional development from local schools to the central office can render professional development less relevant for a given school. Providing principals with autonomy to use literacy coaches in ways that are sensitive to local needs is one way to guard against this sort of irrelevancy. Yet, as our findings demonstrate, a number of principals used this autonomy to deploy literacy coaches in ways that ran counter to the primary purpose of the initiative, namely, improving the literacy instruction of teachers.

DESCRIBING DISTRICTWIDE VARIATION IN COACHING IMPLEMENTATION

This section reports the results of a survey of literacy coaches which describe districtwide patterns in coaching practice. We begin by comparing the amount of time coaches spend on interactive work with teachers to the amount of time they spend on other leadership functions. We then present the results of exploratory regression analyses that examine whether coaches are more likely to engage in direct, interactive coaching when three factors are present: clear expectations about coaching, quality professional development, and support from literacy specialists.

While the DPS coach role focused primarily on direct, interactive coaching activities, there is a wide range of potential leadership functions that coaches might perform. Camburn, Rowan, and Taylor (2003) developed a set of scales that measure leadership functions that might be performed by formally designated leaders in schools, such as principals, assistant principals, department/subject area chairs, and teacher leaders in various roles. Among the scales developed for that study were measures of leaders' work on building operations, goal setting, and direct instructional support for teachers. Camburn et al. (2003) found that instructional coaches were more likely than any other kind of leader, including principals and assistant principals, to perform a function they called "developing instructional capacity." That function reflects the extent to which leaders provide direct support to teachers about instruction.

We compared DPS coaches' emphasis on developing instructional capacity with their emphasis on two other leadership functions investigated by Camburn et al. (2003): administration and setting goals. Administration refers to the amount of time coaches spend completing routine paperwork and coordinating and administering programs in the school. Goal setting refers to the degree to which coaches frame and communicate school

improvement goals, clarify expectations or standards for student performance, and develop plans intended to improve instruction. As mentioned
previously, developing instructional capacity refers to direct work with teachers with the intention of improving their instructional practice.

We can get an overview of the range of the kinds of work performed
by coaches in the Davis district by looking at how often coaches performed
specific leadership activities. Figure 7.1 displays the means for the items
making up the three leadership scales. A score of 2 indicates a coach worked
on an activity "a few times throughout the year," 3 indicates they worked
on the activity "a few times per month," and 4 indicates they worked on
the activity "1–2 times per week." As Figure 7.1 illustrates, coaches reported working on most activities "a few times per month." The coaches
devoted considerably more time to three activities: coordinating programs,
demonstrating instructional practices, and completing routine paperwork.

Figure 7.1. Mean scores for items measuring coaches' work on
administration, goal setting, and developing instructional capacity.

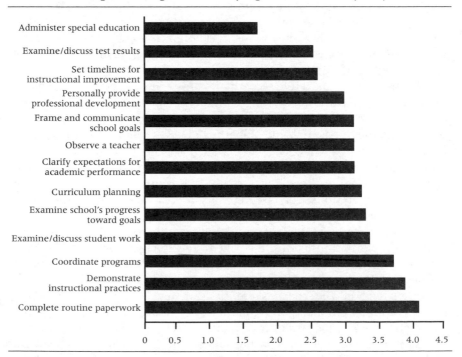

Note: 1 = never; 2 = a few times throughout the year; 3 = a few times per month;
4 = 1–2 times per week; 5 = more than 2 days per week.

Two of these activities—coordinating programs and completing routine paperwork—are what we consider to be administrative work. In fact, completing routine paperwork was the activity coaches performed the most frequently, engaging in that task about once or twice a week. Activities associated with developing teachers' instructional capacity were performed less frequently. While coaches said they demonstrated instructional practices nearly once or twice a week, they examined students' work, observed teachers, and provided staff development only a few times per month, and examined and discussed test results even less frequently.

We next examined coaches' relative emphasis on the three leadership functions and looked at how much coaches in the Davis district varied in their performance of these functions by comparing their scores on the administration, goal setting, and developing instructional capacity scales.

We found that DPS coaches placed a similar overall emphasis on administration, goal setting, and teacher capacity-building in their work. The average for the developing instructional capacity scale is slightly higher than the average for the other two scales, but this difference is not substantial. Despite the fact that the DPS guidelines for the coach role clearly placed a higher priority on direct interactions with teachers around instruction, the survey responses suggest that coaches did not prioritize their efforts in this way, but instead, spread their attention across a range of leadership functions. Indeed, we found that 25% of the coaches reported that they worked to develop teachers' instructional capacity less than a few times per month.

Though the overall frequency with which Davis coaches performed the three leadership functions were quite similar, patterns of variation between coaches were different for each of the three scales. While some coaches performed administrative tasks only a few times per year on average, others performed such tasks more than 2 days per week. There was less variation among coaches in their development of teachers' instructional capacity, with 50% of the coaches on this scale scoring between 3 and 3.5 (a score of 3 means they worked on this function a few times per month while a score of 4 means they worked on it a few times per week). In general, coaches were less variable (i.e., more consistent) in their emphasis on developing instructional capacity, and more variable in their emphasis on administration and goal setting.

INVESTIGATING FACTORS THAT SUPPORT
INSTRUCTIONAL COACHING

To test the theory of action of the DPS literacy coach initiative, we performed two linear regression analyses. The first analysis examined factors that are related to the clarity of coaches' understanding of role expectations. Such clarity might have resulted from specialists communicating role expectations to coaches and from professional development that communicated district standards. The second analysis examined factors related to coaches' use of "direct coaching" practices.

Based on our understanding of the DPS coach initiative design, we hypothesize two key influences on coaches' practice and their understanding of role expectations. Clearly, the interaction between specialists and coaches is potentially an influence. We examined the effects of such interactions with a variable indicating whether a coach met with a specialist 3 or more times. A second potential influence is professional development. We tested the effect of this factor with a measure of coaches' assessment of the quality of their professional development. We also examined the effect of the clarity of role expectations, conjecturing that coaches would be more likely to use direct coaching practices if interactions with specialists and professional development had served to clarify district priorities. We attempted to account for competing explanations of the outcome variables by controlling for coaches' experience level in literacy coaching and the average reading achievement levels in coaches' schools.

Neither the number of years of coaching experience nor the overall reading achievement level in a coach's school had a significant effect on coaches' understanding of role expectations or their use of direct coaching practices. After controlling for these factors, we found that coaches who met with literacy specialists three or more times were no more likely than coaches who met with specialists fewer times to have a clearer understanding of the expectations of the coach role. The second regression model also predicted that the frequency of coaches' interaction with literacy specialists was not a significant determinant of coach engagement in direct coaching practices.

Coaches who rated the quality of their professional development more highly were more likely to feel they had a clear understanding of expectations regarding the coach role. Similarly, in the second regression analysis, we found that coaches were more likely to engage in direct coaching if they perceived their professional development to be of higher quality. The second analysis also predicted that coaches were more likely to provide direct coaching to teachers when they believed that expectations for the coaching role were clearer, though the effect of this variable was slightly above a .05 significance threshold (.056). The variables measuring the clarity of expectations and the quality of coaches' professional development were by far the strongest predictors in both regression models.

These statistical results provide suggestive evidence that to a partial degree, the coach initiative may have worked in a manner consistent with the initiative's theory of action. The DPS initiative relied upon professional development provided by literacy specialists to communicate district objectives and expected coaching practices. Evidence from the first analysis suggests that coaches' professional development communicated the district's expectations regarding direct coaching practices. Results from the second analysis suggest that a substantial number of coaches not only had a clear understanding of expectations, but also translated those expectations into practice. The regression results also suggest that the *amount* of time literacy coaches spent with the specialists was not an important determinant of coaches' understanding of role expectations and their practice, but perhaps the *quality* of these interactions was important. The positive effect of the quality of coaches' professional development in both models suggests that specialists might have influenced coaches through the professional development they provided. It is important to note however, that literacy coaches had access to other professional development beyond that provided by specialists.

AN IN-DEPTH LOOK AT IMPLEMENTATION: TWO CASE STUDIES

We probed the supports and constraints for the literacy coach initiative in greater depth with case studies of two schools. The descriptions of these schools illustrate the enacted roles of literacy coaches, professional development they received and provided, and the nature of their interactions with literacy specialists, teachers and principals. Each case provides examples of coaching as originally intended by the district, and also highlights barriers to this kind of coaching.

Ellington School

Ellington Elementary School is located in a working class neighborhood and enrolls over 460 students from prekindergarten through fifth grade. A majority of the students are African American (81%), while 13% are White, 2% are Hispanic, and about 4% are either Asian or Native American. Over 88% of the students are eligible for free/reduced price lunches and about 20% receive special education services. Recent test scores have shown some decline. On the state reading assessment, 58% of fourth-grade students scored proficient or advanced in 2002, while 55% scored at that level in 2005. Language arts declined from 70% of students proficient or advanced in 2002 to 55% in 2005.

Teachers were involved in the hiring process for the current literacy coach, Sandra. The first coach served in the position for 2 years, but left the school "abruptly" when it was clear that the newly appointed principal, with the encouragement of teachers, intended to change the role to be more involved with direct coaching and collaborative teaching. The prior coach concentrated on providing school-level professional development and providing literacy materials. The new principal sought input on what teachers wanted from a literacy coach, and it was clear that more hands-on work with teachers was desired. The principal noted that he was aware of other principals assigning duties unrelated to literacy coaching, and that he believed principals should be held accountable for using coaches in the manner intended by the district.

Sandra had a total of 14 years in the classroom, primarily as a fifth-grade teacher. She completed a master's degree in curriculum and instruction, but did not receive formal literacy training. She chose to become a coach because she wanted to have an impact beyond her classroom. As an informal teacher leader in her previous position, Sandra felt the literacy coach opportunity was a natural extension for her. As she stated, "I saw a need for, you know, certain things that work in my classrooms, other teachers were struggling with, so I would lend support to them and offer different strategies for teaching and learning. So that is what really pushed me to go on."

In her first five months, Sandra encountered teacher resistance, with some teachers less willing to welcome her into their classrooms. She managed to earn the respect of most teachers, but still had difficulty with a few. She believed she faced this resistance because she came to Ellington as an outsider and because some teachers felt they already possessed literacy expertise. The principal recognized this tension and encouraged Sandra to constructively work with the resisting teachers.

Coach activities. Sandra was hired for her writing expertise and worked directly with teachers on writing strategies. As one teacher explained, "This is the first year in which the literacy coach has been in the classroom to develop the writing on an ongoing process." The teacher provided the following example of her work with the coach:

> We've done two specific writing prompts; we've done brainstorming in the first session; we have worked on and completed introductory paragraphs, the body of the composition, and the conclusion.
> We have worked one-on-one with the children, and we have brainstormed and edited their work.

Although Sandra supported all teachers, at the time of the interview, her focus was on third- and fifth-grade writing, the two grades subject to an upcoming district writing test.

With writing as the school's focus, Sandra worked to bring a number of professional development opportunities to teachers. She stated that writing instruction was difficult for teachers at each grade level; therefore "we're constantly in-servicing our staff, you know, just to change the thinking." Teachers spoke of helpful in-services either conducted or arranged by Sandra. As one explained, "she also has worked with us with the reading series because . . . it has reading and writing and language arts combined in one, so she helps us to align that and how we should better instruct it to make sure that the writing piece was in all areas."

Sandra fulfilled other responsibilities beyond the direct coaching of teachers. These included work as a cofacilitator for the school's professional leadership team, which met twice per week and focused on student learning and faculty professional development needs across content areas, and on budgeting. Sandra also led the design of a new grading system for the school and mentored new teachers. She organized an action research team of teachers as part of a literacy grant, which she administered. In addition, she ordered all instructional materials and worked with the assistant principal to administer assessments. Finally, Sandra facilitated periodic family nights at the school. Although many of these roles might fit within the district parameters of the literacy coach role, they illustrate that the position can involve much more than direct work with teachers on literacy instruction.

Influences on practice. Sandra cited various sources of training she received during her short time as literacy coach. Training primarily came from the literacy specialists and district content specialists and was seen as helpful. However, she was torn between attending training and working with teachers. She characterized the tension as follows: "I'm supposed to be at [a training] right now, but you know, I have to look at where my responsibilities lie. Though they're doing their job by in-servicing us, I'm doing my job by staying in the building and working with my teachers." Not all requirements to leave the building were related to the literacy coach initiative. Sandra explained that literacy coaches often had to attend district meetings for various school grants they administered.

Teachers noticed when Sandra was out of school for district training and felt that impinged on their time. As one said, "The one drawback is that the literacy coach could be pulled for an in-service and then we won't have that amount of time with her. That happened the other day so I took it upon myself to move on from the point that we had left off and moved forward. You have to be flexible."

Despite her previous experience as an informal teacher leader, Sandra did not feel adequately prepared to assume the position. When asked what would have been more helpful, she explained:

If maybe [the district] had done some type of extensive training of what my role was prior to me taking the position. So once I was hired as the literacy coach in the district, I think there should have been, maybe a 2-week training so I knew exactly what my role would look like. But they don't do that for teachers either. You come in as a new teacher and you pretty much learn on the job.

According to teacher interviews, the coach's activities were largely dictated by the principal. One stated that "my understanding is that the directives come from him." Despite the presence of an assistant principal at the school, Sandra explained:

I feel like I'm responsible for everything. I mean even purchasing of textbooks. You know, teachers are in need of textbooks or materials, it's my job to locate these textbooks or materials for the teachers . . . for all content areas.

When asked where the responsibility for all the noncoaching activities came from, Sandra responded: "It's a directive [from school administration]. I mean, . . . we have no reading resource person, so if you don't have a reading resources person in your building, the literacy coach assumes that position." She continued, "When I look at what the literacy coach job description is, a lot of the things that I do [are] not in there." The literacy coach was "third in command" after the principal and assistant principal. She explained, "The principals think that they can do just about whatever they want. Whatever they want to utilize the literacy coach for they can. . . . You know, I am supposed to be modeling best practices in classrooms, but I should never take over teacher instruction, but I do."

Teachers, the principal, and Sandra believed that her work in classrooms was having an impact on literacy instruction. Yet, her first year of experience led her to question how long she could continue. Sandra's primary frustration was the unrealistic time demands of the position. She described her days as "overly long," considering that coaches do not receive higher pay for their role. Under these conditions, Sandra was unsure whether the position was worth the sacrifices. She concluded, "It's definitely a burnout role. Because whatever we do, there is never enough unless we are working from sunup to sundown. It's a lot of responsibility for one person."

Brubeck Elementary School

Brubeck is a Pre-K through fifth-grade school serving over 670 students. The student population is 75% Hispanic, 11% African American, 8% White, and 2% Asian. Eighty-five percent of the students are eligible for subsidized meals. Brubeck offers a bilingual program for English language learners, who represent 31% of the school population. Achievement data suggest that the school has struggled to improve literacy scores on the fourth-grade state standardized test. The percent of students at advanced or proficient dropped from 69% in 2002 to 60% in 2005. Language arts scores followed a similar downward trend, decreasing from 61% proficiency in 2002 to 52% in 2005.

The literacy coach, Beth, had been in the position for 4 years. Prior to that, she taught first grade, both at Brubeck and another school in the district. Beth had extensive training in reading, holding a reading specialist license. She explained that while her comfort level with emerging reader strategies when she began was already high, she needed "to beef up" her skills at supporting teachers in the intermediate grades. Nevertheless, teachers who were interviewed remarked that "she knows her stuff."

Coach activities. As the primary facilitator for a new curriculum adopted by the school, Beth focused her energy on coaching seven new teachers in the building. She supported the new teachers by acquainting them with the school, the profession, and the new curriculum. For these teachers, she observed and modeled instruction and provided feedback. She explained, "I need to give more of my attention to the new people because they are the ones that need it." Her goal was to observe or model in at least one classroom per day.

Beth's coaching work was not limited to one-on-one interactions. The principal described her work during leadership team meetings as facilitating discussions about curriculum and instruction. Planning and facilitating professional development was viewed as another important aspect of her job. According to the principal, she "plays an integral role in structuring all of that." Whether in groups or individually, engaging teachers in conversations about improving their literacy practices was pivotal to her work as a literacy coach. Unfortunately, both she and teachers complained that other responsibilities took time away from her direct work with teachers.

Beth took on various other roles in the school. As the assessment coordinator, she facilitated the administration of all testing. She also analyzed the various achievement data generated in the school and trained teachers in their use. The principal reported a long list of both formative and summative tests taking place throughout the year, all of which required Beth's coordination. Beth explained that recent testing had taken a significant amount of time away from her duties as a coach.

Additional duties added up over her years as a teacher leader in a busy building. As a former special education teacher, she also served as a resource for special education teachers, helping them with logistical concerns like scheduling and with strategies for struggling students. Beth also coordinated the Reading First grant and was responsible for organizing and providing grant-related accountability measures. One teacher observed that, "she does a lot of different things that I'm not sure fall under the title of literacy coach."

Beth's time with teachers was also reduced due to required district-level meetings. One of the teachers interviewed remarked on the encroachment of district meetings and assessment coordinator responsibilities on Beth's time:

> I think the amount of time that the literacy coach is expected to be out of the building is too much. I mean, she's gone at this meeting, that meeting. . . . If she could just focus on literacy, that would be a lot more helpful, too, rather than finding pencils for the state standardized test . . . a lot of other jobs have fallen upon her because of budget reasons.

Influences on practice. When Beth first became a coach, she relied on the support of her district-level specialist to teach her the ropes. She also cited initial district trainings on the literacy framework and cognitive coaching as helpful. She explained that recent changes in the structure of the district-level training made her feel disconnected from the district. Although she had been assigned a new literacy specialist, she had not built a relationship with her, relying instead on a cohort of literacy coaches, all of whom worked with the Reading First grant. She also worked closely with her former literacy specialist, who was no longer part of the district, but who assumed an informal support role with several schools.

Both the principal and teachers remarked on the role Beth plays as a district messenger. The principal explained that "the literacy coach position has kind of become this umbrella position where the district funnels information and its expectations for various initiatives that are coming down the pipe through the literacy coach position." One teacher described this role as complicating her ability to coach, stating, "I know that she gets quite a bit of grief from some people . . . and a lot of things that she has to hand out come from the district, but because she's the messenger, she takes a lot of the heat . . . she's just pulled in way too many directions." Expectations from the district to implement district policies at the school level confounded her role as a support for teachers and took time away from coaching.

Despite the conflicting demands on her time, Beth saw herself as having "a better situation than a lot of people do." She attributed this to her working relationship with the principal, whom she described as supportive of her and her work. She said, "Of everyone on the staff, I work most closely with him. Our philosophies are very much aligned, we do a lot of planning together, we do a lot of problem solving together . . . we have a really good line of communication." She believed his reading background was invaluable when it came to standing up for her and found that his authority was a regular source of support.

Although she described some backlash from teachers unwilling to change, she explained that overall, teachers were willing to work with her. The two teachers interviewed both voiced their respect for her knowledge and supported her work. Both expressed an appreciation for the difficulty of her role, and one commented, "I think it would be very hard to work with so many different personalities . . . and you know, we're always knocking on her door, I mean, we're really impressed with how she handles everybody." The other said, "She would be the first person I would go to if I have a concern regarding reading and she's very approachable, very easy to get along with, and she'll help you any way she can."

Despite these positive responses to her work and the support of the principal, Beth still felt the strain of walking the line between teacher and administrator. She explained that as a coach, "you don't fit anywhere. You're kind of out there by yourself. . . . I'm not an administrator, but yet I'm not really part of the teaching ranks either, and it just gets you after awhile."

SUMMARY AND CONCLUSIONS

By examining the literacy coach initiative through multiple conceptual lenses using multiple methods, a comprehensive picture of this teacher leadership strategy in Davis Public Schools emerged. As designed, the initiative fit well within recommendations from research on instructional coaching and professional learning and had strong potential to promote the use of coaching to improve literacy instruction. When viewed from the perspective of research on district decentralization, the initiative also held promise to support the use of coaching practices given the large commitment of human and financial resources, the provision of new curricular guidelines for literacy, and ongoing training tied to the guidelines. Our findings demonstrated that literacy specialists worked hard to support coaches, who in turn, were perceived as valuable resources in many DPS schools. The findings also showed, however, that coach efforts to provide direct instructional support to teachers was limited by a number of factors. In this final section, we summarize key findings and reflect upon their broader implications for literacy coaching and teacher leadership in general.

Our school case studies demonstrated a number of positive examples of coaching that reflected DPS expectations and professional standards for coaches. Yet, there was ample evidence of forces that eroded time spent on direct coaching, with principals using coaches for local school needs and time spent at district meetings. Our school case studies also provided evidence that the literacy specialist role was not being used to its full capacity. In two of the eight schools where Direct Instruction was utilized, the coaches felt the initial specialists were not supportive of that program's approach. In one of our featured cases, Brubeck School, the new district literacy specialist was seen as less helpful than the former specialist. In fact, both the principal and coach explained that they found a way to keep working with their former literacy specialist instead of their assigned specialist.

The shortage of literacy specialists presented a substantial structural problem that may have weakened the impact of the literacy specialists. With only four of six positions filled, the specialists simply had too many schools to support. Most only visited half of the schools assigned to them. These problems are consequential because the literacy specialists played a central role in the design. Specialists were to support coach development and communicate district priorities and expectations of the coaching role. Without school-level support from specialists, coaches had to increasingly rely on training at the district level.

As coaches and specialists reported, district-level training became increasingly focused on district priorities and consequently became less sensitive to the needs of local schools. In a sense, an attempt at "recentralization" occurred, whereby district priorities were given greater attention than local school priorities. Coaches and specialists reported that coaches were used to deliver district mandates for school level curriculum alignment, facilitate school improvement planning, and develop classroom formative assessments.

At the same time, specialists reported frustration in their ability to hold coaches accountable for compliance with literacy coach logs, and the unwillingness or inability of the district to hold principals accountable for how coaches were used in schools. Both the district- and school-level cases provided evidence of principals trumping district priorities in order to use coaches in ways that often departed from the original intentions of the initiative. As we observed, many literacy coaches took on roles that were outside the original vision for the position. Lack of an evaluation tool tailored to the coach role and its unique set of responsibilities may have contributed to generally weak accountability over the use of coaches in schools.

Survey reports of how coaches allocated their time across a range of activities aligned well with the results of the case studies. The survey data showed that there was widespread use of direct, interactive coaching across the district. However, the survey data also demonstrated that coaches devoted considerable amounts of time to other leadership functions such as administration and goal setting. Consequently, direct coaching did not receive a clear majority of coaches' attention, even though this was the intention of the DPS coach design. We did, however, find suggestive evidence from survey results that direct coaching can be supported through effective professional development and by clarifying expectations for coaches.

It was also evident that the effectiveness of teacher leaders in our study depended on the support of school principals. As both coaches and specialists indicated, principals have a large impact on the roles coaches play and the extent to which coaches focus on direct support to teachers. A related finding is that teacher leaders often get drawn into other leadership roles, such as de facto assistant principals, grant administrators, or test administrators. The fact that coaches are often tapped by their principals for additional responsibilities is not terribly surprising if one considers the administration and leadership demands associated with the complex constellation of curricula, assessments, and programs that is typical in public schools.

Taking stock of these findings, we are reminded of arguments that, in order for instructional improvement initiatives to succeed in decentralized districts, there needs to be clear guidance and supports, and authority and accountability provided by the district (Elmore, 1993; Odden, 1998). The DPS initiative attempted to provide guidance through district standards, support through literacy specialists, and accountability over the initiative through coach logs. Yet we found examples of coaches declining to complete logs or attend training, and frustration on the part of specialists who could not enforce compliance with these requirements. Further, specialists expressed dissatisfaction with the district's inability or unwillingness to hold principals accountable for assigning roles unrelated to literacy support. Based on the evidence, it is our opinion that district accountability was weak, and that district expectations were often overridden at the local level. Often this meant that coaches spent time on work that did not involve direct interaction with teachers in the service of instructional improvement.

This is not to say that the lack of accountability had uniformly negative consequences. Indeed, we saw ample evidence that some schools took advantage of both the guidance and support provided by the district and the autonomy afforded in the district, implementing coaching practices aligned with district expectations and professional standards. However, we conjecture that allowing so much local autonomy appears to create a situation where schools with greater capacity for instructional improvement might be able to take greater advantage of available flexibility to support existing initiatives. Lower capacity schools, on the other hand, may not be as well positioned to take advantage of these resources, and could perhaps use greater scaffolding. Our study does not resolve the fundamental dilemma facing decentralized districts about the optimal balance between central control and local autonomy. Nonetheless, while documenting less productive uses of teacher leadership resources, we also provide concrete evidence of productive ways in which district guidance and assistance can support the implementation of teacher leadership initiatives. We recommend that future research in this area attempt to shed light on how teacher leadership initiatives can most effectively capitalize on the strength of both central guidance and local initiative.

NOTE

    The authors wish to thank Anthony Milanowski at the Wisconsin Center for Educational Research for his invaluable input at various stages of the work. Sarah McKinney, Mina Kim, and Kristin Schomisch provided research assistance on this study. We also wish to thank the teachers, principals, literacy coaches, literacy specialists, and other district staff who generously gave of their time to participate in the research. Research reported here was supported in part through a grant from the Carnegie Corporation of New York and a contract from the local school district.

REFERENCES

Ashworth, D. (1999, Winter). Effects of Direct Instruction and basal reading instruction programs on the reading achievement of second graders. *Reading Improvement, 36*(4), 150–156.

Bandura, A.(1977). *Social learning theory.* Englewood Cliffs, NJ: Prentice Hall.

Brown, J. S., Collins, A., & Duguid, P. (1989). Situated cognition and the culture of learning. *Educational Researcher, 18*(1), 32–42.

Camburn, E., Rowan, B., & Taylor, J. (2003). Distributed leadership in schools: the case of elementary schools adopting comprehensive school reform models. *Educational Evaluation and Policy Analysis, 25*(4), 347–373.

Corcoran, T., & Christman, J. B. (2002). *The limits and contradictions of systemic reform: The Philadelphia story.* Philadelphia: Consortium for Policy Research in Education.

Cohen, D. K., & Ball, D. L. (1999). *Instruction, capacity, and improvement* (CPRE Research Report No. RR-443). Philadelphia: Consortium for Policy Research in Education.

Elmore, R. (1993). School decentralization: Who gains? Who loses? In J. Hannaway & M. Carnoy (Eds.), *Decentralization and school improvement: Can we fulfill the promise?* (pp. 33–54). San Francisco: Jossey-Bass.

International Reading Association (IRA). (2004). *The role and qualifications of the reading coach in the United States: A position statement of the International Reading Association.* Newark, DE: Author.

International Reading Association (IRA). (2006). *Standards for middle and high school literacy coaches: A Project of the International Reading Association.* Newark, DE: Author.

Joyce, B., & Showers, B. (1980). Improving inservice training: the messages of research. *Educational Leadership, 37*(5), 379–385.

Lave, J., & Wenger, E. (1991). *Situated learning: legitimate peripheral participation.* Cambridge, UK: Cambridge University Press.

Mazmanian, D. A., & Sabatier, P. A. (1981). *Effective policy implementation.* Lexington, MA: Lexington Books.

Newmann, F. M., Smith, B., Allensworth, E., & Bryk, A. S. (2001). Instructional program coherence: what it is and why it should guide school improvement policy. *Educational Evaluation and Policy Analysis, 23*(4), 297–321.

Odden, A. (1998). How to create and manage a decentralized education system. In *New American Schools: Getting better by design* (Vol. 2). Arlington, VA: New American Schools Development Corporation.

Putnam, R. T., & Borko, H. (2000). What do new views of knowledge and thinking have to say about research on teacher learning? *Educational Researcher, 29*(1), 4–15.

Showers, B., & Joyce, B. (1996). The evolution of peer coaching. *Educational Leadership, 53*(6), 12–16.

Smylie, M. A., Lazarus, V., & Brownlee-Conyers, J. (1996). Instructional outcomes of school-based participative decision making. *Educational Evaluation and Policy Analysis, 18*(3), 181–198.

Sykes, G., King, C., & Patrick, J. (2002). Models of preparation for the professions: implications for educational leadership. In M. Tucker & J. Codding (Eds.), *The principal challenge: Leading and managing schools in an era of accountability* (pp. 143–200). San Francisco: Jossey-Bass.

CHAPTER 8

Instructional Influence in American High Schools

Jonathan A. Supovitz

STUDIES OF school leadership have typically focused on the efforts of those who hold positions of formal authority. Most prominently, investigations of the roles and influence of school principals abound (Hallinger & Heck, 1998; Leithwood, 1994; Marks & Printy, 2003; Murphy & Datnow, 2003). The teacher leadership literature, as well, tends to focus on the formal roles of those who hold specific appointed positions such as lead teachers, co-ordinators, and coaches (Frost & Harris, 2003; York-Barr & Duke, 2004). While it is well established that formal leaders play important roles in introducing instructional improvements and catalyzing school effectiveness efforts, their work captures only a portion of the important leadership activity in schools (Riggan & Supovitz, 2006; Spillane, 2006).

In this chapter I seek to use a broader notion of leadership as "influence" to explore the range of individuals who are providing instructional leadership in a national sample of 14 high schools. My central research questions are: (1) Who plays instructional leadership roles in high schools? (2) What are their positions and characteristics? (3) How do they differ from other school staff? (4) Why do teachers report going to others for instructional assistance?

This chapter unfolds in a fairly typical sequence. First, I present a brief literature review to conceptually frame the study. Second, I describe the data and analysis techniques employed for this study, including a description of the sample of schools, the measures used to collect data, and the techniques used to analyze the data. Third, I identify the instructionally influential individuals and the reasons why colleagues turn to them for assistance. In the final section I discuss my interpretation of the results in relation to the literature and their implications for practice.

CONCEPTIONS OF LEADERSHIP IN THE LITERATURE

Explications of the distribution of leadership across the range of faculty members in school organizations—both those holding formal leadership positions and those without—are being driven by the conceptual work of Gronn, Spillane, and others. Gronn (2000) urges a reallocation of the tasks and activities that constitute the division of labor in school organizations such that "joint performance" and "tool-mediated activity" replace the rigid boundaries currently in place. Spillane has written extensively on the distributed perspective of leadership. In his view, leadership arises out of the interactions between individuals, tasks, and situations rather than being imbued in any formal title or responsibility (Spillane, 2006). A perspective on leadership that is consonant with the distributed perspective comes from conceptions of leadership arising out of authority and influence of leaders over followers. In this view, leadership is not solely positional but rather is rooted in the act of establishing influence over others. Schneier and Goktepe (1983) define such informal leadership as influence over other group members. Pescosolido (2001) argues that informal leadership that develops within a group plays a key role in defining the group's sense of efficacy. Research from organizational sociology indicates that informal leaders have a strong influence on group processes, norms, and outcomes (Bass, 1990; Wheelan & Johnston, 1996). De Souza and Klein (1995) showed that "emergent leaders" have a strong influence on group goals. Yet there is relatively little research on the roles of informal leaders, their characteristics, and the behaviors and mechanisms they use to affect group change (Druskat & Pescosolido, 2002).

Heifetz (1994) defines *authority relationships* as "conferred power to perform a service" for others (p. 57). Heifetz explored the sources of authority for political leaders who did not carry formal positions of power. For example, Heifetz analyzed the authority of Martin Luther King that arose from his ability to carry moral suasion with large numbers of Americans across racial boundaries. As Heifetz points out, the implications of this definition are twofold: First, authority is not immutable, but rather it is given consensually and can therefore also be effectively revoked. Second, authority is conferred as part of an exchange between leaders and followers. Heifetz's framing of leadership has at least two implications: First, it opens up the possibility that leadership can come from any member of an organization at any time. Second, it accentuates the sway of the follower in the leader-follower relationship because the authority of leadership is derived from the consent of the follower. Gronn (1996) captures this difference nicely when he distinguishes between headship and leadership and quotes Lantis (1987) in saying "a head may be a leader but is not one inevitably" (p. 9).

French and Raven (1959) developed a typology based on the notion that authority results from a transaction in which influence is given in exchange for some service. French and Raven defined *social influence* as changing the behavior, opinions, attitudes, goals, or values of a person. Their typology of the bases of power for social influence consisted of the following kinds of power: (1) *reward power*, based on B's perception that A has the ability to "mediate rewards for him"; (2) *coercive power*, based on B's perception that A has the ability to "mediate punishments for him"; (3) *legitimate power*, based on B's perceptions that A has "a legitimate right to prescribe behavior for him"; (4) *referent power*, based on B's identification with A; and (5) *expert power*, based on B's perception that A has "some special knowledge or expertness" (pp. 155–156). Raven (1965) later added a sixth power base, *informational power*, whereby A influences B through the information of her message.

The bases of power typology has been empirically investigated many times across industries, including several times in educational contexts (see Erchul & Raven, 1997, for a summary). Cienki (1982) conducted a videotaped consultation with 68 teachers and found that both expertise and identification were correlated with perceptions of effectiveness. Short, Moore, and Williams (1991) found that training, experience, and expertise were associated with perceived effectiveness. Roberts (1985) found that consultant expertise and referent power correlated with measures of educators' satisfaction and perceptions of problem resolution. These and other studies suggest that the power bases are important sources of influence independent of an individual's job title.

DATA SOURCES AND ANALYSIS METHODS

The data for this study come from a sample of high schools that were examined by the Consortium for Policy Research in Education (CPRE) as part of its Study of High School Strategies for Instructional Improvement. In CPRE's study, the research team focused on the interactions between local high school culture and organization and five different external support providers that are fostering instructional improvement interventions in the areas of literacy, whole school reform, and data use. The sample of schools for the CPRE study were purposefully chosen in consultation with the support providers to represent a range of schools in early and mature stages of reform implementation. (While CPRE's high school study contains 15 high schools, the data for this chapter were based on 14, as one school joined the CPRE study after these analyses were conducted.) The CPRE research study focused on high schools for two reasons: First, relatively little is known about instructional improvement efforts in high schools compared to elementary schools. Second, high schools are understood to be distinctive educational organizations (McLaughlin & Talbert, 2001; Siskin, 1994).

The sample for this chapter represents a diverse set of 14 high schools. A selection of the demographics of the sample of high schools is shown in Table 8.1. These schools were located in 10 states around the country. Two of the schools were in rural areas, two in midsized cities, six were located in urban fringe areas, and four were urban (i.e., in large cities). The sample averaged 44% students receiving lunch assistance. On average, the schools were 45% minority but, with a standard deviation of 37%, they included a broad range. Four of the schools were 90% or more White, while three

Table 8.1. Demographics of sample.

School	Urbanicity/ State	Percent of Students at Standard in Reading	School Size (number of students)	Percent of Students Receiving Free or Reduced-Price Lunch	Percent Black	Percent Hispanic
1	Rural (GA)	92	1,436	25	1	2
2	Urban fringe (MI)	86	1,648	4	0	0
3	Urban fringe (PA)	83	569	0	0	1
4	Urban fringe (PA)	83	1,372	0	12	2
5	Urban fringe (TX)	71	4,778	35	28	38
6	Urban fringe (NJ)	57	923	37	1	2
7	Large city (TX)	53	2,164	86	11	78
8	Urban fringe (PA)	53	1,904	33	46	8
9	Midsized city (IA)	50	1,142	35	22	4
10	Rural (MS)	39	415	99	77	0
11	Midsized city (NY)	39	478	82	71	25
12	Large city (PA)	14	1,150	91	47	6
13	Large city (KY)	11	1,113	41	50	2
14	Large city (LA)	9	1,470	51	99	0

of the schools were more than 90% minority. Of the schools that were majority minority, six were predominantly Black, while two were largely Hispanic. Finally, the sample ranged in performance levels. Three of the schools had less than 15% of their students performing at standard on their state reading assessment, while four of the schools had over 80% of their students reading at the state proficiency level.

Instruments

The CPRE study included three rounds of data collection from the sample of schools. These included a round of previsit phone interviews conducted with the school's principal or vice principal in the winter of 2004, a 2-day visit by a two-person team in the spring of 2005, and a follow-up 2-day visit in the spring of 2006. The data for this chapter come principally from the school visits in spring 2005.

During the spring 2005 visits, both survey and interview data were collected. First, survey data were collected from all faculty members that had any degree of instructional responsibilities with students. Second, interviews were conducted with a sample of faculty members at each school during 2-day site visits conducted in the spring of 2005. Staff members with both central and peripheral involvement with the reforms of interest were targeted for interviews. In total, over 200 semistructured interviews lasting about 30–60 minutes each were conducted with teachers and school leaders. Each of these data collection methods are described in more detail below.

Survey data. Surveys were administered to all teaching staff (administrators and nonteachers were not included) in each school during a schoolwide faculty meeting. School faculty response rates ranged from 59% to 89%, averaging 73%.

A central focus of this investigation was to ascertain the answers to social network survey questions. Social network survey analysis is a method for the systematic study of social structures and relationships (Degenne & Forse, 1999). The survey focused on three particular instructional networks: curriculum, student discipline, and assisting low-performing students. More specifically, three network questions were asked on the teacher survey:

- *Curriculum network question.* During this school year, to whom *in your school* have you gone for help in selecting and planning course content coverage and pacing?
- *Discipline network question.* To whom, *in your school*, have you turned for advice about classroom management during this school year?

- *Assisting low-performing students network question.* During this school year, to whom *in your school* have you turned for advice on strategies to assist low-performing students?

For each network question on the survey, respondents were asked to name the individuals from whom they sought guidance or advice, the frequency that advice was sought from that individual, and the level of influence the respondent felt that the advice had. There was space for respondents to list up to five names for each network.

Interview data. During each 2-day school visit two CPRE researchers interviewed a range of teachers and school administrators. These interviews focused on general questions related to the reform that was being implemented as well as specific issues related to the contexts of each particular school. For the purposes of this study, interviews with teachers and administrators in each of the schools included questions about whom respondents went to for instructional assistance and why they chose to go to that particular person for instructional assistance. Overall, 205 interviews were conducted.

Analysis

On the survey, the responses to the frequency stem "How often have you sought guidance from this person?" were on a 4-point scale (recoded to represent an approximate number of days in a school year). The responses to the influence stem "How influential is the advice . . ." were also on a 4-point scale (operationalized to represent the proportion of influential conversations with respect to the respondent's practice). To utilize both the frequency and influence dimensions, survey data were combined into a single measure of weighted tie-strength (Frank, Zhao, & Borman, 2004).

To identify individuals whose influence was statistically significant, the actual distribution of influence in each school was compared against the distribution that would be expected to occur by chance alone. Using a technique that was pioneered by Cole and Weiss (2006), this was accomplished by running 10,000 simulations in which each individual's weighted out-ties were randomly assigned to other individuals in the network. Once all of the weighted ties had been reassigned, the influence measure for each individual was recalculated for the new random data. Individuals were considered "statistically significant influentials" if their influence score was higher than their random-ranked counterpart at least 99% of the time. By doing this, influential individuals were those whose influence is statistically significantly greater than random chance while holding constant the number, frequency, and influence of conversations in the network.

The interview data went through a three-stage coding process to develop categories for the reasons people sought assistance from others. First, any data pertaining in any way to leadership were coded as such. In the second step, the questions of whom people went to for assistance and why they sought assistance from others were then separated and assigned to a second database. Third, informed by both the literature and a preliminary reading, the data were recoded into the following categories of why people sought assistance from others: expertise, formal authority, experience, resource access, physical proximity, and social connections. A single interview could, and often did, include multiple codes of whom a person went to for instructional assistance. Additionally, in many cases individuals gave multiple reasons for seeking assistance from a single person.

INSTRUCTIONAL INFLUENCE IN HIGH SCHOOLS

Instructional influence is defined here as receiving significantly more requests for assistance about an instructional topic in a school than would be likely to happen by chance (see analysis methods above). Relatively few faculty members met this criterion. In the curriculum network, only 6% of the faculty members across the 14 schools (103 people out of 1,715 faculty members) were identified as significantly influential. In the discipline and the low-performing student assistance networks, 10% of faculty members were significantly more likely to be recipients of requests for assistance than would be likely to happen by chance. In both the curriculum and discipline networks, there were several schools where no individual was statistically significantly influential.

Roles of Instructionally Influential Individuals

The overwhelming majority of individuals who were identified as instructionally influential were classroom teachers who held no formal leadership designation in their school. Table 8.2 shows the distribution of instructionally influential individuals by role. In each of the three instruction-related networks, teachers were the large majority of instructionally influential individuals. In the curriculum network, two thirds of those who were instructionally influential were teachers, while about a quarter were department chairs. In the discipline network, 56% of those identified as influen-

Table 8.2. Roles of instructionally influential people in high schools (percent of network).

	Curriculum Network	Discipline Network	Low-Performing Student Assistance Network
Teachers	66	56	64
Department chairs	27	15	7
School administrators	2	18	9
Counselors	5	3	11
Other		8	9
	(*n* = 103)	(*n* = 159)	(*n* = 166)

tial were teachers and 15% were department chairs. School administrators, including both principals and vice-principals, were significantly more likely to be asked for assistance about discipline issues than about the other issues.

Of those who were significantly more likely to be sought for advice about low-performing students, 64% were teachers. The teachers who were statistically influential in this network can be further broken down into content area teachers (35%) and special education teachers (29%). Eleven percent of the individuals who were influential in the low-performing student assistance network were counselors, while only 9% were school administrators.

Instructional Transcenders

Relatively few of the individuals who were identified as influential in one of the three instructional networks appeared as influential in one of the other instructional networks. As shown in Figure 8.1, of the 428 people who were influential across the three networks, 301 of these, or 68%, were influential in just one of the three networks. Sixty-five individuals, or 22%, were influential in two of the three networks. Only 10% of the influential individuals, 31 people, were influential in all three of the instructional networks. This suggests that instructional influence, which we saw before was held largely by teachers without formal leadership positions, was distinctive depending on a particular instructional domain.

Figure 8.1. Proportion of people influential in multiple instructional networks (*N* = 428).

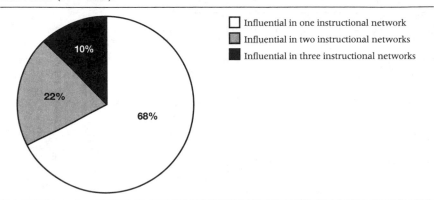

Characteristics of Instructionally Influential Individuals

Individuals who were instructionally influential in the sample of high schools were more likely to be female, to have been in their schools longer, and to be members of other groups or committees in their schools. Table 8.3 presents a comparison of characteristics collected on the survey of those individuals identified as instructionally influential in their schools to other faculty members in their schools. These data are based solely on teachers, not administrators, because there were only survey responses from those individuals.

Almost 70% of those who were significantly more likely to be influential on one of the three instructional networks in the study were female, as opposed to 56% of the general population of teachers in the 14 sample schools. There were no differences in overall experience between those who were instructionally influential and other teachers, but the instructionally influential individuals were more experienced in their schools. Finally, they were more likely to play other leadership roles in their schools. The survey asked whether they held leadership positions on any faculty committees or school groups. Seventy-one percent of those who were influential indicated that they participated in such leadership activities, as compared to about half in the general teaching population.

Power Bases for Instructional Influence

As detailed earlier, French and Raven (1959) developed a taxonomy for bases of power for social influence which included reward, coercion,

Table 8.3. Characteristics of instructionally influential individuals.

Characteristic	Influential Individuals	Noninfluential Individuals
Female	69%*	56%
Total years of experience		
Mean	13.88	13.28
SD	10.2	10.55
Years of experience at the school		
Mean	9.11*	7.99
SD	8.47	8.34
Member of faculty team [a]	0.71*	0.51
	$(N = 371)$ [b]	$(N = 1,411)$

[a] Includes school improvement teams, advisory boards, committees, and so on.

[b] The sample size for this analysis was reduced from 428 to 371 because not all respondents provided information about these characteristics.

* $p < 05$.

legitimacy, identification, expertise, and information. Using this taxonomy as a starting point, a similar series of rationales were developed as to why teachers would go to others for instructional assistance. These included categories of expertise, formal authority, experience, resource access, physical proximity, and social connections. Several of these comport with the French and Raven taxonomy, although French and Raven's approach requires more psychological interpretation of the rationale of the requestor.

Using the interview data from teachers, teacher responses to questions about whom they went to for assistance on instructional issues and why they sought assistance from those individuals were examined. While there were 205 interviews, there were 437 explanations of why people sought assistance from others. The number of mentions exceeds the number of interviews because a respondent could, and often did, mention more than one person who they went to for instructional assistance and more than one reason why they sought assistance from that individual. Therefore, the counts of why people sought assistance from others are not directly proportional to the number of interviews.

Before exploring the reasons why respondents sought assistance from others, several things are important to note. First, who is sought for assistance tended to be issue specific. Individuals choose where to go for assistance based upon the kind of assistance needed. For example, one ninth-grade science teacher said,

> It depends on what it is. If it's a content question [I'll go to] col-
> leagues in the department. And it even depends on how specific
> the question is. If it's physics, I'll go to _____. If it's about some
> sort of enrichment or as far as reading or literacy, _____ and
> _____ are both obviously always available for that.

This is likely why the individuals who were instructionally influential were mostly influential in one, but not multiple, of the instructional networks; cases of instructional transcenders were relatively scarce.

Second, assistance not only depends on the assistor being *able* to provide something of value to the requestor, but also being *willing* to provide it. There were several cases in the data where someone described another person as having expertise but not being accessible, and therefore not tapped. Third, the interview data suggested that assistance often is requested and received casually. As one teacher explained about how she sought instructional assistance, "Sometimes it is just other teachers, colleagues, that I'm friends with that are in other subject areas, often just in conversation, sort of trying to enrich the others' classroom a little just by doing what we can." Fourth, there are often multiple reasons for seeking assistance from a single individual. In many cases, respondent's used multiple rationales within the same explanation as to why they sought assistance from someone.

There was a wide array of reasons as to why people sought instructional assistance from others, although a few reasons predominated. Figure 8.2 shows the frequency of the different reasons that teachers explained why they went to a particular individual for instructional assistance. The two most frequently identified reasons for why a respondent sought assistance from another individual were expertise and the formal position of the recipient. Expertise was cited over 140 times by the 205 teachers interviewed and formal position was cited 131 times by those interviewed. There were 58 examples of teachers describing the experience of another person as their rationale for going to them for instructional assistance. Resources, proximity, or social reasons (largely friendship) were cited about 25–30 times by the 205 respondents. These were less common reasons for seeking assistance from others.

Expertise. The notion of expertise, which stems from B's perception that A possesses knowledge or expertise in a particular area, was the most commonly mentioned reason why an individual sought assistance from an-

Figure 8.2. Reasons why people sought instructional assistance from others (number of mentions by 205 interviewees).

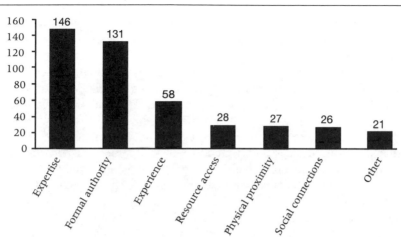

other. For example, one mathematics teacher explained why she went to a colleague for help:

> She is a real talented, knowledge-wise, content-wise teacher. I mean, I have a master's degree in math education. She's got her master's degree in core mathematics. So she definitely has deeper insight into the bigger picture and how certain pieces of the curriculum relate a bit stronger than I do.

For this respondent, content expertise in mathematics provided the rationale for seeking assistance.

According to another mathematics teacher, she went to a peer for instructional assistance because "_____ is a resource of knowledge." She explained:

> This guy to me is probably the best teacher I've ever seen teach. If I have questions, I go to him. The greatest thing about the guy is he is more than willing to teach anybody. He doesn't care who he is teaching. He just loves to teach, and it's fantastic.

This explanation combines both expertise and approachability or willingness to provide assistance. Finally, one teacher viewed expertise in terms of a peer getting results with her students. "We probably look to _____ sort of as our leader, just because of her results within her classroom," the teacher explained. For this teacher, expertise was associated with improved student outcomes.

Formal authority. French and Raven (1959) ascribe legitimate power as B's sense of obligation to accept A's influence due to B's perception of A's right to influence "perhaps because of A's position within the organization" (p. 160). In the interviews, teachers often described gravitating to formal school leaders as those providing assistance, using the leaders' formal positions as the explanations of why they sought assistance from them. One social studies teacher, when asked to name the top three resources for subject-specific information, asked, "Do they need to be administrators?" indicating that she thought she was expected to associate subject-specific resources with formal leaders, even though she may not have believed this was the case. A mathematics teacher, when asked who are the curriculum leaders for the school said, "Well, I know it's supposed to be the principal. And our principal happens to be a former math teacher. So it should be the principal and it is." This teacher also associated formal authority with expertise and seemed to be relieved that in her particular case her formal leader also had instructional expertise in mathematics. Another teacher viewed the department chairs in her school as the natural curriculum leaders, based on their position as department chairs. As she said, "Well, for instance in science it would be _____ just because he's the head of the science department. Generally, it's just the head of the department . . . I guess the heads of the departments would be the natural curriculum leaders."

Experience. In 58 cases teachers also cited experience as a reason why they sought assistance from a colleague. Experience is not identified as a base of power in French and Raven's typology, but it may be related to legitimacy, as experience may confer a sense that a person has developed special knowledge over time. In their explanations as to why they sought assistance from an individual, teachers used such explanations as the following:

> She's a veteran, she's been doing this for almost 30 years.

> He's been a great resource. He's been around the school. I think he's been teaching here 32 years. He knows everyone. He knows the system.

> She's been teaching a long time. She's a wealth of information.

> He is a senior person in the social studies department. He's been here a long time. He actually taught me when I was a student here.

As implied in the second and third examples above, experience was often used in combination with some other reason for seeking assistance from that individual, indicating that experience is at least implicitly associated with some other perceived quality of value.

Resource access. Teachers mentioned material resource access 28 times as a reason for seeking assistance from another. Resource access may be similar to French and Raven's reward power, as control of resources may be a basis for influence due to the tangible benefits associated with the source of assistance. As one teacher said, "I go to _____, she is Ms. Resource." Another said, "I go to _____. She has been very helpful and very proactive. It's things as simple as getting me the resources I need."

Physical proximity. Physical proximity was mentioned in 27 cases as a rationale for seeking assistance from others. Physical proximity has been shown in other research to foster the type of relationships that contribute to social networks. According to Brass (1985), "Employees tend to develop informal relationships with others who work close to them" (p. 329). As with experience, proximity tended to be mentioned in combination with other reasons as to why individuals sought assistance from others. Examples of proximity as a reason for why someone chose to go to a particular person for assistance included the following:

> INTERVIEWER: Can you think of people that you've gone to for assistance around curriculum, pedagogy, classroom management?
> RESPONDENT: _____ is an English teacher, _____, the science teacher, those are people that more than others I talk to regularly.
> INTERVIEWER: These are the ones across the hall?
> RESPONDENT: That's probably true, I tend to talk more to my immediate neighbors.

> ANOTHER RESPONDENT: _____, because she's right next door to where my classroom is. I ask her a lot of stuff too, and she's been here a long time.

> INTERVIEWER: Who among your colleagues do you usually talk to about your classes?
> RESPONDENT: I have a mentor, and just whoever shares the classrooms near my classroom, proximity.

Social connections. Finally, social relationships were identified as a reason for seeking assistance from others. Social relationships tend to be one of the strongest predictors of network patterns. Several studies have shown that people who are friends are likely to discuss professional issues (Frank et al., 2004; Rogers, 1979). In CPRE's study with the same data used for this chapter, it was found that "friends" networks were denser than either instructional networks or networks focused on external programs (Weinbaum et al., 2006). In the interview data explaining why people sought instructional assistance from others, social explanations were evident in 26 cases. As one teacher said when asked to whom she went for instructional assistance, "I would probably ask people I'm . . . friendlier with. I don't know how to put it any other way." Perhaps because of the substance of instructional questions, while social relationships may have been a factor in whom people sought for assistance, it was not a major factor in explaining why people sought assistance from others.

IMPLICATIONS FOR THE STUDY AND PRACTICE OF SCHOOL LEADERSHIP

Principals and other designated school leaders are often exhorted to practice instructional leadership (Fink & Resnick, 2001: Heck, 1992; Supovitz & Poglinco, 2001). The findings of this study suggest, however, that much instructional leadership—at least if it is defined as the provision of support, advice, and assistance around instructional issues—comes more informally from colleagues and peers than from the top down or even through formal leader-follower channels.

There could be several reasons for this finding. First, authority relationships tend to discourage candor about problems that teachers may be having (Supovitz, 2006). Thus teachers may feel more comfortable sharing their instructional challenges with peers rather than superiors. Second, as Elmore (2000) has noted, as formal school leaders naturally spend less of their time engaged in instructional matters, they are less experienced in these issues than teachers. Instructional expertise, the number one reason that people reported for seeking assistance from a particular other, is more likely to reside in teachers rather than administrators.

The rich view of instructional assistance networks offered in this chapter challenges us to rethink several leadership concepts. First, when we think of what it means for formal school leaders to be instructional leaders, these findings suggest that we might need a broader perspective. Rather than formal leaders directly providing instructional support themselves, instructional leadership for formal leaders might mean identifying those who are both willing and capable to provide instructional support, facilitating the opportunities for these informal leaders to interact with other school faculty members, and providing organizational resources in support of these interactions. While formal leaders may provide some direct assistance themselves in areas in which they have expertise and experience, they are more likely to coordinate the provision of assistance in content areas for which they have less depth of knowledge.

Second, this study provides impetus for us to develop a wider conception of the range of leadership activity that goes on in schools. The findings support the notion that instructional leadership is being provided from members of high schools well beyond those typically thought of as school leaders. Based on these findings, expanded conceptions of instructional leadership might include a far broader cast of players supporting different aspects of the instructional improvement puzzle. While formal leaders may be introducing and marshalling support for reform ideas, the interactions around the meaning of those reforms may be facilitated by more complex networks of both formal leaders and selected classroom teachers. Informal leaders are playing important and different roles in the deepening of instructional engagement in schools.

A third implication from this study is that the assistance networks in schools, or at least in high schools, appear quite distinct depending on the issue at hand. It was surprising in these data to find that relatively few of the individuals who were influential in one of the three instructional networks appeared as influential in another instructional network. In fact, two thirds of the instructional leaders were significantly influential in only one of the three instructional networks, suggesting that the instructional networks in schools are distinct from one another depending on the particular issue. This adds another dimension of complexity to the picture beyond subject matter differences that are often seen as distinctive (Burch & Spillane, 2003; Stodolsky, 1988).

The reasons why teachers in this study sought assistance from others followed an expected pattern. Expertise and formal authority were the two dominant reasons why people sought out specific individuals for instructional advice, with experience also a substantial explanation of why. These rationales comport quite nicely into the French and Raven typology, confirming other studies that have employed this framework in educational settings. The frequency of seeking assistance from formal leaders may be masking either the legitimate or coercive powers described by French and Raven (1959). In either case, this would seem to reflect the cultural expectations embedded within schools as organizations with well-established patterns and routines around relationships between individuals.

The recognition of the distinct contribution of informal leadership to school improvement suggests several channels for future inquiry. Additional research should examine the distribution of informal leadership across high school departments to explore variation by subject matter. Future research might also illuminate how informal leaders perceive their leadership activity and what influences them to take on leadership roles. Additionally, further investigations should also examine the interrelationships between formal and informal leaders and how these combinations work to spread and deepen improvement efforts. As the study of leadership practice expands beyond the confines of those traditionally labeled as leaders and burrows deeper into the complex interactions between individuals that produce changes in organizational activities, studies of the full range of organizational staff can contribute to a more robust understanding of effective leadership activity.

NOTE

This chapter was prepared under the Consortium for Policy Research in Education's grant (R308A960003) from the Institute of Education Sciences, U.S. Department of Education. Opinions expressed in this chapter are those of the author and do not necessarily reflect the views of the Institute of Education Sciences, the United States Department of Education, CPRE, or its institutional members. The author would like to thank Matthew Riggan, Russell Cole, and Michael Weiss of the Consortium for Policy Research in Education for their contributions to different aspects of this chapter.

REFERENCES

Bass, B. M. (1990). *The Bass and Stogdill handbook of leadership* (3rd ed.). New York: Free Press.

Brass, D. J. (1985). Men's and women's networks: A study of interaction patterns and influence in an organization. *Academy of Management Journal, 28,* 327–343.

Burch, P., & Spillane, J. P. (2003). Elementary school leadership strategies and subject matter: Reforming mathematics and literacy instruction. *Elementary School Journal, 103*(5), 519–535.

Cienki, J. A. (1982). Teachers' perceptions of consultation as a function of consultants' use of expert and referent power. (Doctoral dissertation, University of Pennsylvania, 1982). *Dissertation Abstracts International, 43*(3-A),725.

Cole, R., & Weiss, M. (2006, November). *Follow the leader: Identifying organizational leaders using network data.* Paper presented at the Teacher Network Conference, Evanston, IL.

Degenne, A., & Forse, M. (1999). *Introducing social networks*. Thousand Oaks, CA: Sage.

De Souza, G., & Klein, H. (1995). Emergent leadership in the group goal-setting process. *Small Group Research, 26*, 475–495.

Druskat, V., & Pescosolido, A. (2002). The context of effective teamwork mental models in self-managing teams: Ownership, learning, and heedful interrelating. *Human Relations, 55*(3), 283–314.

Elmore, R. (2000). *Building a new structure for school leadership*. New York: Albert Shanker Institute.

Erchul, W. P., & Raven, B. H. (1997). Social power in school consultation: A contemporary view of French and Raven's bases of power model. *Journal of School Psychology, 35*(2), 137–171.

Fink, E., & Resnick, L. (2001). Developing principals as instructional leaders. *Phi Delta Kappan, 82*(8), 598–606.

Frank, K. A., Zhao, Y., & Borman, K. (2004). Social capital and the diffusion of innovations within organizations: The case of computer technology in schools. *Sociology of Education, 77(2)*, 148–171.

French, J. R. P., & Raven, B. (1959). *The bases of social power*. In D. Cartwright (Ed.), *Studies in social power* (pp. 150–167). Ann Arbor, MI: Institute for Social Research.

Frost, D., & Harris, A. (2003). Teacher leadership: Towards a research agenda. *Cambridge Journal of Education, 33*(3), 479–498.

Gronn, P. (1996). From transactions to transformations. *Educational Management and Administration, 24*(1), 7–30.

Gronn, P. (2000). Distributed properties: A new architecture for leadership. *Educational Management and Administration, 28*(3), 317–338.

Hallinger, P., & Heck, R. H. (1998). Exploring the principal's contribution to school effectiveness: 1980–1995. *School Effectiveness and School Improvement, 9*(2), 157–191.

Heck, R. H. (1992). Principals' instructional leadership and school performance: Implications for policy development. *Educational Evaluation and Policy Analysis, 14*(1), 21–34.

Heifetz, R. A. (1994). *Leadership without easy answers*. Cambridge, MA: Harvard University Press.

Lantis, M. (1987). Two important roles in organizations and communities. *Human Organization, 49*(5), 8–12.

Leithwood, K. (1994). Leadership for school restructuring. *Educational Administration Quarterly, 30*(4), 498–513.

Marks, H. M., & Printy, S. M. (2003). Principal leadership and school performance: An integration of transformational and instructional leadership. *Educational Administration Quarterly, 39*(3), 370–397.

McLaughlin, M. W., & Talbert, J. E. (2001). *Professional communities and the work of high school teaching*. Chicago: University of Chicago Press.

Murphy, J., & Datnow, A. (Eds.). (2003). *Leadership for school reform: Leadership lessons from comprehensive school reforms*. Thousand Oaks, CA: Corwin Press.

Pescosolido, A. T. (2001). Informal leaders and the development of group efficacy. *Small Group Research, 32*(1), 74–93.

Raven, B. H. (1965). Social influence and power. In I. D. Steiner & M. Fishbein (Eds.), *Current studies in social psychology* (pp. 371–381). New York: Holt, Rinehart & Winston.

Riggan, M., & Supovitz, J. A. (2006, April). *They come in all shapes and sizes: Leaders and high school reform efforts.* Paper presented at the annual meeting of the American Educational Research Association, San Francisco, CA.

Roberts, L. A. (1985). School psychological consultation outcomes and perception of consultant power base (Doctoral dissertation, University of Connecticut, 1984). *Dissertation Abstracts International, 46,* 382A.

Rogers, E. M. (1979). Network analysis of diffusion of innovations. In P. W. Holland & S. Leinhardt (Eds.), *Perspectives on social network research* (pp. 137–164). New York: Academic Press.

Schneier, C. E., & Goktepe, J. R. (1983). Issues in emergent leadership: The contingency model of leadership, leader sex, and leader behavior. In H. H. Blumberg, A. P. Hare, M. V. Kent, & M. F. Davies (Eds.), *Small groups and social interaction* (Vol. 1). Chichester, UK: Wiley.

Short, R. J., Moore, S. C., & Williams, C. (1991). Social influence in consultation: Effect of degree and experience on consultees' perceptions. *Psychological Reports, 68,* 131–137.

Siskin, L. S. (1994). *Realms of knowledge: Academic departments in secondary schools.* Washington, DC: Falmer Press.

Spillane, J. P. (2006). *Distributed leadership.* San Francisco: Jossey-Bass.

Stodolsky, S. S. (1988). *The subject matters: Classroom activity in math and social studies.* Chicago: University of Chicago Press.

Supovitz, J. A. (2006). *The case for district-based reform: Leading, building, and sustaining school improvement.* Cambridge, MA: Harvard Education Press.

Supovitz, J. A., & Poglinco, S. M. (2001). *Instructional leadership in a standards-based reform.* Philadelphia: Consortium for Policy Research in Education.

Weinbaum, E. H., Supovitz, J. A., Gross, B., Cole, R., Weiss, M., & Ricalde, B. (2006, April). *Going with the flow: Communication and reform in high schools.* Paper presented at the annual meeting of the American Educational Research Association, San Francisco, CA.

Wheelan, S. A., & Johnston, F. (1996). The role of informal member leaders in a system of containing formal leaders. *Small Group Research, 27,* 33–55.

York-Barr, J., & Duke, K. (2004). What do we know about teacher leadership? Findings from two decades of scholarship. *Review of Educational Research, 74*(3), 255–316.

Student Services Practices as a Model for Data-Driven Instructional Leadership

Richard Halverson and Christopher N. Thomas

THE IDEA of accountability is not new in educational institutions, but the emphasis on using student achievement data to hold schools accountable is a recently emergent phenomena. No Child Left Behind (NCLB) outlines many of the same aspirations as previous initiatives, such as Goals 2000, but with demands for local schools and districts to measure performance with student achievement data. For many of us in education, NCLB represented the first time that student data had been presented to us in such a way. Meeting Adequate Yearly Progress (AYP) goals forces school leaders to understand how to develop local systems to translate summative testing data into the kinds of information teachers and staff can use to improve student learning. This change has pushed school leaders into the new data-driven paradigm, which calls on schools to understand and use this new data to inform instruction. This is not an easy transition, considering that most educators are only now beginning to receive training on the use of data in schools.

As part of a 5-year National Science Foundation study, we have been collecting data that examines how school leaders create social and technical systems to help teachers use achievement data to improve instruction at their school. In this research it has become apparent that school leaders have turned to the practices and expertise of student services personnel in their efforts to develop schools that use data effectively. We found that while schools already had significant capacity to design curriculum-level interventions to address the needs of groups of students, leaders we studied turned to special education practices and professionals to provide the in-house expertise necessary to create a variety of student-level interventions. This chapter will highlight one of the schools in our study, the Harrison School in the Easton School District (both pseudonyms), to understand how the roles and practices of student services staff shifted to help use data to improve learning. Harrison provides a picture of the increased role that student services staff has had in developing and maintaining program- and student-level support programs. Specifically, we will investigate two central issues:

1. *Student services practices provide a precedent for student-level intervention design.* School leaders are reshaping special education practices to help all students and teachers meet the demands of high-stakes accountability. The emergence of problem-solving teams provides a good example of how special education practices, specifically the Individualized Education Program process, is being adapted for general educational issues with individual students.
2. *Student services staff play new roles as data-savvy instructional leaders.* Student services staff are trained in using data to diagnose and guide learning plans for individual students. The need for data-driven student-level interventions invites a new range of staff, including social workers and school psychologists, to play key leadership roles in revising core instructional practices of schools.

In addition to showing how schools utilize expertise at hand to build data-driven instructional systems, our findings begin to provide insight into how schools might unite internal instructional systems, such as instructional and student services staff, that have been historically separated. This new melding of practices promises to reshape both instructional leadership and special education. As school leaders draw data-driven special education practices into the core instructional program, student services staff offer access to a better range of services to children. The capacity to identify and help students before they fail not only fulfills accountability demands but also changes how schools view teaching and learning.

STUDENT SERVICES AND INSTRUCTIONAL LEADERSHIP

The press to use assessment data has led school leaders to seek out data analysis and implementation expertise. Some of this expertise, to be sure, has been provided by district assessment specialists and external consultants. Student services staff such as special educators, school psychologists, and social workers had been trained in using achievement data for years prior to NCLB. Since the 1997 reauthorization of Individuals with Disabilities Education Act (IDEA), educators have been trained to write measurable annual achievement goals for individual students on each child's federally mandated Individualized Education Programs (IEP). IEP goals must address both academic and functional needs of the child to measure progress through the general school curriculum. Special education teachers and school psychologists are typically responsible for the assessment activities that contribute to developing IEPs.

Student services staff have often received training in the use of assessments and data collection as a part of their professional training programs, which is not the case for many teachers and administrators receiving their general education licensure. Student services staff have also acquired additional data analysis expertise as a result of the IDEA and NCLB mandates that all students participate in state and districtwide assessments. In the past, students with special needs were often tested out of grade level when taking state achievement tests. Now NCLB requires that all students be assessed using achievement tests at their grade level. Independent of the 1% of students with the "most significant cognitive disabilities," all special education students are expected to take grade-level achievement tests (Huefner, 2006). While IDEA 1997 required state-level testing for special education students, it was not until the requirements of NCLB that testing of special education students truly became a school concern.

STUDYING DATA-DRIVEN INSTRUCTIONAL LEADERSHIP

Our study was designed to investigate the practices of schools with strong records for improving student achievement scores and reputations for using data effectively. We focused our site selection on the practices of elementary and middle schools leaders in a midwestern state. We also collected information on data-based practices at the district level for each school. Elementary and middle schools with increasing test scores and school leaders with a reputation for effectively helping teachers use data were included in the sample.

Our data analysis draws on data sets collected at each school composed into individual school case studies. Yin (1994) proposes a variety of data be collected to insure the accuracy of case study representation. We conducted 52 interviews, 53 field observations, and examined a variety of artifacts from each school. In our initial paper on this research project (Halverson, Grigg, Pritchett, & Thomas, 2005) we developed a Data-Driven Instructional System (DDIS) framework (see Figure 9.1) to trace how school leaders design for data-driven organizations. As described, these functions include:

Figure 9.1. The data-driven instructional system model.

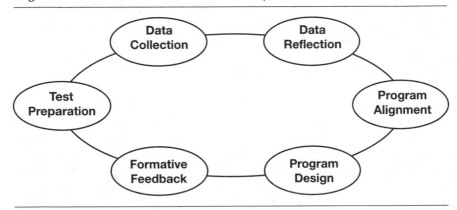

Note: From Halverson et al., 2005.

1. *Data collection.* How schools collect, store, and represent the variety of information used to guide student learning
2. *Data reflection.* How schools make sense of the data collected and set instructional goals
3. *Program alignment.* How schools use data to determine instructional program adequacy and coherence
4. *Program design.* How schools develop new program initiatives based on data-driven discussions
5. *Formative feedback.* How schools develop processes to measure the success of program design in terms of student progress
6. *Test preparation.* How schools prepare students to generate new achievement results

To make sense of our field notes and artifacts collected, we used a qualitative data analysis computer program. The data we present here reflects the practices of formal and informal leaders and staff who took on key roles in facilitating data-driven conversations, reflections, or redesign efforts in their schools.

ADAPTING STUDENT SERVICES PRACTICES
AT HARRISON SCHOOL

Our DDIS study at Harrison revealed several kinds of social and technical systems school leaders developed for using data to improve learning. The student services staff appeared to play important roles in the program design and formative feedback DDIS functions. The short description of the school's context that follows was developed as a result of our data analysis.

Harrison School is a culturally diverse K–8 school serving more than 500 students in a large, urban midwestern city. Harrison serves a diverse population with nearly 30% Asian, 10% African American, 20% Hispanic, and 50% White students. 70% of Harrison students qualify for free or reduced-price lunch, and 30% have English as a second language. Once identified as a "school in need of improvement" under the NCLB criteria, the Harrison staff applied for and received a Comprehensive School Reform grant to reorganize the school around the Direct Instruction curriculum. Harrison's transformation began with a focus on literacy and curriculum alignment while at the same time developing an elaborate academic and behavioral support system that used data to help determine program- and student-level intervention needs. The school piloted a districtwide initiative to use the problem-solving method to provide schoolwide support for struggling children. Harrison's use of the problem-solving model provides insight into how special education practices are used for the purposes of schoolwide data-driven decision making. Harrison's student services staff, particularly the school psychologist, helped the school progress in its data-driven model.

Our research at Harrison illustrated how student services staff are relied upon to provide data-driven instructional leadership services beyond traditional job descriptions. To be sure, much of the work of school psychologists and social workers in the school has persisted. However, we found that staff members in each of these areas—staff with expertise in using data to help customize and implement student learning plans—were acting as instructional leaders in the schools. In these next sections of the chapter, we will describe how first the practices, then the roles, of student services staff are being transformed by the need to develop capacity for data-driven instructional practices. We will then describe the implications for these changes in the instructional practices of the school.

Individualized Education Programs as a Precedent

Special education's Individualized Education Program served as a powerful precedent for organizing student-level data-driven instructional practices at Harrison. IEPs have served as core practices for providing special education services since the advent of the 1975 Education for All Handicapped Children Act. An IEP describes the services customized to meet the special needs of a student. Broadly speaking, prior to the advent of the

IEP, school instructional interventions were primarily assembled at the curricular level. Student support staff, such as school psychologists or social workers, helped students meet the demands of the instructional program. If students struggled with their courses they would be tracked into remedial classrooms, moved to another school, or they would simply be failed. The IEP, in particular, and special education in general, constituted an important, data-driven precedent for individual student program planning. With the IEP, schools could legitimately pursue a student-centered path to instructional interventions by customizing existing (and new) resources to the needs of individual students.

The significant aspects of the IEP we wish to highlight are the mandatory, data-driven components of the process: identification and evaluation, staffing, plan construction, and plan review. In the identification and evaluation processes, teachers or school staff members use classroom assessment data and informal observational data to determine that students struggling in the general education program receive more comprehensive evaluation, often in the form of specialized assessments. The assessment results are then referred to a "staffing" team. IDEA requires that each team include parents, regular education teachers, special education teachers or service providers, and a school representative, often a school leader, who is qualified to commit the resources and sign off on the IEP. Often school psychologists or social workers serve as the members of the team responsible for communicating evaluation results. The team reflects on the data and the perceived needs of the student in order to determine the student's eligibility for special education services and develop an action plan that includes (a) a statement of the student's present levels of performance, (b) annual achievement goals, (c) a description of services, (d) the setting in which services will be provided, and (e) when the services will be provided. The team then agrees to a means of evaluation and a process for revisiting the goals and services specified in the IEP.

To be sure, the IEP as implemented in many schools is far from a model practice. IEPs have been used to overidentify students of color as qualifying for special education services (e.g., see Blanchett, 2006; Losen & Orfield, 2002; Zhang & Katsiyannis, 2002). In practice, the IEP process was often merely seen as a step toward assigning a student for special education. This reactive model is often referred to as the "wait to fail" model of special education because if classroom interventions did not change student outcomes, then the next step was to wait for the child to fall far enough behind for him to qualify for special education. Even if used effectively to identify students, IEPs have often been used to marginalize students into pull-out programs that cut off access to general education classrooms (Capper, Frattura, & Keyes, 2000). For the purposes of this chapter, we are less interested in the history of IEP usage than in the precedent IEPs provide for using data to address student-level learning issues. The now commonplace IEP process illustrates a powerful prototype of how school staff use data to design learning plans for individual students. In our research, we found examples of how schools extended quasi-IEP processes into schoolwide programs designed to use data to identify, design, and evaluate new kinds of student-level interventions. The Problem-Solving Team at Harrison fulfilled this function.

Problem-Solving Teams: Taking the IEP Schoolwide

Problem-solving teams extend the IEP process to address learning issues for students across the school. We found there were different understandings and uses of the problem-solving model at the district and school levels. Reschly, Tilly, and Grimes (1999) describe problem solving as a systemic, noncategorical approach to delivering special education services. In a traditional special education model, students need to be assigned to disability categories in order to receive services. Problem-solving processes allow schools to diagnose learning issues with the assessment tools used with all students and customize learning plans for students based on the existing instructional program (Jankowski, 2003; Ysseldyke & Marston, 1999). Although problem solving, like the IEP, is rooted in special education, many districts have extended the scope of problem-solving activities to address planning and student learning activities across the school.

In Harrison's district, leaders approached problem solving as "a school improvement initiative based on the problem-solving process." Problem solving at the district level is described as

> a collaborative, outcome-based intervention process that utilizes continuous progress monitoring to drive instructional decision making and resource allocation based on student needs.

The advent of NCLB pressed Easton's problem-solving process from a special education intervention to a schoolwide data-driven decision-making model that integrated school improvement planning, aligning resources with standards and instructional priorities and developing professional learning communities. One Easton district leader noted:

> I think that data use is something that's evolving in a positive way. I think that the No Child Left Behind with all of its weaknesses— one of the really positive things that it has fostered is an increased

awareness of . . . data in general. It fostered an increased awareness of and appreciation for accuracy in data.

NCLB has pushed the district schools to take data seriously and to understand how measures of student achievement are linked to core instructional processes. The district leader explained:

> Understanding how [data use] fits into the whole strategic planning process for the school, I really think that this is a result of No Child Left Behind. . . . We really wouldn't have been able to create that kind of urgency for schools to pay attention to it if it weren't for No Child Left Behind.

NCLB pushed the district to develop a model to integrate problem identification, planning, solution development, and assessment into a schoolwide process. The urgency to meet the demands of high-stakes accountability called for the capacity of schools to change instructional practices accordingly (Abelmann & Elmore, 1999). Adapting the problem-solving model from a student-level to a school-level intervention pointed toward how schools might integrate these processes across the school.

At the school level, Harrison's implementation of problem solving demonstrated the link between current practices in special education and traditional classroom practices. While the district model used problem solving to describe a more general, schoolwide intervention strategy, the problem-solving team (PST) at Harrison was more firmly rooted in the special education model. Starting with the 1997 reauthorization of IDEA, schools had been required to collect data on students before placing them in special education. Many schools responded by developing school-based teams, modeled on IEP staffing teams, that were composed of the classroom teachers and student services staff members such as the school psychologist and special education teachers (Reschly et al., 1999). Harrison's version of problem solving echoed the IEP process of referral, team staffing, and intervention plan that includes data-based criteria for success. The following narrative synthesizes our experience with the PST process at Harrison.

According to the Harrison school psychologist, "anyone in the school can make a PST referral . . . based on either [student] learning or behavior." When a teacher observes academic or behavioral problems with a student, a referral is made to the school psychologist. The psychologist then uses available information to assess the condition and specific needs of the child and will decide who should be present at the PST meeting and when the problem will be discussed. A team composed of the school psychologist, special education teachers, classroom teachers, and the parent will meet to determine which kinds of data will help to construct a learning plan for the student.

The school psychologist will begin the meeting by providing a summary information packet for each student referred to the team. As a Direct Instruction (DI) school, Harrison teachers and staff use a variety of formative assessment tools to assess student learning and determine student learning goals. This data-rich environment allows the school psychologist to develop a sophisticated data profile of how a student is learning in terms of the DI curriculum. The discussion is further strengthened—in terms of data use—through the use of the readily available district and promotion data kept in district data warehouses. This data is often used to make a correlation between the student's current problems and past attendance, standardized testing, and so on. This information supplements the team's experiential knowledge of the student.

The team will then review the information packet compiled by the school psychologist. The PST delves into whether anyone had observed anything different in the student's recent behavior. The classroom teacher reports whether there are any behavioral disturbances recorded through the DI marking process. The social worker describes the student's behavioral record, and the parent, if present, is asked about issues at home. The psychologist will then hone in on the behavioral problem in terms of academic achievement by comparing current DI measures with other assessments, such as DIBELS[1] testing. These measures are checked with the perspectives of classroom teachers.

The PST develops a series of measurable academic and behavioral goals and interventions for the student. Because the PST works in the data-rich DI environment, many of these goals can be measured in terms of the school's existing assessment tools. The PST then sets up a follow-up meeting to monitor the student's progress toward these learning or behavioral goals. If the goals are met, then the student will be released from the PST plan. If the student has not made adequate progress toward the PST plan goals, the PST will develop further intervention, including the possibility of a special education placement.

The PST thus acts as an intermediate structure intended to provide a noncategorical customization of the school instructional resources to meet the needs of students. The PST serves as an intermediate adaptation of the IEP that allows the school to develop data-based interventions to address emergent student behavioral and learning issues. One teacher commented that "certainly anyone involved in a PST is discussing data on some level because you have to keep track of some kind of data." The central role of the PST is evident in both how the student is discussed, as well as in the data used to look at a respective student. According to the school's social worker, problem solving

> brings it all down to the individual student level . . . every problem-solving team meeting involves deciding what kind of data we're going to collect on that particular issue and then usually in 3 or 4 weeks we all meet back together to look at it and figure out what to do with it.

In the past, the staff might have assumed that something was wrong with the student when meetings such as this were held. The data-based PST meetings have started to change the conversation to focus on the supports students need to be successful. A Harrison kindergarten teacher summarized the influence of problem solving at Harrison this way: "Problem solving is the overall way to approach everything in the building."

The transition to problem solving at Harrison has highlighted the difficulties of bringing together the previously separated roles of teachers, special educators, and school psychologists to create student learning plans in the PST. The psychologist acknowledged that many teachers continued to struggle with the transition from reading achievement data to diagnosing student learning issues. "Even though my brain works that way, I find it very confusing that other people don't get the sort of logical connections between it, but everyone's different." The psychologist described the difficulty of getting teachers to integrate data into the student evaluation process:

> [I] try to keep people on track of "Why do you think that we're getting this particular data?" and "What do you want to be different?" and then "What is our plan?" and "How are we going to make it different?" So, any discussion that I'm involved in, I try to focus it back to data because it leads us beyond just admiring the kids or [saying], "We're working really hard and yet it's not coming out" to focusing on [who] didn't do well.

Another problem in using data to address student learning issues across the school was the current role-bound "silos" in which existing data were organized. The psychologist described how "trying to get the data . . . out from pockets of people to the broader staff . . . continues to be a big problem because some people really get it now and really know how to use it, but it is often times not the classroom teachers." Reconciling the tension between traditional instructional practices and the data-driven problem-solving process is a continuous aspect of her work at Harrison. "It's not so much that people aren't capable of analysis," she explains, "but a lot of times they just want to jump to 'Okay, what are we going to do and how are we going to fix it?' and this, unfortunately, leads to lousy solutions."

Part of the psychologist's difficulty was helping teachers shift to a special education perspective of data use from a more informal approach to assessing students. Here the gap between special education and general education training became apparent. One teacher commented:

> When we were first trained in problem solving, we were unfortunately trained from more of a special education point of view instead of the overall school [approach] and so we're still struggling to get everyone looking at how we deal with problems and that method because there's still people who think that it's special ed—it's not a way of how we work in the school so it's something that we're still learning how to do.

Emphasizing the data-driven practices both in DI and in other parts of the school has helped teachers make the transition to the special education model. Teachers have used several kinds of formative assessments to gauge the success of reading interventions. The principal described their problem-solving model:

> [It gives us] a bigger picture of a kid. Rather than just saying, "The kid can't read," we can ask "What are we going to do?" Now we have a couple snapshots of how kids are doing: maybe it's a grade-level thing, or maybe a classroom-level thing. Maybe it's a schoolwide-level thing.

Situating the PST process in this data-rich environment has helped teachers and staff see how assessment data can be used across the instructional program to shape plans for student learning.

Adapting Student Services Roles for Instructional Leadership

The new PST leadership roles put additional pressure on Harrison student services staff. Behavior and learning problems that were once dealt with through informal processes are now subject to PST interventions. The PST structure allows for a small group of teachers and parents to work together in developing a data-driven plan with the assistance of student services staff with extensive training in working with data. The Harrison student services staff have taken on these roles. However, the assessment and intervention expertise of the school psychologist and the social worker is stretched thin in efforts to evaluate learning for all students in terms of achievement data. The school social worker, for example, described that, as a result of PST, "there's not a real clear line between psychologist and social worker." While the psychologist "provides guidance [and] does IQ tests" and the social worker continues to do "home visits for attendance," when it comes to working with assessing student learning, "both of us are involved." This emphasis on the use of data and the PST has meant that some of student support services responsibilities have been pushed to the margins: "If you mean clinical therapy . . . [then], no, that doesn't happen here because neither of us has the time that we could commit."

Student services staff have also taken on more formal leadership roles in the school. Another Easton district initiative calls for the establishment of Learning Teams at each school. The Learning Team is organized to use data to improve student learning through developing the school education plan, organizing professional learning for teachers, and cultivating a safe learning environment. Learning Teams must include the principal, the literacy coach, and at least six teachers. The Harrison Learning Team also includes the school psychologist, the social worker, and a special education teacher. The Learning Team plays a central role in coordinating how data are used to support learning through the school. The school principal explains:

> I know our Learning Team is really key [for] looking at data. . . .
> They're the ones who develop the planning for the school. The
> people on the Learning Team . . . are familiar with it, are trained in
> data collection and analysis, and [they] can help to move the
> others along.

The student services staff play central leadership roles in the Learning Team. A part of this formal leadership role has been to help colleagues learn to use data effectively to develop and analyze the school educational plans. The school psychologist, for example, sees her role as helping the Learning Team to become more data focused:

> We do a pretty good job of using [data] in problem-solving teams.
> . . . We're now using it a little bit more in the Learning Team. That
> has been a bit of a challenge, to tell you the truth, despite the fact
> that that's really what [the Learning Team] is trying to do—

problem solve all the time and use the data and what the data tells us [to do]. It's coming, but that's been kind of a slow process.

Although she served in a leadership role to help the Learning Team use data effectively, the school psychologist was still limited by her position to do anything about the ways other committees, primarily the teacher-driven grade-level teams, used data to inform their practices. Part of the problem in using data at this level was the gulf between the data expertise of the student services staff and the teachers. The school psychologist described the situation:

> It was very frustrating because I think, "here's this great data and we're not using it." I said "Let's look at where the kids are falling apart on the test. . . ." There was a small [teacher] committee that looked at it [last year]. They looked at the math test . . . they discovered a pattern which I had been aware of for a number of years.

Fortunately, the school principal has been able to build links between the support staff and the teachers. As the school literacy coach commented, "I'd say the principal always gives the direction. . . . She's a great thinker who always sees the big picture."

The PST process at Harrison has made student services practices and staff central to the school instructional program. The need to meet accountability challenges pushed school leaders to develop instructional programs that could yield predictable results in terms of student learning. Analyzing the role and function of the PST demonstrated how the school relied upon the IEP precedent and student services expertise as critical resources for developing the capacity to diagnose and address student learning issues. The school principal emphasized how Harrison worked to develop a program to serve all children:

> It depends on what the PST figures out (about) where we're really struggling. Is it just looking at the data, and trying to figure out what's going on with this child and then figuring out different strategies and interventions? Are we effective with every single strategy? No, but I've never seen a school that tries so hard. We don't give up because [a student] doesn't qualify for special ed. When I was a teacher in another school, there were these "gray area" kids, and they would just say, "sorry, we can't help you there, they don't qualify for special ed so just deal with it." We don't do that here. We work through the process and all of the kids get supported.

ADAPTING STUDENT SERVICES PRACTICES
FOR DATA-DRIVEN LEADERSHIP

The Harrison case illustrates how formal leaders in schools rely on student services personnel and practices to create data-driven instructional systems in their schools. The pressure to use data effectively means that schools must not only receive reliable student achievement data, but must also develop the capacity to intentionally adjust instructional practices in order to reach accountability goals. Some researchers have emphasized the unsavory nature of this leadership work as a matter of gaming the system, to unfairly categorize students in order to evade the demands of accountability, to spend exorbitant time drilling students on sample test items, or simply to cheat (Jones, Jones, & Hargrove, 2003; Leavitt & Dubner, 2005; Noddings, 2001; Ryan, 2004). Our research on how leaders build data-driven instructional systems revealed that, in some schools, leaders and teachers work to create sociotechnical practices for generating and acting on formative data about student learning and behavior (Halverson et al., 2005). We found that school leaders did not create these new practices from scratch; rather, they turned to the local expertise of student services staff and the powerful precedent for organizing student-level interventions, the special education IEP.

In light of these examples, we would like to make a few observations about how data-driven practices are organized around IEP-like structures: (1) While these types of practices might not be new, reframing around data might represent a common solution to an NCLB policy problem; (2) student-centered assessment practices require schools to reallocate internal resources both in terms of human and material capital; and (3) if special education practices are being adapted for new purposes, why are school psychologists' and social workers' roles changing, but not necessarily those of special educators?

Common Solution to a New Design Problem

The 1997 IDEA required schools to describe prior interventions put into place to aid student learning as a part of the referral/evaluation process. This need pressed the student services staff to develop practices for documenting the interventions used to support students. Schools throughout the country created team structures to evaluate and discuss whether these interventions were successful. Some of these programs were called Teachers Helping Teachers, Student Study Teams, Building Consultation Teams, or, as in Harrison's case, Problem-Solving Teams. However, since special education continued to serve as a method to pull students out of the schoolwide assessment system, these team conversations remained largely in the realm of special education and did not affect the general education program (Frattura & Capper, 2007).

NCLB changed the function of these team conversations about intervention success. Previously, teams may have engaged in perfunctory conversations about adequacy of the school's interventions as a preliminary step to special education assignment. Now, with NCLB, simply assigning students to special education does not help evade the whole school-level accountability requirements. IDEA 1997 required that all students with disabilities be tested, and with NCLB, schools were required to have at least 95% of the total school population take the state exam. With many schools assigning 10–20% of students to special education, this meant most students assigned to special education would have to take the state exam.

The quality of the interventions taken to improve learning for students who struggled now mattered at the school level, and those responsible for designing and measuring the success of these interventions took on a new schoolwide leadership prominence. In fact, the very students who may have been written off before as special education students are now the group for which the school receives the most attention. Schools are judged by their ability to move as many of these "bubble students," as described by Jennifer Booher-Jennings (2005), across the line from basic to proficient performance on the exams. While researchers debate whether this form of "educational triage" offers an effective model for organizing school practice, in our cases, we have seen how the social workers and school psychologists played a central role in developing these quasi-IEP student assessment processes to build learning plans for students who struggle. We suggest that as schools continue to develop new capacities for using data to improve teaching and learning, structures like the PST and positions like school psychologists and social workers will become more prominent aspects of the general education program.

Reallocating Internal Resources

The cost estimates of NCLB are often modestly calculated in terms of testing and constructing an external accountability system (e.g., see Hoxby, 2002). For local school leaders, however, accountability costs need to include resources for reallocating existing assessment and instructional expertise. Allan Odden's work on resource reallocation (Odden, 2004; Odden & Archibald, 2001) suggests schools may already have the resources necessary for making this transition. Odden and Archibald (2001) describe how schools create several kinds of specialist positions to deliver services to students who traditionally struggle, including categorical specialists, such as special educators, to provide remedial instructional services directly to students, and pupil-support specialists, such as school psychologists, social workers, and assistant principals, to address students' nonacademic issues. In the schools we studied, leaders repurposed the practices of categorical specialists and the roles of pupil-support specialists, to create new forms of data-driven student interventions. Instead of focusing only on students designated for special education, the IEP process at Harrison was adapted to serve as an intervention strategy for proactively developing learning plans before students were assigned to special education. In this school, psychologists and social workers adapted their assessment expertise to provide critical instructional assessment support for students in need before they were placed into special education, rather than noninstructional assessment services after students had already received special education services.

No gain in organizational capacity comes free. At Harrison, for example, the social worker commented that her caseload for individual student counseling had disappeared, and she did not say whether anyone had stepped in to provide this vital service. The student support staff we interviewed appeared to have high levels of dedication and a commitment to reframe their practices. Still, the principal pursued and received comprehensive school reform funding to train teachers and staff in new practices, and was able to redesign staff positions to engage in the quasi-IEP initiatives. Since the previously existing resources, in the form of faculty and staff positions, were already encumbered and embedded in existing school cultures, resource reallocation at Harrison was as much about changing professional culture as drafting a new budget. The ability to reallocate (and redeploy) existing staff resources to provide a critical instructional support system for all students pointed toward a significant aspect of principal leadership expertise (Halverson, 2004; Halverson & Rah, 2005). The costs, here, can be figured in terms of the human capital, the expertise of the school leadership team to recognize which staff members would be able and willing to step into new instructional leadership roles in the school. As with other examples of leadership expertise, it is difficult to translate this ability into a cost estimate or to construct a model that would scale to effect similar practices in other schools.

Special Education Practices, but Not Special Educators?

We began our study with the hypothesis that special educators, as well as special education practices, would play a key role in these new data-driven, student instructional support systems. Instead, we found that categorical staff played a surprisingly small leadership role in the PST program. We suggest that the ability of special educators to redefine their roles says more about their current job responsibilities than their willingness to engage in schoolwide leadership. Like classroom teachers, the special educators in our case schools defined their job responsibilities in terms of time spent with the specific students in their care. Some of this time was spent working with students in inclusive classrooms, and other time was spent serving students in resource rooms and keeping up with the considerable paper trail required to deliver special education services. The special educators at Harrison found little discretionary time to participate in schoolwide leadership activities.

The school psychologists and social workers, also intimately involved in the special education IEP process, framed their job responsibilities in terms of providing services to students as needed. Psychologists and social workers often treated acute student needs on a day-to-day basis. Students who needed more intensive services were referred to the PST processes, largely conducted by the student services staff, and, if necessary, assigned to special education. In the IEP process, student services staff, especially the school psychologist, already provided diagnosis and assessment expertise in identifying students for special education. By intervening in classrooms across the school with a wider variety of students than the special education staff, student services staff were able to develop a schoolwide perspective on the strengths and weaknesses of the instructional program. And since the student services staff in this school had already served in leadership roles by creating schoolwide learning and behavioral reports and helping staff interpret the results of standardized tests, it appeared to be a relatively small step for them to assume the new schoolwide role of developing learning plans for struggling students.

LESSONS FOR INSTRUCTIONAL LEADERSHIP

Schools and districts have faced growing pressure to use data for improving student learning. These pressures have come from high-stakes accountability in NCLB as well as from research supporting the use of data-based decision making. The shift toward data use has brought student services staff to the forefront because of their expertise in working with data. Understanding data and how to use it has become a part of the way schools are doing, or being required to do, business. This shift toward data has pushed school leaders to rely on data-savvy staff members. Several members of a school community, such as social workers and school psychologists typically have considerable experience generating data to measure and improve student learning. The practices of special education, for example, are framed by the assessment and diagnostic processes of the IEP. School psychologists and social workers, typically trained in both psychology and education, help students through counseling, evaluation, and designing interventions for academic and nonacademic issues. These practices and positions comprise a significant resource for school leaders to design systems for using data to improve student learning.

This new melding of practices promises to reshape both instructional leadership and special education. As school leaders draw data-driven special education practices into the core instructional program, student services staff can provide a better range of services to children. The capacity to identify and help students before they fail not only fulfills accountability demands but also changes how schools view teaching and learning. A new wrinkle, the Response to Intervention (RtI) model, was added to these challenges with the 2004 reauthorization of IDEA:

> In determining whether a child has a specific learning disability, a local educational agency may use a process that determines if the child responds to scientific, research-based intervention. (§ 1414(b)(6)(B))

The RtI model suggests a continuum of services that serves all students based on their current needs. The move to RtI represents a major shift in how we will view the role of special education in schools today. School leaders must recognize the possibilities that exist for change through this model because they will be expected to build RtI-like structures at their schools. RtI is a proactive model that works to identify students in need of interventions from the time they enter school and determines the instructional or behavioral interventions a student needs to be successful in the general education classroom. We suggest that the case we described above provides an example of a program that anticipates how schools might change to meet the demands of RtI and of how the practices of special education diagnosis, assessment, and intervention might come to characterize the general education program in schools.

NOTES

The research reported in this chapter was supported by the National Science Foundation (Award 0347030) and by the Wisconsin Center for Education Research, School of Education, University of Wisconsin–Madison. Any opinions, findings, or conclusions expressed in this chapter are those of the authors and do not necessarily reflect the views of the funding agencies, WCER, or cooperating institutions.

1 . DIBELS, or Dynamic Indicators of Basic Early Literacy Skills, are a set of standardized, individually administered measures of early literacy development.

They are designed to be short (one minute) fluency measures used to regularly monitor the development of prereading and early reading skills.

REFERENCES

Abelmann, C., & Elmore, R. F. (1999). *When accountability knocks, will anyone answer?* Philadelphia: Consortium for Policy Research in Education.

Blanchett, W. (2006). Disproportionate representation of African American students in special education: Acknowledging the role of White privilege and racism. *Educational Researcher, 35*(6), 24–28.

Booher-Jennings, J. (2005). Below the bubble: "Educational triage" and the Texas accountability system. *American Educational Research Journal, 42,* 231–268.

Capper, C. A., Frattura, E., & Keyes, M. (2000). *Meeting the needs of students of all abilities: How leaders go beyond inclusion.* Newbury Park, CA: Corwin Press.

Frattura, E., & Capper, C. (2007). *Leading for social justice: Transforming schools for all learners.* Thousand Oaks, CA: Corwin Press.

Goals 2000: Educate America Act of 1992, H.R. 1804, 102d Cong. (1992).

Halverson, R. (2004). Accessing, documenting and communicating the *phronesis* of school leadership practice. *American Journal of Education, 111*(1), 90–122.

Halverson, R., Grigg, J., Prichett, R., & Thomas, C. (2005). *The new instructional leadership: Creating data-driven instructional systems in schools.* (Wisconsin Center for Educational Research Working Paper, No. 2005-9.) Madison: University of Wisconsin. Retrieved July 24, 2006, from http://www.wcer.wisc.edu/publications/workingPapers/Working_Paper_No_2005_9.php

Halverson, R., & Rah, Y. (2005). Representing leadership for social justice: The case of Franklin School. *Journal of Cases in Educational Leadership, 8*(2). Retrieved October 1, 2006, from http://www.ucea.org/html/cases/V8-Iss2/

Hoxby, C. (2002). The cost of accountability. In W. M Evers & H. J. Wahlberg (Eds.), *School Accountability.* Stanford, CA: Hoover Institution Press.

Huefner, D. (2006). *Getting comfortable with special education law: A framework for working with children with disabilities.* Norwood, MA: Christopher-Gordon.

Individuals with Disabilities Education Act (IDEA 1997), 20 U.S.C., Sec. 1400 (1997).

Individuals with Disabilities Education Improvement Act of 2004, Pub. L. No. 108-446, 118 Stat. 2647, (2004).

Jankowski, E. (2003, Fall). Heartland Area Education Agency's problem solving model: An outcomes-driven special education paradigm. *Rural Special Education Quarterly, 22*(4), 29–36. Retrieved October 10, 2006, from http://findarticles.com/p/articles/mi_qa4052/is_200310/ai_n9241552/

Jones, G., Jones, B., & Hargrove, T. (2003). *The unintended consequences of high-stakes testing.* Lanham, MD: Rowman & Littlefield.

Leavitt, S. D., & Dubner, S. J. (2005). *Freakonomics: A rogue economist explores the hidden side of everything.* New York: Harper Collins.

Losen, D. J., & Orfield, G. (2002). *Racial inequity in special education,* Cambridge, MA: Harvard Education Press.

No Child Left Behind Act of 2001, Pub. L. No. 107-110, 115 Stat. 1425 (2002).

Noddings, N. (2001). Care and coercion in school reform. *Journal of Educational Change, 2,* 35–43.

Odden, A. (2004). *Summary and reflections on 14 years of CPRE school finance redesign research* (CPRE-UW Working Paper No. SF-04-01). Madison: University of Wisconsin, Wisconsin Center for Education Research, Consortium for Policy Research in Education.

Odden, A., & Archibald, S. (2001). *Reallocating resources: How schools can boost student achievement without spending more.* Thousand Oaks, CA: Corwin Press.

Reschly, D. J., Tilly, W. D., III, & Grimes, J. P. (Eds.). (1999). *Special education in transition: Functional assessment and noncategorical programming.* Longmont, CO: Sopris West.

Ryan, J. E. (2004). The perverse incentives of the No Child Left Behind Act. *New York University Law Review, 79,* 932–989.

Yin, R. K. (1994). *Case study research: Design and methods.* London: Sage.

Ysseldyke, J., & Marston, D. (1999). Origins of categorical special education services in schools and rationale for changing them. In D. J. Reschly, W. D. Tilly, III, & J. P. Grimes (Eds.), *Special education in transition: Functional assessment and noncategorical programming* (pp. 1–18). Longmont, CO: Sopris West.

Zhang, D., & Katsiyannis, A. (2002). Minority representation in special education: A persistent challenge. *Remedial and Special Education, 21,* 180–187.

Drawing Conclusions About
Instructional Teacher Leadership

Sara Ray Stoelinga and Melinda M. Mangin

THIS VOLUME presents research on nonsupervisory, school-based, instructional teacher leader roles. The contributors have examined these roles from a variety of theoretical perspectives, using a diverse set of research methods, and in an array of contexts. In this chapter, we use a common framework to examine and discuss the results of the studies in this volume. The framework comes from the theoretical analysis set forth by Taylor in Chapter 2 and addresses two points of evaluation: (1) the propensity for instructional teacher leadership to influence teachers' instruction and (2) the contextual factors that influence instructional teacher leadership. Using these two foci we examine the lessons learned, gaps in our knowledge, and areas for future research.

A FRAMEWORK FOR ANALYSIS

Taylor states that the rationale for investing in instructional teacher leader positions is based on the understanding that teachers' instruction profoundly influences student learning. Thus a key way to improve student learning and performance is to design reforms that directly influence instructional practice. School reform policies that aim to change school governance structures or teacher credentialing can be too distant from instruction; professional development may be overly generalized and removed from the classroom context. Teacher leaders, through classroom-based coaching and an intensive focus on individual teachers' needs, perhaps represent a more direct path to improving teachers' practice.

According to Taylor, there are three pathways between instructional teacher leaders and enhanced teaching. First, instructional teacher leaders can help teachers develop an understanding of desired teaching practices. Second, instructional teacher leaders have the ability to influence teachers' motivation to improve their practice. Finally, instructional teacher leaders can contribute to teachers' knowledge and skill development. On this basis we ask the question, What can the findings from the studies in this volume teach us about the influence of instructional teacher leaders on teacher thinking, motivation, and knowledge?

Taylor also describes five contextual factors that researchers identify as influential on the character, depth, and functioning of instructional coaching roles. These include (1) formal and informal school leadership; (2) alternative instructional guidance, such as professional development, technical support, and peer collaboration; (3) the goals, design, and understandings of larger school reform efforts at the school, district, state, and national levels; (4) faculty norms, such as trust and professional community; and (5) the availability of supporting resources including time, logistics, training, and expertise. Given the wide range of potentially influential contextual components, we ask a second question, What do these studies teach us about how context influences instructional teacher leadership?

INFLUENCING INSTRUCTIONAL PRACTICE

Three studies directly examine how instructional teacher leaders can influence teachers' instructional improvement: those by Manno and Firestone (Chapter 3); Lord, Cress, and Miller (Chapter 4); and Halverson and Thomas (Chapter 9). Here, we examine what the findings from these studies tell us about teacher leaders' influence on instructional practice.

Manno and Firestone demonstrate that teacher leaders' content knowledge positively influences the three instructional improvement pathways described by Taylor. Content experts were able to recognize deficiencies in teachers' content knowledge and to focus their work on those areas, contributing to deeper understandings of both desired practice and the necessary knowledge and skills to enact that practice. Manno and Firestone also found that teacher leaders' content knowledge enhanced teachers' perception of teacher leaders as advocates for children's learning, leading to increased trust between teachers and teacher leaders. This, in turn, influenced teachers' motivation to use services provided by the teacher leader. Thus the findings presented by Manno and Firestone support the notion that instructional teacher leadership, enacted by content experts, can influence instruction by helping teachers acquire the motivation, knowledge, and skills necessary to identify and develop desired practices, as specified by Taylor.

Lord, Cress, and Miller also provide new evidence of the relationship between teacher leader roles and teachers' instructional improvement. Teacher leaders approached their work "as teachers" and used "show and tell" strategies to contribute to individual teachers' instructional improvement. Instructional teacher leader roles were effective in promoting change in teacher practice and improvement in teacher knowledge and skills, demonstrating the three pathways in Taylor's framework. While promising in terms of individual teacher development, the teacher leader–teacher relationship lacked the "hard" feedback necessary for "establishing the kind of collegial critique or reflection that serve as engines for continuous improvement." Lord, Cress, and Miller conclude that building and sustaining learning communities that critically examine practice is vital in designing a teacher leader role that can both deepen work with individual teachers and promote change at a wider level.

Halverson and Thomas contend that instructional leadership is not limited to formal teacher leader roles but is distributed across a variety of positions. They describe the part that student services staff can play in using student achievement data to identify instructional needs in the general population and tailor instructional services accordingly. The analysis and utilization of data to identify student instructional needs and to design appropriate interventions is an essential component of the pathways to instructional improvement described by Taylor.

THE INFLUENCE OF SITUATIONAL CONTEXTS

Four chapters focus explicitly on the relationship between instructional teacher leadership and situational context: those by Mangin (Chapter 5); Stoelinga (Chapter 6); Camburn, Kimball, and Lowenhaupt (Chapter 7); and Supovitz (Chapter 8). In this section, we examine how findings about situational context can inform instructional teacher leadership.

Mangin demonstrates that the design of initiatives influences teacher leadership enactment. Mangin analyzed teacher leadership design in five school districts, examining the extent to which effective designs were optimized. Mangin found that contextual constraints, such as the limited number of qualified applicants and insufficient funds, forced district leaders to make choices about the design of their initiatives. These choices involved trade-offs, resulting in district leaders' having to choose one benefit of teacher leadership over another. This finding substantiates the influential nature of resources such as time, logistics, training, and expertise (Taylor's fifth contextual factor). Moreover, Mangin provides evidence that factors beyond the school, such as the district and larger policy contexts, also influence teacher leadership (Taylor's third contextual factor).

Camburn, Kimball, and Lowenhaupt illustrate the challenge of implementing school-level literacy coach roles in the context of a large, urban, decentralized district. They found that district decentralization policy influenced implementation (Taylor's third contextual factor), causing district leadership to oscillate between lesser and greater degrees of control over the initiative. Like Mangin, they also found that insufficient resources (Taylor's fifth contextual factor) hindered the initiative. At the district level, lack of qualified human resources personnel affected the hiring and retention of the district-level literacy specialists. At the school level, differential enactment of the coach position compromised the role's instructional focus and a lack of time for coaches to attend meetings, meet with specialists, or complete time logs further hindered effectiveness.

Stoelinga's contrasting case studies of the relationship between formal and informal teacher leaders demonstrate Taylor's first and second contextual factors. Existing informal teacher leaders and informal teacher communication networks shaped the character of the institutionalization of teacher leader roles, both positively and negatively. Thus the extent to which informal and formal teacher leaders shared similar goals determined the level of acceptance of or resistance to formal teacher leaders. At the same time, the harmony between existing school values and the values underlying formal instructional teacher leader roles also influenced institutionalization, illustrating the influence of faculty norms (Taylor's fourth contextual factor). For example, when school staff did not have norms of sharing instructional practice, institutionalization was compromised. Similarly, the aims of the larger school reform effort, and the extent to which it focused on instruction, determined teacher leaders' propensity to influence instructional practice (Taylor's third contextual factor).

Supovitz's analysis of instructional leadership in high schools demonstrates the dynamic of formal versus informal leadership, the variety of sources of instructional guidance in schools, and the influence of faculty norms. Working on the presumption that leadership is distributed, Supovitz demonstrated that leadership in high schools was largely enacted informally (Taylor's second contextual factor). The emergence of these informal teacher leaders was based on others' perceptions of their expertise and openness to providing support. Supovitz also found evidence of the influence of faculty norms (Taylor's fourth contextual factor). In high schools, authority relationships and departmentalization distanced formal school leaders from instructional matters and led to norms of informal problem solving among colleagues, promoting reliance on informal leaders.

While the primary evidence for contextual influences on instructional teacher leadership is to be found in Chapters 5 through 8, all the empirically based chapters provide some evidence of situational influence. Manno and Firestone (Chapter 3) show how the larger school reform context, focused on standards-based curriculum materials, influenced the character of coaching provided by content expert teacher leaders. Halverson and Thomas (Chapter 9) demonstrate how policy contexts such as the No Child Left Behind Act (NCLB) and the reauthorization of the Individuals with Disabilities Education Act (IDEA), prompted school leaders to turn to student services staff as leaders in data analysis. Lord, Cress, and Miller (Chapter 4) explain how contextual factors such as lack of training, norms of private practice, role definitions that prohibit evaluation, limited time, and inadequate scheduling all limited teacher leaders' efforts at meaningful critiques of teacher practice. Taken together, all of these chapters present a convincing argument for increased attention to the context of instructional teacher leader initiatives.

IMPLICATIONS FOR FUTURE RESEARCH

We have applied Taylor's framework as a means to discuss important findings from the studies in this volume. As a result, the ways in which instructional teacher leadership represents a path to instructional improvement and the contextual factors that influence this path are highlighted. At the same time, the frames draw our attention to areas in need of further study and aspects of instructional teacher leadership that remain unexamined. Here we ask, What new studies might be conducted to further our understanding of nonsupervisory, instructional teacher leadership? In response, we examine the gaps in our knowledge as an indication for future development.

Increasing Knowledge and Skills

Studies in this volume identify the kinds of knowledge and skills that instructional teacher leaders need to increase their influence. From Manno and Firestone we know that content knowledge influences the work of instructional teacher leaders; the effectiveness of content experts differed significantly from that of nonexperts. What remains unexplored is the relationship between subject area, content expertise, and effective instructional teacher leadership. Does teacher leadership in the areas of math or science, as studied by Manno and Firestone, require a different type of content knowledge than teacher leadership in literacy or another subject area? New studies focused on documenting instructional teacher leadership in different subject areas are necessary to extend our understandings of the influence of content knowledge and subject area.

In addition to content knowledge, instructional teacher leaders need procedural knowledge to foster instructional improvement. Lord, Cress, and Miller demonstrate that teacher leaders must be able to move their work beyond nonconfrontational one-on-one relationships to extend their influence. Accordingly, knowing how to facilitate collaboration, dialogue, and trust may be directly related to teacher leaders' success. Manno and Firestone found that teachers leveraged their content knowledge differently with novice teachers than with those who were more experienced. This finding implies that tailoring procedural strategies on the basis of contextual factors may constitute a critical component of effective instructional teacher leadership. Similarly, Halverson and Thomas demonstrate the importance of procedural knowledge in the form of data analysis skills, which can be used to target instructional improvement efforts. To date, we know little about the form and function of procedural knowledge. Additional research is needed on how these skills are learned and enacted, the degree to which such skills are considered in the hiring process, and the extent to which procedural knowledge is necessary for effective instructional teacher leadership.

In identifying the need for additional research related to content and procedural knowledge, this volume also reveals the need to further examine the training of instructional teacher leaders. Mangin describes training as an important design component that influenced teacher leaders' knowledge and teachers' perceptions. Similarly, Camburn, Kimball, and Lowenhaupt demonstrate how variation in training prompted uneven implementation across a large, decentralized school district. Little is known about effective training for instructional teacher leaders. How frequently should professional development occur? Who should provide the training? What content should be presented and in what format? Future studies that include evaluation of the form and content of teacher leader training can facilitate a better understanding of the connections between preparation, enactment, and outcomes.

Improving Enactment

The studies in this volume contribute important insights about instructional teacher leader role enactment at the school level. Lord, Cress, and

Miller explain that norms governing access and accountability presented challenges to teacher leaders' ability to move beyond one-on-one relationships, constraining the potential of teacher leadership to contribute to widespread instructional improvement. This finding leads to questions about the necessary conditions for effective teacher leader role enactment. What kinds of professional norms might facilitate the development of teacher leadership and can these norms be created to increase the effectiveness of enactment? Alternately, can mandates and high-stakes accountability practices promote teacher leader enactment? Future research that explores the influence of professional norms and authoritarian mandates can lead to deeper understandings of the conditions that facilitate and constrain teacher leadership initiatives.

Another school-level factor that influences the enactment of formal teacher leadership is the structural context. From Supovitz we learn that the highly departmentalized structure of high schools presents a unique context for the enactment of formal teacher leader roles, raising the question of how organizational structure influences enactment. Lord, Cress, and Miller provide additional information on school structures that facilitate the deepening and broadening of the work of instructional teacher leaders, for example, collegial observation and critique, clear role expectations, and a focus on organizational development. Examining these and other structural factors can lead to the identification of supporting contexts for effective teacher leadership enactment.

Improving teacher leadership enactment may also be contingent upon our understanding of school-level leadership. The findings of Supovitz and of Stoelinga indicate that other informal and formal leadership roles can undermine or call into question the validity and usefulness of formal instructional teacher leader positions. As such, distribution of leadership, formal and informal, and its influence on instructional teacher leader roles is an important area for future research. In particular, the role of the principal in developing and supporting teacher leadership is unexamined in this volume. Such studies can promote teacher leadership designs that fit in the existing school context and yet have the potential to promote instructional improvement by contributing to changes in school norms and structures.

Finally, the improvement of teacher leader role enactment requires an examination of the assumptions that underlie these roles. Taylor's conceptual overview underscored the need to clarify what teacher leadership is and what it isn't. For example, this volume has deliberately focused on roles that are nonevaluative. Nonevaluative teacher leader positions are based on the assumption that they are more conducive to teacher leader–teacher trust, which is fundamental to promoting change. Yet teacher leaders' presence in classrooms provides them with intimate knowledge of teachers' strengths and weaknesses, and they have access to formal leaders who conduct potentially high-stakes evaluations of teacher practice. How do teacher leaders negotiate the tension between assessment and assistance? Can they respect teachers' confidentiality while simultaneously meeting the pressing need for instructional improvement? Further research is needed on the assumptions behind these roles including the nonevaluative nature of instructional teacher leadership and its relationship to role enactment, teachers' receptivity, and interaction with other school leaders.

Expanding the Context

The findings in this volume point to the district as a critical context in the development of instructional teacher leadership. Mangin's work reveals the district's role in selecting, developing, and distributing teacher leaders as well as the need for district-level communication structures that facilitate these processes. Camburn, Kimball, and Lowenhaupt describe how variation in implementation in the context of a large, urban district with a multilevel structure resulted in diluted effectiveness of the teacher leader role. Both these studies raise questions about how district demographic factors such as district size, population density, economic resources, and history influence the design, implementation, and effectiveness of instructional teacher leader positions. Future research should situate the evaluation of teacher leadership initiatives within the context of district demographic factors.

The findings in this volume also underscore the influence of the larger policy environment on instructional teacher leader roles. Most prominently, the NCLB policy context and the resulting emphasis on accountability have profoundly influenced the development of teacher leader positions. While chapters in this volume explore the influence of policy on teacher leader roles, deeper investigation of both national and state policy contexts is needed. For example, the current focus on "data-driven instruction" and "high-quality" teaching has implications for teacher leader roles. Also, trends in "standardized testing" and "instructional differentiation" contribute to new ways of thinking about teacher leadership. Studies focused on the influence of the policy environment can situate teacher leader role development within the current reform context.

Evaluating Effectiveness

Effectiveness of an intervention is measured by the extent to which its goals are realized. The chapters of this volume measure the effectiveness of teacher leader roles in relation to a range of goals, including teacher leaders' influence on instructional practice (Chapters 3 and 4), teacher leader role enactment (Chapter 5), the depth of institutionalization of teacher leader roles (Chapter 6), and the integration of the role into a coherent initiative for school reform (Chapter 7). While assessing these outcomes is informative, measures of influence on instructional improvement and student achievement are needed. A critical next step for scholars is to design studies that investigate the relationship between instructional teacher leader positions, instructional practice, and student outcomes.

Another aspect of formal teacher leader positions that requires further investigation is financial cost. Teacher leader–based initiatives are expensive and cost-benefit analyses are needed to develop better understandings of the financial cost in relation to the potential for positive outcomes. As Mangin (Chapter 5) and Camburn, Kimball, and Lowenhaupt (Chapter 7) indicate, limited resources lead to trade-offs in the design of reform initiatives. Analyses of what is sacrificed to pay for teacher leader positions can promote more informed initiative design.

THE PROMISES OF INSTRUCTIONAL TEACHER LEADERSHIP

Teacher leader roles were a prominent part of the conversation about education reform during the late 1980s and early 1990s. After a period of silence, teacher leader roles have reemerged. What has changed in the interim? What remains the same?

The policy context of school reform has certainly changed. The NCLB legislation and increased focus on accountability constitute a major shift in the context for teacher leadership. As a result, the teacher leader roles described in this volume differ from their predecessors in significant ways. No longer are these positions intended as a pathway to individual improvement. Instead teacher leadership is focused on collective improvement through the mentoring of colleagues, marking a shift in the purpose of the role and the overarching goals of reform.

The scope of school reform initiatives has also changed. The trend toward broader and deeper reforms has grown, in part, out of high-stakes accountability, a need for replicable improvements, and research indicating the dependency of reform on programmatic and structural coherence. This focus on "scaling up" reform has resulted in an increase in the number, and expansion of the function, of teacher leader positions. Moreover, the work of these teacher leaders is intended to reach a larger number of teachers, promoting deep and lasting change.

The aspirations of school reform have become more demanding and expectations for teacher leaders have increased in parallel. This new wave of teacher leadership focuses increasingly on instructional improvement: leading district initiatives, designing and offering professional development, analyzing data, creating learning communities, and negotiating complex mentoring relationships. As such, the teacher leader of the 1980s has reemerged to find an entirely new set of expectations requiring more sophisticated skills.

Given these new contexts, it is not surprising that investigative efforts are needed to design, understand, implement, and evaluate these new teacher leader roles. What remains from the 1980s is the enduring commitment to the importance of teacher leadership in the school reform process—the notion that teachers, as those closest to student learning, should be instrumental in improving schools, instruction, and achievement.

The work of instructional teacher leaders must focus on the promise of improvement that emerges from findings in this volume. As practitioners and school leaders, we must use these new understandings to revise and refine teacher leader roles to make their work more meaningful. As researchers, we must use the cases, conclusions, and recommendations presented here to deepen inquiry and understandings, open doors to conversation with practitioners, and promote more effective teacher leadership.

About the Editors and the Contributors

MELINDA M. MANGIN is an Assistant Professor of Educational Administration at Michigan State University. She received her PhD from Rutgers University, where she conducted research at the Center for Educational Policy Analysis. Mangin's career in education began as a public high school Spanish teacher in New York City. Presently, her research focuses on the contexts that influence teacher leadership and instructional improvement.

SARA RAY STOELINGA is a Senior Research Analyst at the Consortium on Chicago School Research at the University of Chicago. She received her PhD in sociology from the University of Chicago. She previously worked as an Assistant Research Professor at the University of Illinois–Chicago, conducting education evaluation in Chicago public schools. Her research focuses on teacher leadership in school reform efforts, the sociology of education, and organizational change in schools.

ERIC M. CAMBURN is an Assistant Professor at the University of Wisconsin–Madison. His current research focuses on the measurement of teaching and leadership practice and the investigation of factors that support and constrain the improvement of educational practice.

KATE CRESS served as a Senior Research Associate at Education Development Center, Inc., in Newton, Massachusetts, from 1999 to 2004. During that time she conducted research on teacher leadership and provided technical support to teacher leadership programs and university-school district partnerships. She has written on a variety of education topics, most recently instructional coaching. Currently, she is a seminarian at the Boston University School of Theology, studying for the ordained ministry.

WILLIAM A. FIRESTONE is a Professor of Educational Policy and Administration in the Graduate School of Education at Rutgers University. He recently coedited *A New Agenda for Research in Educational Leadership* (with

Carolyn Riehl) and *The Ambiguity of Teaching to the Test* (with Roberta Schorr and Lora Monfils).

RICHARD HALVERSON is an Assistant Professor in Educational Leadership and Policy Analysis at the University of Wisconsin–Madison. He received his PhD from Northwestern University in Learning Sciences, after 10 years' experience as a school teacher and administrator. He is a founding member of the University of Wisconsin Learning Sciences program and the Games, Learning and Society Research Group. His research integrates cognitive psychology, classical philosophy and instructional technology to study and communicate expert school leadership practice.

STEVEN M. KIMBALL is a researcher with the Consortium for Policy Research in Education (CPRE) and the Wisconsin Center for Education Research at the University of Wisconsin–Madison. Prior to joining CPRE, he held legislative analyst positions in the U.S. House of Representatives, the U.S. Senate, and the Texas State Office in Washington, D.C. His research and publications focus on teacher evaluation and compensation, principal evaluation, and instructional leadership.

BRIAN LORD is Co-Director of the Center for Leadership and Learning Communities at Education Development Center, Inc., a research and development organization in Newton, Massachusetts. He has directed research on teachers' professional development, teacher leadership, instructional coaching, and lesson study and has led technical assistance initiatives in mathematics and science education reform. His research focuses on teacher collegiality, teacher learning communities, and the critique of instructional practice.

REBECCA LOWENHAUPT is a PhD candidate in the department of Education Leadership and Policy Analysis at the University of Wisconsin–Madison. She is interested in the role literacy coaches play in effective on-site teacher learning. Her other research interests include school reform practices in a climate of rapid demographic shift and the school experience of recent immigrants as they navigate new languages, cultures, and literacy practices.

CHRISTOPHER M. MANNO is currently the Superintendent of Schools of the P–12 Burlington Township School District, New Jersey. Previously, he was a mathematics teacher, district math supervisor, director of curriculum, and assistant superintendent for curriculum and instruction. He earned a doctorate in Educational Administration from Rutgers University.

BARBARA MILLER is Co-Director of the Center for Leadership and Learning Communities at Education Development Center, Inc., in Newton, Massachusetts. She has directed a number of projects focusing on teacher leadership, including research studies, evaluation efforts, and technical assistance projects on the design and implementation of teacher leadership programs. She has authored casebooks on teacher leadership and school reform issues.

JONATHAN A. SUPOVITZ is an Associate Professor in the Graduate School of Education at the University of Pennsylvania and a senior researcher at the Consortium for Policy Research in Education. His research examines the structures and cultures of learning both within and by organizations and investigates the array of leadership across education systems.

JAMES E. TAYLOR is a Senior Research Analyst at the American Institutes for Research (AIR) in Washington, D.C. Prior to joining AIR, he conducted research on the study of instructional improvement at the University of Michigan. His research focuses on instructional leadership, coaching, and teacher professional development as well as school improvement and accountability policy.

CHRISTOPHER N. THOMAS is an Assistant Professor in the Department of Leadership Studies at the University of San Francisco. He has had 10 years of experience as a teacher, principal, and administrator in California and Wisconsin. His research interests include special education and urban school leadership.

Index